ASEAN, Sovereignty and Intervention in Southeast Asia

Lee Jones
Lecturer in International Relations, Queen Mary, University of London, UK

First published 2012 by
PALGRAVE MACMILLAN

Palgrave Macmillan in the UK is an imprint of Macmillan Publishers Limited, registered in England, company number 785998, of Houndmills, Basingstoke, Hampshire RG21 6XS.

Palgrave Macmillan in the US is a division of St Martin's Press LLC, 175 Fifth Avenue, New York, NY 10010.

Palgrave Macmillan is the global academic imprint of the above companies and has companies and representatives throughout the world.

Palgrave® and Macmillan® are registered trademarks in the United States, the United Kingdom, Europe and other countries

ISBN 978-0-230-31926-4

This book is printed on paper suitable for recycling and made from fully managed and sustained forest sources. Logging, pulping and manufacturing processes are expected to conform to the environmental regulations of the country of origin.

A catalogue record for this book is available from the British Library.

A catalogue record for this book is available from the Library of Congress.

10   9   8   7   6   5   4   3   2   1
21   20   19   18   17   16   15   14   13   12

Printed and bound in Great Britain by
CPI Antony Rowe, Chippenham and Eastbourne

Critical Studies of the Asia Pacific Series

Series Editor: **Mark Beeson**, Winthrop Professor of Political Science and International Relations at the University of Western Australia

Critical Studies of the Asia Pacific showcases new research and scholarship on what is arguably the most important region in the world in the twenty-first century. The rise of China and the continuing strategic importance of this dynamic economic area to the United States mean that the Asia Pacific will remain crucially important to policymakers and scholars alike. The unifying theme of the series is a desire to publish the best theoretically-informed, original research on the region. Titles in the series cover the politics, economics and security of the region, as well as focussing on its institutional processes, individual countries, issues and leaders.

Titles include:

Stephen Aris
EURASIAN REGIONALISM
The Shanghai Cooperation Organisation

Toby Carroll
DELUSIONS OF DEVELOPMENT
The World Bank and the Post-Washington Consensus in Southeast Asia

Aurel Croissant and Marco Bunte *(editors)*
THE CRISIS OF DEMOCRATIC GOVERNANCE IN SOUTHEAST ASIA

Shahar Hameiri
REGULATING STATEHOOD
State Building and the Transformation of the Global Order

Lee Jones
ASEAN, SOVEREIGNTY AND INTERVENTION IN SOUTHEAST ASIA

Hiro Katsumata
ASEAN'S COOPERATIVE SECURITY ENTERPRISE
Norms and Interests in a Regional Forum

Erik Paul
OBSTACLES TO DEMOCRATIZATION IN SOUTHEAST ASIA
A Study of the Nation-State, Regional and Global Order

Joel Rathus
JAPAN, CHINA AND NETWORKED REGIONALISM IN EAST ASIA

Barry Wain
MALAYSIAN MAVERICK
Mahathir Mohamad in Turbulent Times

Robert G. Wirsing and Ehsan Ahrari (editors)
FIXING FRACTURED NATIONS
The Challenge of Ethnic Separatism in the Asia-Pacific

Critical Studies of the Asia Pacific Series
Series Standing Order ISBN 978–0–230–22896–2 (Hardback) 978–0–230–22897–9
(Paperback)

You can receive future titles in this series as they are published by placing a standing order.
Please contact your bookseller or, in case of difficulty, write to us at the address below with
your name and address, the title of the series and one of the ISBNs quoted above.

Customer Services Department, Macmillan Distribution Ltd, Houndmills, Basingstoke,
Hampshire RG21 6XS, England

To my parents, Diane and Paul

Contents

Acknowledgements

The greatest pleasure in seeing this book finally come to press is the opportunity to acknowledge all the help and support I received in researching and writing it. Scholarship can seem a rather lonely, individuated task at times but, like all production, intellectual production is actually an intensely social activity. It involves not only standing 'on the shoulders of giants' to contribute to ongoing debates, but it is also enabled and enriched by countless discussions, arguments, criticisms, and acts of kindness.

I will forever be grateful to Allan Patience who first introduced me to the study of International Relations (and ASEAN) in his course at the University of Tokyo in 2002. As a working-class youth who was the first in my family to attend university, without Allan's encouragement and mentorship, I would never have even embarked upon graduate study, let alone written this book. He has been a superb teacher and friend, lending unstinting support since we first met.

This book emerged out of research subsequently undertaken for my postgraduate studies at the University of Oxford, where I had the privilege to be supervised by Andrew Hurrell. Andy's kind and supportive, yet critical and rigorous approach taught me a great deal and is, I hope, reflected here. Yuen Foong Khong's robust guidance and help in arranging fieldwork was also much appreciated. Rosemary Foot's advice was also extremely useful, both at the formative stages of my project and when she later became my internal examiner. My external examiner, the late Fred Halliday, was not only a source of intellectual inspiration but also rightly pushed me to develop my theoretical framework much further when writing this book. His passing was a great loss to us all.

At Oxford, I was particularly fortunate to meet other, far more talented graduate students who became close friends and collaborators. Conversations with Alastair Fraser, Chris Bickerton and Phil Cunliffe profoundly changed the way I thought about the world. I cannot express my debt to them enough. Our collaboration in the 'Sovereignty and its Discontents' BISA working group, alongside other valued interlocutors including David Chandler, James Heartfield and Rahul Rao, inspired an interest in sovereignty and intervention that will probably persist for a lifetime. A host of other friends also made Oxford an intellectually stimulating and enjoyable place to be. I am particularly thankful for the companionship of Emily Paddon and Vidya Kumar.

As will become apparent to readers, this book emerges out of a particular 'political economy' approach to understanding Southeast Asian politics. This approach was pioneered by scholars based at or linked with the Asia Research Centre at Murdoch University, Perth. At its most basic, this book tries to apply their insights about the nature of state power in Southeast Asia to deepen our understanding of international relations in that region. Whether I have done this successfully or not, I greatly admire their work and owe them a significant intellectual debt. Two directors of the Centre, Garry Rodan and Richard Robison, have provided valuable comments on my work and have been very supportive and generous. The Centre's Shahar Hameiri has also significantly influenced my thinking and research agenda, becoming a friend and close intellectual collaborator.

Many other individuals and institutions helped make this book possible. The Economic and Social Research Council and Nuffield College, Oxford, financed the fieldwork. Ambassador Barry Desker, dean of Singapore's S. Rajaratnam School of International Studies, graciously provided a base for me there, while Beth Dunlap generously housed me in Jakarta. Many people kindly gave their time to be interviewed. Hannah Chandler at Oxford's Bodleian Library and the excellent librarians at Nuffield College worked tirelessly to help me access far-flung research materials. The warmth, encouragement and advice of my colleagues at Queen Mary was very important to me as I wrote the book. I am particularly grateful to Ray Kiely, James Dunkerley, Jeremy Jennings, and Rick Saull, and especially to Toby Dodge, who has unselfishly helped me in countless ways. The editor of this series, Mark Beeson, showed consistent faith in the manuscript and has been critical in bringing it to press, as have Christina M Brian and her colleagues at Palgrave. My thanks also to Palgrave's anonymous reviewer, and to the reviewers for *The Pacific Review, Cambridge Review of International Affairs,* and *Asian Security*, where some of the ideas and material in the book were explored for the first time.

The text used in the epigraphs is reproduced by kind permission of their respective publishers. The sources are indicated in the text. Thanks also to the United Nations' Cartographic Section for the use of their map of Southeast Asia. Every effort has been made to trace rights holders, but if any have been inadvertently overlooked the publishers would be pleased to make the necessary arrangements at the first opportunity.

Above all, I am grateful to my family for all their love and support. My mother and grandmother in particular instilled in me an inspirational love of learning for its own sake and a rejection of injustice and oppression in all its forms. Along with my partner, Ian, and many good friends, my family have supported me constantly.

Whatever is good about this book, then, I really owe to others – even if none of them may actually agree with very much of what I have written. Its shortcomings, however, are of course mine alone.

Note on Citations

UN Documents are cited as follows. 'A' indicates a General Assembly document. 'C.', followed by a number, indicates a committee of the General Assembly, the most commonly cited being C.4, the decolonisation committee. 'BUR' denotes the General Committee. 'E' denotes the Economic and Social Council, under which the UN Human Rights Commission (C.3) used to fall. 'S' indicates a Security Council document. 'PV' indicates a Provisional Verbatim record and 'SR' a Summary Record. They are preceded by the session number in the case of General Assembly records, or by the meeting number in the case of Security Council records. Page numbers follow. E.g., 'A/35/PV.4, p. 2' indicates page two of the provisional verbatim record of the 35th session of the UN General Assembly. RES indicates a resolution, followed by the number of the resolution for the Security Council, or by the session number and resolution number for the General Assembly. E.g., S/RES/688 (1990) indicates Security Council Resolution 688, passed in 1990; A/RES/45/3 indicates General Assembly Resolution 3 of the 45th session. 'L' denotes a draft resolution. 'Add.' and 'Rev.' following a reference denote additions and revisions to the original document.

British Foreign and Commonwealth Office documents are cited by their title, where one exists, followed by their location in the British National Archives at Kew, as follows: FCO folder number/subfolder number/document number. # is substituted for missing document numbers.

List of Acronyms

AFTA	ASEAN Free Trade Area
AIETD	All-Inclusive East Timorese Dialogue
AIPMC	ASEAN Inter-Parliamentary Myanmar Caucus
AMM	ASEAN Ministerial Meeting
APCET	Asia-Pacific Conference on East Timor
APEC	Asia-Pacific Economic Cooperation
APODETI	*Associação Popular Democratica Timorense* (Timorese Popular Democratic Association)
ARF	ASEAN Regional Forum
ASA	Association of Southeast Asia
ASDT	*Associação Social-Democrata Timorense* (Timorese Social-Democratic Association)
ASEAN	Association of Southeast Asian Nations
ASEM	Asia-Europe Meeting
BAKIN	*Badan Koordinasi Intelijen Negara* (State Intelligence Coordinating Agency)
BCP	Burmese Communist Party
CGDK	Coalition Government of Democratic Kampuchea
CIA	Central Intelligence Agency
CLMV	Cambodia, Laos, Myanmar and Vietnam
CPP	Cambodian People's Party
CPT	Communist Party of Thailand
DK	Democratic Kampuchea
EEC	European Economic Community
EU	European Union
FRETILIN	*Frente Revolucionária de Timor-Leste Independente* (Revolutionary Front for an Independent East Timor)
FUNCINPEC	*Front Uni National pour un Cambodge Indépendant, Neutre, Pacifique, et Coopératif* (National United Front for an Independent, Neutral, Peaceful and Cooperative Cambodia)
GDP	Gross Domestic Product
GOLKAR	*Partai Golongan Karya* (Party of the Functional Groups)
ILO	International Labour Organisation
IMF	International Monetary Fund
INTERFET	International Force for East Timor

IR	International Relations
JIM	Jakarta Informal Meeting
KPNLF	Khmer People's National Liberation Front
KR	Khmer Rouge
MAC	*Movimento Anti-Communista* (Anti-Communist Movement)
MCP	Malayan Communist Party
MILF	Moro Islamic Liberation Front
MNLF	Moro National Liberation Front
NAM	Non-Aligned Movement
NGO	Non-Governmental Organisation
NLD	National League for Democracy
PAP	People's Action Party
PAS	*Parti Islam SeMalaysia* (Pan-Malaysian Islamic Party)
PKI	*Partai Komunis Indonesia* (Indonesian Communist Party)
PPA	Paris Peace Agreements
PPP	People's Power Party
PRB	*Partai Rakyat Brunei* (People's Party of Brunei)
PRK	People's Republic of Kampuchea
R2P	Responsibility to Protect
SEATO	South East Asian Treaty Organisation
SLORC	State Law and Order Restoration Council
SNC	Supreme National Council
SPDC	State Peace and Development Council
SRP	Sam Rainsy Party
TAC	Treaty of Amity and Cooperation
TRT	Thai Rak Thai
UDT	*União Democrática Timorense* (Timorese Democratic Union)
UMNO	United Malay National Organisation
UN	United Nations
UNAMET	United Nations Mission in East Timor
UNCHR	United Nations Commission for Human Rights
UNDP	United Nations Development Programme
UNESCO	United Nations Educational, Social and Cultural Organisation
UNGA	United Nations General Assembly
UNHCR	United Nations High Commission for Refugees
UNMISET	United Nations Mission of Support in East Timor
UNSC	United Nations Security Council

UNTAC	United Nations Transitional Administration in Cambodia
UNTAET	United Nations Transitional Authority in East Timor
US	United States of America
VCP	Vietnamese Communist Party
ZOPFAN	Zone of Peace, Freedom and Neutrality

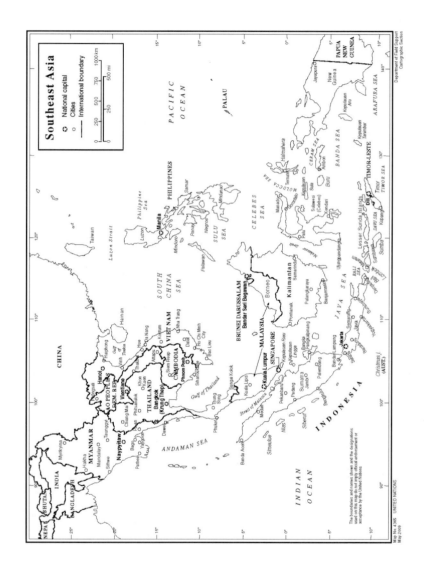

Introduction

> ASEAN countries' consistent adherence to this principle of non-interference is the key reason why no military conflict has broken out between any two ASEAN countries since the founding of ASEAN... Let us maintain it in the twenty-first century.
>
> – *S. Jayakumar, Singaporean Foreign Minister* (1997)

> Frankly, we have been interfering mercilessly in each other's internal affairs for ages, from the very beginning.
>
> – *Bilahari Kausikan, Permanent Secretary, Singaporean Foreign Ministry* (2008)

In 1975, Indonesia invaded East Timor and, backed by its partners in the Association of Southeast Asian Nations (ASEAN), forcibly annexed the territory, killing up to 182,000 people during its occupation. Three years later, in response to Vietnam's toppling of Cambodia's Pol Pot regime, ASEAN states pursued a proxy war against Hanoi and the new Cambodian government, championing the deposed Khmer Rouge in the United Nations (UN), hosting, re-arming and resupplying their guerrillas, manipulating foreign aid to fuel the war, and forming a new coalition government-in-exile to manoeuvre its clients back to power in Phnom Penh. After the Cold War, ASEAN states and state-linked business elites tried to export their capital and governance models to neighbouring states, bolstering authoritarianism in Burma and fuelling an ongoing civil war in Cambodia, culminating in the collapse of the coalition government there in 1997. ASEAN then imposed political conditions for Cambodia's membership of the Association. Two years later, core ASEAN states promoted and joined a humanitarian intervention in

1

East Timor. And, particularly since 2003, ASEAN has repeatedly sought to insert itself into Burma's democratisation process.

Oddly, all of these incidents – and more – occurred in a region where governments are famed for their strict adherence to the principle of non-interference in the internal affairs of other states. ASEAN elites regularly invoke their mantra of 'non-interference' to explain ASEAN's success as the leading instantiation of third-world regionalism. Academics have almost universally accepted this mantra as fact, agreeing, whatever their other theoretical quarrels, that ASEAN states strictly adhere to this 'cherished' norm. Journalists, accepting the elite and scholarly consensus as read, have turned the media into a confirming echo chamber from which there seems no escape.

This book begs to differ. Rather than denying or downplaying the reality of ASEAN states' interventions, it recovers the marginalised history of those actions, using elite interviews, archival evidence, official documents and many other primary and secondary sources. It also explains these interventions through a theoretical framework that transcends the dominant realist-constructivist debate on ASEAN, drawing on research on the political economy of Southeast Asian politics and regionalism that is usually neglected by ASEAN scholars. The book argues that we cannot understand state interests or norms in abstraction, but only as part of an ongoing process of social conflict – in important part, transnational in nature – which gives rise to specific state forms, regimes and ideologies. It shows that both intervention and the non-interference principle can be explained as the outcome of struggles between and within ASEAN's most powerful social forces as they seek to impose their interests as *raison d'état*.

ASEAN and non-interference: A misplaced consensus

The study of Southeast Asian regionalism has been dominated by a long-running debate between realist and constructivist scholars, recently leavened with liberal and English school contributions. Strikingly, despite their other disagreements, scholars from all these approaches agree on the absolute centrality of the non-interference principle for ASEAN states. This consensus, however, is badly misplaced. It fails to reflect the reality of regional politics, and has deflected attention away from the facts of ASEAN state intervention. When these facts become too difficult to ignore, prevailing theoretical approaches have merely tried to downplay them or explain them away, producing serious, unresolved inconsistencies.

Realist scholars emphasise material capabilities, international anarchy and power-balancing strategies to explain outcomes in international politics. They have analysed ASEAN as a somewhat incoherent grouping of weak states that has little influence on regional order relative to the great powers, serving largely as a sub-regional mechanism for reconciliation after intra-mural conflicts in the early 1960s (Leifer, 1989; Jones and Smith, 2006). Nonetheless, many realists see ASEAN's norm of non-interference in states' internal affairs as central to the limited role the Association has played in dampening down regional tensions. They describe it as a 'cherished principle' that has been broken only twice in ASEAN's history (Leifer, 1999, pp. 35–6). Unusually, realist scholarship on ASEAN has thus admitted a modest role for norms in sustaining regional order.[1]

Later constructivist scholarship developed this basic realist position into a far more ambitious and sophisticated theoretical argument. They maintained that ASEAN created regional order by articulating principles of interstate conduct into a bundle of norms dubbed the 'ASEAN way'. Constructivists argue that these norms – 'the single most important of which is the doctrine of non-interference' – do not merely 'regulate' behaviour; once established, norms acquire a 'life of their own', producing a 'cognitive transition', redefining states' interests and identities through 'socialisation' (Acharya, 2009a, pp. 70, 26, 23–32; see also Caballero-Anthony, 2005). Over time, they argue, an incipient 'regional identity' or 'security community' has thereby been formed, allowing the region to transcend international anarchy by entrenching norm-governed interaction.

While this thesis is not universally accepted, there continues to be remarkable consensus on the central role played by non-interference. In rebutting the 'security community' argument, realists have merely solidified the underlying consensus on ASEAN's commitment to sovereignty, arguing that 'the only "institutional principle" to which ASEAN adheres is that of non-interference' (Jones and Smith, 2006, pp. 167–8). Scholars outside the realist-constructivist debate also agree. A pioneer of the international society or 'English school' approach, for instance, argues that, contrary to constructivist expectations, some ASEAN principles have been broken by member-states – but only in defence of their own sovereignty (Narine, 2006, pp. 212–13).

This scholarly consensus corresponds very closely to the rhetoric used by regional elites to explain their own behaviour. A typical example is the claim made by Singapore's prime minister that 'we don't set out to change the world and our neighbours. The culture of ASEAN is that we do not interfere' (Economist, 1992). Indeed, ASEAN governments often do appear hyper-sensitive to any 'intervention' or 'interference' in their internal affairs (terms they use interchangeably). For instance, in 1982 Indonesia's suggestion of Philippine-Malaysian talks to settle a territorial dispute saw Indonesia's ambassador expelled from Manila for 'undue interference' (Antolik, 1990, p. 79). Protests in Malaysia and Indonesia against a 1986 Israeli presidential visit to Singapore were denounced as 'interference' in Singapore's domestic affairs (Antolik, 1990, p. 43). More recently, Singapore's senior minister was attacked by Indonesian politicians for having 'intervened in other people's affairs' by simply commenting critically on Indonesia's anti-terrorism policy (Cotton, 2003, p. 153).

ASEAN's non-interference principle is thus apparently seen by both scholars and policymakers to impose extraordinarily strict limitations on state behaviour, prohibiting even verbal commentary on domestic affairs to avoid disrupting regional order. Antolik (1990, p. 156), states that non-interference brooks 'no public challenges, comments or criticisms of other regimes' legitimacy, domestic systems, conduct, policies, or style'. Acharya (2009a, p. 72) further elaborates the norm as demanding the following conduct:

1. Refraining from criticising the actions of a member government towards its own people, including violations of human rights, and from making the domestic political systems of states and the political styles of governments a basis for deciding their membership in ASEAN;
2. Criticising the actions of states which were deemed to have breached the non-interference principle;
3. Denying recognition, sanctuary, or other forms of support to any rebel group seeking to destabilise or overthrow the government of a neighbouring state;
4. Providing political support and material assistance to member states in their campaign against subversive and destabilising activities.

Today, when such a tight conception of sovereignty norms is increasingly seen as outdated, Asian states are said to remain 'at the forefront of resistance to post-Westphalianism' (Acharya, 2009b, p. 74); indeed, it is argued that a 'naked pursuit of Westphalian sovereignty epitomise[s] the essence of Asian security today' (Moon and Chun, 2003, p. 107).

However, reality does not necessarily correspond to this scholarly and elite consensus. As even some ASEAN elites occasionally admit, their fabled commitment to non-interference is actually far from rigid in practice. For example, ASEAN's former secretary-general, Rodolfo Severino (2006, p. 94), insists that the application of non-interference is governed by 'pragmatic considerations' and accordingly 'has not been absolute'. The permanent secretary of Singapore's foreign ministry admits that, 'frankly, we have been interfering mercilessly in each other's internal affairs for ages, from the very beginning' (Kausikan, 2008).

So far, however, interventionist behaviour by ASEAN states has received little systematic exploration, despite *prima facie* evidence of dramatic violations of non-intervention (Khoo, 2004). Typically, only quite petty deviations from the principle are admitted, creating the impression that nothing more serious has occurred. For example, Caballero-Anthony (2005, pp. 212–13) rightly states that non-interference 'has not been strictly observed' since 'several cases in the past... contradicted this norm'. However, she notes only fairly minor exceptions – a joint statement on unrest in the Philippines in 1986, and a few undiplomatic comments traded between governments – concluding that despite 'exceptions to the rule, ASEAN has essentially observed this principle'. Haacke (2003, p. 168) makes a virtually identical argument, citing the same examples. Indeed, the general view is that non-interference has been 'maintained' in the face of repeated challenges (Ramcharan, 2000).

Thus, rather than exploring the gap between ASEAN's rhetoric and reality, the usual approach is simply to paper over it, reaffirming its fundamental role in Southeast Asian regionalism. Scholars have either downplayed or marginalised discrepant evidence that challenges their theoretical interpretations, or have simply presented evidence of intervention alongside contradictory restatements of the power of non-intervention, rendering their accounts incoherent.

Constructivists often ignore or downplay evidence of interventionist practices. Their primary theoretical goal is to 'prove', *contra* realism, that norms 'matter'. This creates an incentive to minimise evidence of norm violation in order to sustain the argument that norms govern state behaviour. Constructivists thus tamely describe interventionist behaviour by ASEAN states as merely 'testing' non-interference (Acharya, 2009a, pp. 127–34). Acharya notes some recent deviations from non-interference and concedes that ASEAN has apparently 'shed some of its rigidity'. Nonetheless, he still asserts that it 'has not significantly departed from the non-interference doctrine' and that 'ASEAN remains wedded to these norms'. Indeed, adherence to non-intervention is said to have 'thwarted ASEAN's ability to respond to the East Timor crisis and apply genuine pressure on Burma', and rendered ASEAN 'functionally deficient in coping with transnational dangers such as financial volatility, environmental degradation or terrorism' (Acharya, 2009a, pp. 258, 276–7, 290, 297).

Jürgen Haacke's more pluralist approach, which acknowledges the role of norms alongside other factors, more openly explores the contradictions of the 'ASEAN way'. Yet, to sustain the idea that regional norms affect state behaviour, he also seems to downplay interventionist episodes and their implications for our understanding of regional order. Haacke presents defeated attempts to revise non-interference as evidence of the norm's continued influence, while violations of it are invariably accompanied by qualifications that minimise their significance for ASEAN's 'diplomatic and security culture', enabling him to reaffirm that 'centrepieces of this normative terrain... have throughout remained meaningful' (Haacke, 2003, ch. 7–8, p. 214).

However, the weight of recent developments seems to have forced some constructivists to acknowledge more significant shifts in ASEAN states' behaviour. Notwithstanding her assessment of ASEAN's past practices, Caballero-Anthony (2005, pp. 248–9, 272) argues that ASEAN's contemporary engagement with NGOs on human rights indicates a shift 'away from... the ASEAN way', and even suggests that Indonesian proposals for a regional peacekeeping force in 2003 implied the 'pooling of sovereignty'. In trying to account for ASEAN's increasingly interventionist relations with Burma, Haacke (2010, p. 174) has recently argued that

> the limits of ASEAN's flexibility in practising non-interference... have been set by a shared interest in anchoring Myanmar in the ASEAN community, different levels of motivation to promote democracy and human rights... economic interests, geopolitical considerations, political prudence... and a perceived need to preserve regional cohesion and unity.

Intriguingly, this apparently implies that the operation of ASEAN norms is actually determined by a host of non-normative factors. A similar possibility is proposed by critical scholar Helen Nesadurai (2009a, p. 104), who argues that 'adherence to the ASEAN Way... [is] contingent on whether such practice secures or undermines national socio-political and economic agendas'. Yet, so far, this suggestion has received no systematic exploration.

Realists and others, who might perhaps have been expected to pursue this line of reasoning, have generally failed to do so, instead merely noting deviations from non-interference while simultaneously restating the principle's importance. Realists have little incentive to downplay interventionist behaviour, but 'the non-interference principle' seems to remain too useful an explanatory trope to discard. Realist scholar Michael Leifer, for example, could thus acknowledge egregious breaches of the principle – such as Indonesia's annexation of East Timor – yet incongruously assert several pages later that 'non-violation of national sovereignty is regarded by Jakarta as a central precept of any system of regional order' (Leifer, 1983, pp. 155–9, 167). Others report that ASEAN has interfered in Burma, yet simultaneously claim that it is 'bound by the cherished principle of non-interference' (Ganesan, 2006). Claims that ASEAN's 'emphasis on non-interference has not [changed]' sit alongside acknowledgements of events in which 'member-state sovereignty and non-interference were not barriers to be clearly respected' (Emmerson, 2009, pp. 23, 50). Scholars even contradict themselves within the space of a single page, claiming both that ASEAN's 'security community' rests on the 'ASEAN *modus operandi* of non-interference' while identifying the recent adoption of 'a "soft-interventionist" approach… on seemingly domestic issues' (Chin, 2007, p. 397). Thus, rather than genuinely probing constructivist claims about non-interference or the historical record in a systematic fashion, realists have continued to invoke it in a rather incoherent, haphazard fashion.

These contradictory claims reflect the way in which 'non-interference' has become a useful catch-all explanation for scholars from all theoretical traditions to explain the genesis, evolution and limitations of ASEAN regionalism. Analysts consistently use it to explain ASEAN's failure to address serious regional issues such as military misrule in Burma, humanitarian crises like East Timor in 1999, and transnational security threats like piracy, environmental degradation, transnational crime, and epidemic diseases (e.g. Rahim, 2008; Huxley, 2002; Emmers, 2003; Caballero-Anthony, 2008). Yet if the non-interference principle has not been absolute, can it really be used with such ease and regularity to explain ASEAN's every shortcoming? If not, it seems we do not yet really understand the reasons why ASEAN engages as it does with these vital international issues. Understanding and explaining the actual role of non-interference is necessarily prior to analysing a range of other questions, and is required to avoid the frequent implication that ASEAN is simply irrational for adhering to non-interference. It is also necessary to avoid poor policy prescriptions. Scholars who ignore previous interventions often recommend repeating these same practices, despite their failure to produce the desired outcomes, or they propose weakening non-interference without appreciating the damage already wrought by violations of the norm.

Therefore, to set the record straight is not simply an act of scholastic pedantry; it is also to cut through elite rhetoric to the reality of state practice, to disrupt the major area of scholarly consensus on ASEAN, to question the most common explanations given for the form Southeast Asian regionalism takes, and to provide a sounder basis for policy-making. It is also to provide firmer ground for a political critique of ASEAN. If it can be shown that ASEAN states have intervened in some areas and not others, 'non-interference' cannot simply be invoked to explain and justify inaction on a given issue. If non-interference operates selectively, then the basis of that selectivity is exposed as the proper object for critique and contestation.

Structure of the book

Chapter 1 explains how the book understands the basis of the selective application of non-interference, laying out a theoretical framework for the analysis of ASEAN's sovereignty regime. It argues that sovereignty norms are best understood as a technology of power, used by domestic groups to help determine the scope of political conflict in a way that best suits their interests. 'Non-interference' can be both invoked and discarded by powerful social groups to defend their particular interests, ideologies and strategies. In order to understand when and why this happens, it is therefore necessary to disaggregate the state, rather than treating it as a coherent actor as much as International Relations (IR) theory does. Indeed, sovereignty norms are often implicated in struggles over what sort of state should emerge, and whose interests it should advance.

The book then divides into two parts, covering the Cold War and the post-Cold War period respectively. Each part is introduced with a chapter outlining the most politically important cleavages and conflicts within Southeast Asian societies and their relationship to ASEAN's theory and practice of (non)interference (Chapters 2 and 5). Major interventions by ASEAN states are also identified within their historical context. The development of ASEAN's sovereignty regime and member-states practices of (non)intervention are analysed as a technology of power. Their strategic intention and effects are traced back to the attempt of dominant forces and state managers operating on their behalf to maintain or advance their interests, ideologies and political projects within evolving social, economic and (geo)political contexts.

Each part of the book then deepens the analysis using case studies of interventions by ASEAN states in neighbouring countries. For the Cold War, the case studies cover East Timor and Cambodia (Chapters 3 and 4), and for the post-Cold War period, Cambodia, East Timor and Burma (Chapters 6, 7 and 8). These case studies reconstruct the neglected history of ASEAN interventionism, explaining what was felt to be at stake, and advancing the argument that they are best understood as political outcomes of the social conflicts in ASEAN states.

1
Theorising Sovereignty and Intervention

Sovereignty is the foundational concept of modern international relations. In declaring that national governments are the supreme authorities within their geographical territories, sovereignty divides the globe into the principal actors and subjects of international politics, states. It demarcates the 'domestic' sphere from the 'international' and, by identifying and authorising its key agents, makes international politics thinkable and possible. The corollary norm of non-interference in states' internal affairs also implies the exclusion of all rival authorities to the state. This creates the possibility of a state accountable to its own people, thereby enabling the practice of self-determination and democracy. Sovereignty is thus vitally important, both conceptually and politically, which is why it has attracted so much scholarly attention from many different disciplines.

However, much of this attention has recently been devoted to exploring the various ways in which sovereignty does not do what it is supposed to. The autonomous sovereign state is often said to have emerged via the 1648 Treaty of Westphalia, which terminated decades of internecine religious conflicts by confirming the absolute supremacy of rulers in their own territories. However, recent scholarship has focused on debunking this 'myth', emphasising how Westphalia preserved the Holy Roman Empire and other semi-sovereign entities, enshrined a hierarchy of monarchies, principalities and republics, legitimised interventions for dynastic aggrandisement, and limited sovereigns' rights to interfere with international trade (Osiander, 2001; Teschke, 2003). Moreover, scholars have emphasised that, since Westphalia, frequent, even systematic intervention in states' internal affairs has occurred, whether by great powers, international organisations or non-state actors. With the 'globalisation' of economic relations, regional integration, and the growing obligations of international law, some scholars even argue that the sovereign state is being eroded or transcended altogether (Strange, 1996). This is the context that makes ASEAN's famed adherence to non-interference so peculiar.

State sovereignty has thus long coexisted alongside interventionist practices. How are we to make sense of this apparently contradictory dual persistence? This chapter proposes an analytical framework, which is later used to explore the specific case of ASEAN. It engages first with the most obvious explanation: that, as Stephen Krasner (1999) argues, sovereignty is merely 'organised hypocrisy', maintained for its benefits but violated whenever it suits rulers' interests. Despite the power and simplicity of this argument, I argue that Krasner's rational choice analysis provides little guide to identify or explain patterns or 'regimes' of sovereignty and intervention. Instead, a deeper analysis of the social, political and economic purposes served by sovereignty is required.

Using insights from historical sociology, political geography and state theory, I propose analysing sovereignty and non-interference as a technology of power. The strategic effect of claiming territorial sovereignty is to define the scope of socio-political conflict by containing it geographically and institutionally, excluding outside influences on domestic struggles for control over state power. Consequently, sovereignty is deeply implicated in helping to (re)produce particular social, economic and political orders and institutions. It is this that generates identifiable patterns or regimes of sovereignty, rather than the free-for-all which Krasner implies. The intimate relationship between sovereignty and social order also means that the scope of sovereignty is constantly subject to contestation by socio-political forces seeking to determine what sort of order should prevail. What emerges in practice is shaped by this struggle, which is in turn conditioned by local and global geopolitical and economic developments.

This book thus aims to contribute both to the general study of sovereignty in IR, and to the study of Southeast Asia and ASEAN, where much of the broader literature on sovereignty has been ignored, despite the centrality of 'non-interference' to much theorising about the region. My fundamental goal is not to 'debunk' sovereignty and non-interference, but more concretely to provide the analytical tools necessary to enable us to explain when sovereignty is and is not transgressed.

Organised hypocrisy?

The claim that ASEAN states have often intervened in each other's internal affairs despite professing non-interference may surprise many

ASEAN scholars, but not mainstream realists, for whom glaring disparities between rhetoric and reality are endemic in international politics. Stephen Krasner has powerfully argued that sovereignty is merely 'organised hypocrisy': it is respected or rejected depending on which course provides most 'utility' to rulers. The norm thus formally persists while also being systematically violated. This may appear a plausible explanation of the historical record in Southeast Asia. On closer investigation, however, it becomes clear that Krasner's rational choice model does not provide the analytical depth required to identify and explain patterns of sovereignty and intervention. Through exploring the limitations of Krasner's analysis, this section indicates the need for a historical-sociological approach which analyses the involvement of sovereignty and intervention in (re)producing particular social and political orders.

From a mainstream realist perspective, norms like sovereignty and non-interference have very little purchase over states. In a sweeping historical survey, Krasner identifies countless violations of sovereignty despite the official persistence of the norm. Strong states have coercively intruded on the affairs of weaker ones, sovereignty has been granted to entities lacking the formal requirements of statehood while those possessing them are not recognised, and states have frequently relinquished their sovereignty to other states or international organisations. Krasner explains this using a simple rational choice model: 'At times rulers adhere to conventional norms or rules because it provides them with resources and support (both material and ideational). At other times, rulers have violated the norms, and for the same reasons'. By creating international recognition, sovereignty provides 'resources and opportunities that can enhance [rulers'] chances of remaining in power'. However, opportunities always arise in which rulers may gain more by disregarding sovereignty norms. Rulers then make 'calculations of material and ideational interests' and uphold or violate their own or someone else's sovereignty based solely on which provides the most 'utility' (Krasner, 1999, pp. 223, 24, 7, 64).

For realists, such violations are perfectly normal given the absence of international authority. International norms often clash with domestic interests, and since rulers respond predominantly to domestic audiences, 'a logic of consequences can always prevail over a logic of appropriateness' (Krasner, 1999, pp. 6, 69).

This is a simple yet very powerful argument that can explain both why sovereignty norms persist, and why they are so frequently violated. Krasner's work has been extraordinarily influential in the study of sovereignty and norms, and the concept of 'organised hypocrisy' may appear to fit the ASEAN case quite well. The apparent contradiction between ASEAN's adherence to and violations of non-interference dissolves if we explain both actions as strategic calculations by rulers to maximise their gains. However, there are a number of problems with the 'organised hypocrisy' approach that severely limit its helpfulness.

The first problem is that Krasner's analytical method generates an undifferentiated and consequently inaccurate description of the actual resilience of sovereignty. Krasner demonstrates that violations of sovereignty are entirely commonplace only by establishing an ideal-type of the sovereign state and then chronicling numerous deviations from it. This ideal-typical state is defined as being able to control movement across its borders (interdependence sovereignty), effectively regulate the behaviour of agents within its borders (domestic sovereignty), exclude external authorities (Westphalian sovereignty), and extract recognition from other states (international legal sovereignty) (Krasner, 1999, pp. 3–4). This is a remarkably tall order, amounting to the total mastery of a state's internal territory and external relations. Setting up such an unrealistic ideal-type may allow countless deviations from it to be identified, but this tells us more about the ideal-type than the deviations. Krasner himself admits that 'only a very few states have possessed all of these attributes' (1999, p. 220). Arguably, no state has *ever* possessed them all simultaneously. Setting the bar so high creates an unrealistic impression of a complete free-for-all, in which rulers are constantly violating sovereignty on the basis of short-term, cost-benefit analyses.

In reality, we can identify relatively stable, historical patterns of sovereignty and intervention. They do not correspond to Krasner's ideal-type, but they do involve states exercising predictable degrees of *de facto* autonomy within a clearly identifiable range. For example, in the European Concert period, European states could act autonomously unless threatened with liberal revolution, in which case they were subject to intervention by the forces of the Holy Alliance (Hobsbawm, 1973, chs. 5–7). During the Cold War, the USSR's Brezhnev Doctrine prescribed similar limits for Eastern European states threatened with capitalist 'counter-revolution', while the US Truman Doctrine and its successors allowed states outside the Soviet orbit to enjoy their sovereignty so long as they remained non-communist (Westad, 2005). Since decolonisation, third-world states have achieved a low level of *de facto* sovereignty, circumscribed by international law and international institutions made and dominated by the former colonial powers (Anghie, 2005). The purpose of intervention also seems to have changed over time, from debt collection in the nineteenth-century, to containing revolution in the early nineteenth and mid-twentieth century, to humanitarian intervention today (Finnemore, 2003). We can therefore identify specific historical patterns of *de facto* sovereignty and intervention that do not correspond to the free-for-all implied by Krasner's relentless listing of violations of sovereignty. Rather, they constitute what John Agnew (2009, p. 129) calls 'sovereignty regimes', a 'dominant calculus of rule relative to a given state or set of states'.

The second, related problem with Krasner's approach relates to his explanatory framework. It is clearly very difficult to explain macrohistorical patterns of sovereignty and intervention through a succession of cost-benefit analyses made by individual rulers. For example, European Union (EU) states do not correspond to the Westphalian ideal-type, but nor is their *de facto* sovereignty constantly being flexed or relaxed in a sporadic fashion corresponding to short-term cost-benefit calculations. European states are instead enmeshed in a complex web of institutionalised, dynamic and multi-level relationships that have transformed their practice of sovereignty, and indeed their very statehood, while entrenching particular political and economic policies. The EU has established a form of economic constitutionalism that decentres and fragments traditional centres of political authority. Its emergence has been associated with the large-scale transformation of the global political economy and European societies (Jayasuriya, 2001). These transformations and their effects are simply not captured by a rational-choice model which assumes that, for example, the basic unit of 'the state' is coherent and unchanging.

Of course, one may insist on describing virtually anything in terms of 'rational choice' and 'utility-maximisation' if one loads all the important explanatory content into the terms under which actors define 'costs' and 'benefits'. If one folded issues like global political transformation, the hollowing-out of domestic politics, the influence of neoliberal ideology, and so on, into the matrices that guide rulers' calculations, one could explain European integration using the terms Krasner proposes. But all the explanatory weight would be on the forces that determine the matrices, not the final rational choice.

However, Krasner actually provides no real basis for understanding why rulers make the choices they do. He argues that 'rulers want to stay in power and, being in power, they want to promote the security, prosperity and values of their constituents' (Krasner, 1999, p. 7). However, the precise meaning and content of 'security, prosperity and values' are so highly contested in every society that it is impossible to promote the conceptions of all 'constituents' simultaneously. The key question, then, is *whose* 'security, prosperity and values' are promoted through upholding or violating sovereignty? On this, Krasner is completely silent. This allows every state action to be uncritically rationalised as promoting the interests of its 'constituents' in general, when closer scrutiny may show that particular patterns of sovereignty and intervention systematically favour highly sectional interests. US interventions against left-leaning social forces and governments during the Cold War, for example, were often to safeguard the interests of American capital or even specific businesses (Barnett, 1970; Gibbs, 1991). Like many 'realists', however, Krasner is unwilling to open up the 'black box' of the state.

What is missing from a realist treatment of sovereignty, therefore, is a sense of distinctive patterns of power relations over time – history – and a sense of the forces that animate state behaviour – political sociology. A proper understanding of sovereignty regimes and the interests and values they advance or constrain thus requires a historical-sociological approach. While Krasner's important emphasis on the strategic aspect of sovereignty/intervention should be retained, we need to pay more attention to macro-historical patterns, and make use of state theory to help identify the forces benefiting from particular sovereignty regimes. The next section begins to delineate such an approach by conceptualising sovereignty and non-interference as a technology of power.

Sovereignty as a technology of power

Sovereignty and non-interference play a key role in structuring political life, simultaneously enabling and constraining different political projects. Secessionist groups crave sovereignty to enable them to independently determine their own political future. Cosmopolitans deride sovereignty for trumping liberal values and impeding the realisation of a global political community. Sovereignty is contested in political life, then, because it is deeply implicated in the (re)production of particular political, economic and social orders. Through exploring this crucial strategic aspect of sovereignty – hinted at, but never fully explored by Krasner – we can appreciate how it is bound up in social conflicts over what sort of order should emerge. This section thus reconceptualises sovereignty and non-interference as a technology of power, particularly in relation to state-making.

Sovereignty's strategic character can be understood quite straightforwardly. Although states are recognised as sovereign in international law, it is governments which actually speak on their behalf and, so to speak, 'wield' state sovereignty in international politics, on behalf of the populations they supposedly represent. This slippage between people, state and government is, of course, required to enable representative government and self-determination as we commonly understand it, and to enable the basic procedures of international politics to function. However, it also enables a range of political strategies which can be used for highly sectional purposes. Although governments are assumed to represent their whole populations, in practice they may represent only the interests of only a very narrow section of their domestic populations – or even of interests beyond their borders. They can strategically use their unique position to determine *what counts* as sovereignty and intervention within their borders, to help change or uphold particular social, economic and political institutions and orders.

For example, tens of thousands of American 'advisors' and troops were stationed in South Vietnam's territory during the 1960s and 1970s. Although this clearly constrained the state's sovereign autonomy in many ways, the government in Saigon did not rush to the UN Security Council (UNSC) to complain about US intervention, but rather legally sanctioned the American presence while denouncing the attempts of North Vietnam to interfere in its 'internal affairs'. The reason for this is obvious: the US presence was vital to prevent the collapse of the country's capitalist social and economic order, the right-wing Saigon government, and indeed the entire state of South Vietnam. The many South Vietnamese people who were opposed to this particular order, including the alternative 'Provisional Revolutionary Government' and its followers, naturally identified the US presence as a malign intervention, but their voices carried no weight in international law. Conversely, sovereignty can be used to try to ward off influences that the forces behind a particular government would find destabilising or detrimental to their interests. In 2010, faced with a violent crackdown by the Thai army, embattled anti-government 'red-shirt' protestors called for foreign intervention, lobbying the UN and the American and British embassies. By contrast, the Thai government warned the UN and others that it would not tolerate interference in its internal affairs. The government's position triumphed.

At its most basic, then, sovereignty and non-interference can be understood a strategic tool to define the scope of political conflict, to determine which forces are included within a particular struggle for power. This is crucial *and* contested since, as Schattschneider (1960, pp. 2, 3) argues, 'the outcome of all conflict is determined by the *scope* of its contagion. The number of people involved in any conflict determines what happens'. Consequently, 'the most important strategy of politics is concerned with the scope of conflict'. Consider a hypothetical situation wherein a right-wing military dictatorship has seized power to defend the propertied classes against the threat of a communist takeover, and faces a left-wing, rural insurgency. The counterrevolutionary regime will seek to contain the conflict's scope to a level at which it can defeat the insurgents. Domestically, it will try to prevent the conflict spreading into the cities, and to block potential alliances between peasants and workers, for example. Internationally, the regime will also seek to insulate the insurgents from external resources and supporters by demanding that outsiders observe non-interference in the country's internal affairs. By contrast, the insurgents will likely wish to socialise the conflict, both domestically and internationally, to broaden its scope and draw in new participants who might tilt the balance against the regime. If the regime is sufficiently embattled, it too may seek to socialise the conflict by requesting assistance from fellow counter-revolutionaries. The regime only differs from the insurgents here in that it possesses the state apparatus and can thus manipulate the legal norms of sovereignty to help control the scope of the conflict to further its own interests.

Of course, there is nothing automatic about a government's definition of sovereignty and intervention winning out over that of its opponents; the outcome depends on prevailing constellations of power, interests and ideology at the international level. Successfully claiming sovereignty depends to some extent on achieving external recognition. At times of particularly intense social conflict, rival forces within a country may be supported by different external agents, with respect for sovereignty being decidedly secondary to the promotion of particular ideologies and interests (Halliday, 1999). Examples include the Spanish civil war, the Vietnam and Afghanistan Wars, and indeed most significant Cold War-era conflicts in the third world. However, in less intense periods of conflict, well-established procedures of recognition may prevail, underwriting the strategic value of being recognised as a sovereign state's government. This in turn partly explains why modern political conflict is typically oriented towards the capture of the state. As Clapham (1996) observes, post-independence conflicts in Africa have often revolved around rapid wars of movement designed to capture the state apparatus, because of outsiders' tendency to recognise whoever occupies it as the legitimate government, a phenomenon he dubs 'letterbox sovereignty'.

The dominant form in which sovereignty is expressed – the territorial nation-state – clearly enables and constrains particular social, economic and political projects, and thus carries significant consequences for the interests and strategies of different societal groups. To claim territorial sovereignty is to stake a claim to ultimate authority over a bounded space, all the people within it, and the flows across the borders implied in the claim. In the modern era, such claims can only be justified with reference to 'the people', on whose behalf authority is said to be exercised. Since the nineteenth century, this justification has most often taken a nationalist form: the claim that the sovereign state corresponds to some body of people who share certain politically-relevant characteristics (language, ethnicity, culture, etc) in common, can be neatly defined from other such groups, and are thus entitled to self-determination. This can be a progressive development in that the state's remit is clearly defined and, since it is subject to no higher authority, it can at least potentially be held to account by the population upon which it bases its legitimacy (Bickerton *et al.*, 2006). In this sense, territorial sovereignty enables democratic, representative government to exist.

However, the decision to establish political authority on the basis of territory rules out many other possibilities, such as religion, race, and class. As Lawson and Shilliam (2010, p. 664) point out, political projects appealing to non-territorial bases of political community have always flourished and sometimes presented a serious challenge to the sovereign states-system. These include international communism and other forms of international class solidarity, 'the Islamic *umma*, pan-racial movements, various regional formations (such as the Bandung "moment"), anti-colonial internationalism including the Tricontinental movement, transnational diasporic communities, international women's movements, indigenous groupings, and, of course, liberal cosmopolitanism'.

Such challenges have frequently been identified as a 'threat' to state 'security' and violently suppressed. Indeed, the maintenance of political authority in the form of the sovereign, territorial nation-state often requires tremendous amounts of violence and is a highly contested, conflict-ridden process. This is not least because relevant socio-political distinctions rarely, if ever, correspond neatly to state borders. Religion, class, race and other forms of human solidarity frequently overlap territorial borders and, to the extent that they form the basis of an alternative political vision, pose a real challenge to the desire to territorialise political authority. As Agnew (2009, pp. 60–1) argues, given this overlapping, the nation-state is best understood as 'the myth of the nation-hyphen-state', since in reality there is no 'clear "inside" and "outside" to society as such defined by the territorial nation to which every state has become conjoined'. Historically 'nations' have been 'created *after* borders are more or less in place by ethnic cleansing or expulsions, forced assimilation, and other planned and spontaneous efforts at cultural homogenisation'.

The inherent and often violent clashes of interest and ideology involved in territorialising sovereign states are frequently airbrushed by much of the mainstream literature on third-world political development and its relationship to sovereignty. Archetypal is Mohammed Ayoob's 'subaltern realism', which purports to explain and justify third-world elites' attachment to sovereignty. Ayoob observes of the Westphalian norms of 'rigidly demarcated and sacrosanct boundaries, mutual recognition of sovereign political entities, and non-intervention in the affairs of other states' that 'third-world elites have internalised these values to an astonishing degree'. This arises from the challenges they face in 'state-making' in a context characterised by weak 'internal cohesion', a lack of 'unconditional legitimacy of state boundaries, state institutions, and governing elites', susceptibility to internal and external conflicts and 'easy permeability by external actors'. Third-world rulers thus struggle to enhance the territorial control and the coercive and extractive capacities of their state apparatuses. Ayoob sympathetically insists that sovereignty and non-interference are consequently vital to buy rulers the space and time necessary to strengthen state institutions (1995, pp. 71, 22–3, 15, 30–1). Correspondingly, he staunchly criticises phenomena like humanitarian intervention.

Explanations of ASEAN's attachment to non-interference frequently invoke a similar logic, referring to the need of Southeast Asia's post-colonial states to consolidate themselves, to overcome 'internal threats' and enhance 'regime security' (Leifer, 1989, p. 14; Acharya, 2009a, p. 71). Ayoob himself explains ASEAN as a form of cooperation built around 'the convergence of regime interests relating to internal security' to manage 'threats to the security of states and the stability of regimes' (1995, p. 62). Ayoob's work has also been used by ASEAN scholars to explain why 'sovereignty was the cornerstone of ASEAN from the outset': it was 'intended to make its individual members stronger, more viable states' (Narine, 2005, p. 475).

Despite the implication of these authors that the desire to overcome 'internal threats' is entirely natural and unobjectionable, there is actually nothing neutral about constructing sovereign states on a territorial, 'national' basis. It is actually the attempt to establish territorially-based political authority which *constitutes* the 'internal' and the 'external', and which also gives rise to 'internal threats' as some social forces resist incorporation into a state-making project and the social, economic and political hierarchies it always involves. By defining the scope of politics in a particular way, territorialisation rules out other forms of political life that would advance very different interests and ideologies. It involves delegitimising and violently suppressing, for example, class-based political struggles and forms of political authority, insisting that solidarity ends at the border, that politics is only legitimately conducted between people understood as citizens of a 'national' state (rather than members of a religion, race, class, etc), and that all political conflict be oriented towards the national state and mediated through its institutions. The sovereign territorial state thus enables some political projects, yet constrains others.

This is never adequately recognised in the literature on ASEAN. Scholars often mention the importance of non-interference in freeing-up 'resources to fight communist insurgency', but the implication that it was thereby used to defend a capitalist social order is never explored (Narine, 2005, p. 475). Instead, the defeat of communist insurgencies is implicitly depicted as a natural, unobjectionable goal. Scholars thus inadvertently side with the ASEAN's authoritarian regimes, which sought to present left-wing movements as enemies of the state and foreign subversives, rather than as people who simply wished to organise their society, economy and politics in a way that threatened existing power relations. This uncritical approach leads to the defence of highly specific societal interests being glossed as the maintenance of 'internal security' and 'stability'. Yet even the maintenance of 'stability' is never neutral since some social groups always benefit disproportionately from the *status quo*.

The role of non-interference in state-making processes is better understood as defining the scope of contestation over how that process should unfold. If one set of social forces is building state apparatuses to suppress another, demands for 'non-interference' are used to buy space and time for them to impose their will on others. It is invoked to block opponents of these forces and their state-making project from drawing on 'external' resources and support that could alter the balance of forces in their struggle. To succeed in defeating 'internal threats' which oppose the construction of social, political and economic order on a territorial-national basis (or simply on the basis favoured by the forces behind an incumbent regime) is not simply a natural, inevitable and desirable stage of political development. It is to inherently advance some societal interests at the expense of others. Limiting the scope of political conflict to the borders of a nation-hyphen-state helps to pre-serves domestic constellations of power and interest that might other-wise be swept away if the artificial territorial boundaries in which it is implicated were removed.

For the sake of completeness, we should note that the *disavowal* of state sovereignty is also used strategically to define the scope of political conflict and thereby advance specific interests and ideological agendas. For example, in the wake of World War II, European states signed a European Convention on Human Rights which bound them to observe certain liberal and democratic principles in their domestic spheres. This deliberately removed fundamental questions about how societies and economies should be governed from the realm of dom-estic political contestation, insulating the capitalist, liberal-democratic state from challenges from radical political forces (Moravcsik, 2000). More recently, the locus of decision-making on domestic and global economic governance has increasingly shifted to inter-elite institutions such as the G8/G20, the International Monetary Fund, the World Bank, the World Trade Organisation, the European Commission and the Euro-pean Central Bank. By diminishing the sovereign autonomy of states to determine their own economic policies, these institutions have helped lock in a form of 'economic constitutionalism' based on neoliberal orthodoxy (Gill, 1994). Their ascendancy reflects the dramatic weakening of organised labour in Western states, which has historically sought to expose economic policy to wider political contestation at the domestic level.[1]

Struggles over how the scope of conflict should be defined have often taken the form of a fundamental clash between rival principles of political organisation. The Cold War, for example, was in part a confrontation between one set of forces seeking to contain political conflicts within territorially-bounded 'nation-states', and another whose political project was premised on a class war that transcended all borders. There was nothing neutral about either way of organising conflict: 'every change in the scope of conflict has a bias; it partisan in nature' because 'every change in scope changes the equation' between the forces in struggle (Schattschneider, 1960, pp. 4–5). For this reason, as Halliday (1999, p. 16) remarks, normative debates about intervention are inescapably partisan:

> The presumption in favour of security, i.e., of those already in power, entails one conception of world order; the presumption against security

entails the other – solidarity with the oppressed, and, where apposite, non-interference by counter-revolution... What appears as a normative debate about international relations, and the pros and cons of intervention, conceals another, *anterior*, debate about the rights and wrongs of states themselves.

Appreciating the crucial strategic role that sovereignty plays in political life in turns helps us to understand intervention. Intervention is typically seen as the negation of sovereignty, but can also be thought of as a necessary component of particular sovereignty *regimes*. That is, intervention is required to help maintain the specific constellations of power and interest that are embedded within certain arrangements of sovereignty. Great power interventions are frequently implicated in a politics of scope, an attempt to assist embattled ruling groups to manage local conflicts and prevent their further contagion, or vice-versa. During the nineteenth century, embattled aristocratic regimes appealed to and were propped up by the forces of the Holy Alliance, which intervened to prevent liberal-nationalist revolutions from spreading across Europe, while internationally-networked forces agitating for national self-determination appealed to Britain to assist their struggles (Hobsbawm, 1973, chs. 5–7). During the Cold War, the explicit US policy of 'containment' sought to limit the contagion of social conflict across territorial borders, while the Brezhnev Doctrine was enforced by Soviet intervention in the event of 'counter-revolution'. Today's economic constitutionalism is policed at the margin through International Monetary Fund (IMF) interventions which try to enforce conformity to neoliberal economic policies, while the 'liberal peace' is managed through humanitarian and state-building interventions. Sovereignty regimes and intervention can therefore be seen as organically linked, almost as two sides of the same coin.

Part of the reason for this intimate relationship between sovereignty regimes and intervention is that both are used to contain and manage social conflicts in a particular direction. As mentioned earlier, important socio-political distinctions frequently overlap state borders. The institutions of territorial sovereignty attempt to curtail this overlap so as to contain political conflict geographically. They often succeed, particularly when supported sympathetically by external forces. However, at other times, such measures are simply insufficient. It is often necessary to police 'external' forces that have linkages to 'internal' forces that threaten powerful interests within the state. For example, anti-communist interventions during the Cold War were often driven by a desire to suppress leftist forces providing inspiration or material support to their counterparts within the intervening state or its allies. As Rosenberg (1994, p. 35) notes, 'a counter-revolutionary foreign policy is rarely just a foreign policy. To a degree which varies with individual cases it is also directed inwards, a nationalist identification of certain programmes of domestic political change with a foreign threat... however much states are compelled to prepare against the possible behaviour of other states, the "international" has also been very much about the management of change in domestic political orders'. A similar case can be made about, say, Israel's wars against Lebanon, which have partly been about curtailing the external bases and support provided to the Palestinian Liberation Organisation and Hamas.

Not all interventions can be neatly explained by reference to relatively abstract, macro-historical sovereignty regimes. Nonetheless, many can be traced back to the specific interests and ideologies of the dominant socio-political coalitions underpinning intervening state power in the intervening state, which are always related to prevailing regimes of sovereignty. On occasion, interventions may also simply be opportunistic efforts to promote powerful, sectional interests, which can be identified using a historical-sociological approach. When dominant socio-political coalitions are relatively stable, patterns of sovereignty and intervention are still likely to emerge. For example, Part II of this book illustrates that the structural power of ASEAN's business classes is expressed through many interventions designed to promote the interests of specific fractions of state-linked capital.

This section has sought to connect the abstract concepts of sovereignty and intervention to the concrete struggles that actually animate political life, by focusing on the strategic value of sovereignty and intervention as a means of controlling the scope of political conflict. Because defining the scope of conflict inherently advances certain socio-political and economic interests and ideologies over others, the politics of sovereignty and intervention are subject to constant contestation, sometimes of a very violent sort. A focus on the social conflict animating this contestation forms the basis of the explanatory strategy used in this book, which is outlined in the next section.

Explaining sovereignty regimes

Because the practices associated with sovereignty and intervention constrain and enable particular political projects, they will naturally be subjected to conflict and contestation by social groups favouring different projects. To explain the sovereignty regimes that emerge in practice, it is therefore necessary to analyse the socio-political coalitions contesting state power, and how they seek to use (non)intervention to further their aims. Thus, although we are still primarily concerned with *state* sovereignty and interventionist practices by state apparatuses, explaining why historical patterns of sovereignty and intervention emerge requires a *non-statist* approach. This section makes use of state theory which disaggregates the state and enquires into the social forces animating in order to grasp whose interests and ideologies are being promoted. However, the interests of dominant forces do not translate directly into sovereignty regimes in a smooth, uncomplicated fashion. Social conflict is always imbricated in and conditioned by broader processes of geopolitical and economic developments which, along with continual contestation of state power and the difficulty of coordinating policies at the interstate level, shape what emerges in practice.

The rejection of a statist approach and the focus on social conflict as the fundamental driver behind sovereignty regimes stems from a basic ontological assumption that power is not some thing or capacity vested in state apparatuses but rather is widely dispersed and inheres in all social action. *De facto* power does not simply 'belong' to the state or inhere in state institutions. It is widely dispersed among many different social forces, such as classes and class fractions, ethnic and religious groups, and so on. The state's very existence gives rise to new societal groups such as bureaucrats and the military. However, although their interests clearly matter in any overall calculus, they are rarely if ever able to simply impose their whims on society (and if they are, this is something to be explained, not explained away).[2] Well-resourced, well-organised social forces have the capacity to resist state practices unfavourable to their interests and to compel state managers to compromise with them through struggling both within and outside of state institutions. Capitalists can withhold investment; workers can withhold their labour; community leaders can implement their own systems of governance rather than uphold the rule of law; wealthy individuals can corrupt officials and buy votes; citizens can withhold their taxes or resist the draft, and so on.

States are consequently powerful only to the extent that leading social forces can mobilise support for state policies and practices among powerful domestic groups, using a range of techniques including ideology, flows of economic concessions, the threat of force, and so on. State power is always 'power "from below"'... the territorial state draws its power in capillary fashion from social groups and institutions rather than simply imposing itself upon them' (Agnew, 2009, p. 89). From this perspective, the neo-Weberian view of states that dominates mainstream political science and IR, which views states as autonomous, coherent actors that stand above and 'do things' to their societies and engage in relations with other states in a relatively autonomous fashion – has to be rejected. As Jessop (1990) argues, states *qua* mere ensembles of institutions are not real subjects at all, but are rather sets of agencies and inscribed capacities activated by determinate social groups.

Furthermore, the very form that states take is powerfully structured by social conflict. As the earlier discussion of territoriality explored, the form in which political authority is organised has very unequal implications for different societal groups. The same is true of specific forms of state, which offer widely varying access for social forces using different strategies to advance different interests and ideologies. Corporatism generally offers better access to state power for trade unions than military dictatorship, for example. Correspondingly, different social forces naturally struggle against one another to establish state forms that will privilege their interests at the expense of others'. As Jessop (2008), following Poulantzas (1976), has argued, what emerges in practice is a contingent accommodation between social forces, reflecting their relative resources, capacities and opportunities for mobilisation and struggle. Dominant socio-political coalitions then seek to use state power to entrench their advantages and to disorganise their opponents. Consequently, the state 'reflects and essentially underpins the prevailing hierarchies of power embodied in the social order', and takes a 'critical, partisan role' in maintaining it (Hewison *et al.*, 1993, p. 6).

Understanding the dominant socio-political coalitions underpinning states, and the battles they are involved in waging against their rivals, is key to appreciating the sovereignty regimes they seek to create. Social forces will naturally try to use state power to create an international environment that is favourable to their own interests, ideologies and strategies of rule, including through trying to construct sovereignty in particular ways and by intervening abroad.[3] Socio-political coalitions whose domination is fragile or highly contested may opt for a strategy of insisting on non-interference in their 'internal' affairs so as to insulate their opponents from outside sources of support, as in the case of many third-world states, including ASEAN. Alternatively (or indeed simultaneously) they may seek assistance from allies abroad and constitutionalise their preferred systems of rule through regional agreements, thus constraining their domestic opponents, as in

Western Europe following World War II. Likewise, unstable socio-political coalitions may seek to sever sources of external support to their internal enemies through interventions. Like the state itself, regimes of sovereignty and patterns of intervention are the result of societal groups seeking to advance their interests and ideologies while disorganising and weakening their opponents.

Of course, these efforts to construct sovereignty regimes do not occur in a vacuum, such that the interests of dominant forces translate directly and uncomplicatedly into international sovereignty regimes. Two points are relevant here. First, as mentioned earlier, the chance of states' individual strategies succeeding depends on prevailing con-stellations of power, interests and ideology at the international level. Interstate cooperation is required to establish stable sovereignty regimes. Historically, this has taken various forms, including great power pacts like the European Concert and the Holy Alliance, regional groupings like the EU and ASEAN, and global arrangements like the UN Charter. However, under conditions of international anarchy, interstate coop-eration is often difficult to achieve. Moreover, certain geostrategic envi-ronments or moments within the evolution of the global economy will favour particular strategies over others. For example, the post-Cold War environment, which is characterised by US hegemony and neoliberal ascendancy, does not afford the same opportunities for a rigid stra-tegy of emphasising absolute sovereignty and non-interference as the Cold War. The societal forces dominating third-world states can no longer enhance their autonomy by playing superpowers off against each other, and their economies are far less nationally-based and much more dependent upon flows of foreign capital. Many states have had to adjust to the new *Zeitgeist* by stressing their commitment to (neo)liberal norms around human rights and 'good governance'. Socio-political coalitions, or the state managers acting on their behalf, always factor such shifting international dynamics into their strategies to craft sovereignty regimes.

More fundamentally, geopolitical changes and global capitalist develop-ment profoundly shape the very nature of these socio-political coalitions. Societies obviously evolve considerably over time, partly as a result of local developments such as the military defeat of rebel groups or the rise of new classes or class fractions as a result of economic development. These changes to the constitution of society can compel changes in the nature of dominant coalitions, and the strategies of rule they use dom-estically and internationally. However, the development of and balance between local forces are always conditioned by broader, global develop-ments. The rise of new class forces, for example, or the destruction of old ones, is powerfully shaped by the articulation of the local economy within an increasingly 'globalised' world economy. The balance between domestic forces is also often affected by geopolitical circumstances. For example, during the Cold War, left-wing forces were seen as far more threatening to the *status quo* than they are today because of their (real or imagined) linkages to two geopolitically significant states, the USSR and communist China. On the other hand, unconditional Western backing often empowered right-wing regimes to take measures against their domestic enemies that would be unfeasible today. The social conflicts shaping sovereignty regimes therefore have to be analysed in relation to the wider geopolitical and economic developments in which they are articulated.

The second reason why dominant forces' interests do not translate smoothly into sovereignty regimes is that, although states are key actors in international life, they are neither alone nor fully coherent. They are not alone because other powerful agents exist with the capacity to shape *de facto* sovereignty, including other states, international institutions, and socio-economic agents like transnational corporations. Societal groups excluded from state power, such as opposition parties or insurgent forces, are also likely to try to contest or overturn the state's official strategy. Moreover, states are not coherent. This is one of the fundamental insights generated by society-centred state theory that is missed by state-centric approaches. States are extremely complex, exhibiting internal divisions, and it is commonplace that different parts of state apparatuses develop particular relationships with or are even captured by different societal groups. Social conflict therefore plays out not merely outside the state but within and between state apparatuses (Jessop, 2008, pp. 36–7). As Migdal (2001, p. 20) observes:

> The sheer unwieldy character of states' far-flung parts, the many fronts on which they fight battles with groupings with conflicting standards of behaviour, and the lure for their officials of alternative sets of rules that might, for example, empower or enrich them personally or privilege the group to which they are most loyal, all have led to diverse practices by states' parts or fragments. Various parts or fragments of the state have allied with one another, as well as with groups outside, to further their goals. Those practices and alliances have acted to promote a variety of sets of rules, often quite distinct from those set out in the state's own official laws and regulations. These alliances, coalitions or networks have neutralised the sharp territorial and social boundary that the [neo-Weberian] portrayal of

the state has acted to establish, as well as the sharp demarcation between the state as preeminent rule maker and society as the recipient of those rules.

Alliances between powerful societal groups and parts of the state apparatus may consequently pursue strategies around sovereignty and intervention quite at odds with the 'official' state policy.

For example, in the early 1990s, the Thai state's official policy was to cease the support it had provided to rebel groups in neighbouring territories in order to facilitate access to their markets by a politically-dominant business class. However, the business, political and military interests which had benefited economically from lucrative black-market trade mediated through the rebel groups resisted this policy shift and ignored it in practice, such that Thai intervention in neighbouring countries actually continued (Rungswasdisab, 2006, pp. 103–11). As we shall see, the Indonesian elite was similarly divided over Cambodia during the Cold War, the Singaporean autocracy hesitated over whether to support Indonesia's invasion of East Timor, and Thai elites have been divided over how to deal with Burma and China. In situations like these, social conflict conditions practices of sovereignty and intervention in two ways: first, through its influence on the state and in setting the basic contours in which state managers develop their strategies, and second in mediating the actual execution (or not) of policy. The more incoherent the state is, the greater the opportunity for a disjuncture between the theory and practice of sovereignty and intervention by that state.

These factors must all be taken into account in explaining exactly what sort of sovereignty regime will actually emerge in practice at the level of a region like ASEAN. Among the geopolitical developments that state managers will be influenced by in formulating their strategies of rule are undoubtedly social, political and economic developments in their near-abroad, and the strategies adopted by their counterparts in nearby states. Official regionalism can be understood as the attempt of state managers to coordinate and thus enhance the efficacy of their strategies of rule. This coordination process is what the vast majority of the IR literature on ASEAN (and other regions) is predominantly concerned with, yet the 'inputs' to it cannot be properly understood without grasping the social conflicts driving state policy. As IR scholars generally recognise, inter-elite coordination is often difficult under conditions of international anarchy. All of the cases we will consider exhibit varying degrees of conflict between ASEAN governments over how or whether to pursue (non)intervention, with significant consequences for the coherence of Southeast Asia's sovereignty regime. Moreover, because states are not fully coherent, even if relative consensus can be achieved among the bureaucracies of foreign ministries, this can always be undermined by powerful forces located elsewhere in regional states pursuing different interests and agendas (Carroll and Sovacool, 2010). Sovereignty regimes can be highly contested at all levels; what emerges in practice can only be grasped as the contingent and dynamically evolving outcome of social conflict. Their stability and coherence depends ultimately upon prevailing constellations of power and interest.

In conclusion, we can explain patterns of sovereignty and intervention with reference to the strategies used by state managers to advance particular societal interests and ideologies over others. Creating particular sovereignty regimes and engaging in intervention is one important way to achieve this because it helps set the scope of political conflict, and thereby shapes its outcome. However, these practices are open to contestation at every step. Because sovereignty regimes are so closely implicated in the state-making process, they will likely be challenged by those forces resisting the forms of social, political and economic order which are being entrenched by state-makers. The state's own internal fragmentation, and its interpenetration with rival social forces, may also condition the state's actual practice of sovereignty and intervention. External challenges may also issue from other states, international agencies or transnational social forces. The coordination of state managers' strategies at the international level is also complex and conflict ridden. What emerges in practice is therefore the contingent outcome of a struggle between all these forces, which must be considered as dynamic, evolving and often interrelated.

Method, evidence and scope

For the sake of clarity and manageability, the analysis is accomplished in two stages and divided into two periods, the Cold War and post-Cold War eras. In the first stage, the first chapter of each period outlines the most politically important conflicts within Southeast Asian societies and their relationship to ASEAN's practice of (non)interference (Chapters 2 and 5). Here, the scholarly literature on Southeast Asian political economy, political sociology and comparative politics is drawn upon heavily and supplemented where possible using primary sources. The task here is to identify the character, interests and ideologies of the dominant socio-political coalitions operating within key

ASEAN states, and to identify the main challenges to their continued domination, emanating both from their own societies and from changes in the global economy and geopolitics.

In this first stage, major interventions by ASEAN states are also identified within their historical context. The development of ASEAN's norm of non-interference and member-states' interventions in other states' affairs are analysed as a technology of power. Their strategic intention and effects are traced back to the attempt of dominant forces, and state managers operating on their behalf, to maintain or advance their interests, ideologies and political projects within evolving social, economic and (geo)political contexts. This requires a critical reading of ASEAN norms and discourse rather than the more usual approach of taking them for granted as a genuine expression of state identities or leaders' moral commitments. As John Foster Dulles once remarked, 'the slogan of non-intervention can plausibly be invoked and twisted to give immunity to what is in reality flagrant intervention' (Wight, 1978, p. 199).

The second stage of the analysis considers specific cases of ASEAN states' interventions in detail. These case studies have three analytical purposes. The first is to establish beyond any doubt their empirical existence. This alone is worthwhile, given the tendency of IR scholars to ignore or marginalise evidence of intervention. The second is to critically assess any existing scholarly interpretations of these events to establish the value of the historical-sociological approach. The third is to show in some depth how these interventions advanced the specific interests and ideologies identified in the chapters framing each historical period.

The case studies selected for close study are, in the Cold War period, East Timor and Cambodia (Chapters 3 and 4), and in the post-Cold War period, Cambodia, East Timor and Burma (Chapters 6, 7 and 8). The case studies are *not* meant to be representative of ASEAN's behaviour towards all states. As we shall see, ASEAN states frequently operate with a double standard, singling some states out for intervention while collaborating strongly with others. The case studies are intended to illustrate the highly selective operation of the non-interference principle in practice and thus to uncover its foundations as socio-political rather than strictly 'normative'. Importantly, the basis of this selectivity is *not* simply whether target states are ASEAN members or not. The chapters reveal numerous instances of intra-ASEAN interventions. These can be explained in a similar fashion to extra-ASEAN interventions, as attempts to manage socio-political and economic order at home and abroad. Finally, focusing on a small number of cases over the course of several decades helps to show how ASEAN's sovereignty regime has evolved over time rather than remaining static or changing only in minor ways as most existing scholarship typically assumes.

The definition of 'intervention' adopted for this study is a broad one: 'activity undertaken by a state, a group within a state or an international organisation which interferes in the domestic affairs of another state' (Vincent, 1974, p. 13). To restrict studies of intervention to, say, military invasions, is unduly narrow. It obscures the wide variety of other means used to limit or violate sovereignty, such as arms transfers, pressure to adopt specific policies, economic aid or sanctions, electoral manipulation, sabotage, aid conditionality, and so on. A broad understanding of intervention is doubly necessary given ASEAN's own expansive interpretation of the term (see Introduction). ASEAN states deserve to be judged by their own, supposedly high standards. This does not, however, imply documenting every petty insult traded across state boundaries. Not only would this be tedious, it would also falsely imply the absence of far more serious interventions. As will become clear, I focus on important events involving war, annexation, proxy conflicts, military and civil assistance, membership conditionality, and soft-peddled regime change.

Furthermore, I do not consider only collective interventions by ASEAN as a grouping. ASEAN member-states are so rarely capable of acting *en bloc* that they have had to institute formulas that allow 'regional' cooperation to proceed on an ASEAN-minus-*x* or even a two-plus-*x* basis. Focusing solely on what ASEAN agrees on collectively would unduly overlook vast amounts of state behaviour. Moreover, exploring member-states' conduct is the only way to actually test the proposition that they are bound by a regional norm of non-interference. Crucially, member-states' inability to reach consensus does *not* necessarily constitute evidence for this proposition. If we observe some ASEAN states intervening but others not, and no collective agreement on intervention is reached, it is clearly illogical to claim that the lack of a corporate ASEAN policy proves the power of non-interference. It would merely prove member-states' inability to reach consensus – which can be explained by reference to the social conflicts underpinning each state's position and the difficulties of coordinating divergent policies. These difficulties are common to all states in an anarchical environment; there is arguably nothing particularly special about ASEAN in this regard.

A broad definition of intervention also usefully encompasses actions not only official government actions but also behaviour by 'groups within a state'. This is vital given the understanding of state power out-lined above, where particular state apparatuses are often interpenetrated with societal groups and can diverge from official policy. Again, this does not mean, say, counting how many times a merchant crosses a border and calling this 'intervention'. However, serious cases of wilful disregard of state sovereignty by, say, powerful state-linked business interests work-ing with elements of the state apparatus, should be considered as inter-vention. This *wilful* element – the clear (often political) intent to interfere in a state's affairs – is particularly important since it distinguishes the political act of intervention from mere interdependence.

A broad and relatively neutral approach to identifying intervention is also helpful in cutting through some of the contradictions and ambi-guity surrounding ASEAN's specific non-interference principle. We may recall that, along with refraining from criticising foreign governments or supporting rebel groups seeking their overthrow, Acharya (2009a, p. 72) includes as part of his typical definition of non-interference 'providing political support and material assistance to member states in their campaign against subversive and destabilising activities'. It should be clear from the foregoing that this actually constitutes a form of inter-vention in support of prevailing power relations, not non-intervention. The fact that it is welcomed by the government of the target state should not mask the fact that such actions are inevitably intended to preserve or change political arrangements in that territory. That they are apparently not considered by elites or analysts as violations of 'non-interference' indicates that, rather than conveying an abstract commitment to state sovereignty and total non-intervention, it seems to indicate a pact to shore up the *status quo* by any means necessary. Thus, although I do not primarily focus in depth on intra-ASEAN interventions, these will be covered and are considered as a form of intervention.

As the foregoing may suggest, the method used in this study is his-torical and interpretive. It consists largely of historical, analytical nar-rative since, as Rosenberg (1994, pp. 103–4) argues, without narrative, 'it is impossible to recover the dynamic social content of the processes which we study in IR. *Without that content, we cannot see what those pro-cesses are actually about*'. Since these processes are inter-related, 'and *because those real inter-relations are dynamic and transforming, they cannot be grasped except through a narrative format of explanation*'. The evidence used to construct this narrative is necessarily partial. All ASEAN scholars face serious barriers to gathering high-quality data, including the inaccess-ibility of national archives, the blandness of publicly-available official documents, and the reluctance of policymakers to divulge information in interviews. These difficulties were exacerbated by the political sensitivity of (non)intervention. For the project to be viable, as many sources as possible had to be canvassed, including American, Australian and British government archives, elite interviews, official documents, secondary literature, and national and international media. The result is very well grounded by the standards of the field. Nonetheless, its argument and conclusions are necessarily tentative and subject to the discovery of new data.

Finally, the analysis of social reality, historically or otherwise, can only be an interpretive act. While every care has been taken to substantiate arguments and assertions, and to assess the validity of sources using triangulation and comparison with other, stronger sources and the overall context, the facts may support alternative interpretations. Ultimately, readers must judge the account for themselves on pragmatic grounds, asking whether it offers a more convincing description and interpretation of events than existing scholarship.

Brief outline of the argument

Part I covers the Cold War. Chapter 2 delineates the implications of social conflict in ASEAN states for the development of ASEAN and its sovereignty regime. I argue that ASEAN was essentially an alliance of authoritarian, capitalist elites threatened by internal rebellions seen as linked to foreign communist revolutions. Non-interference emerged to reduce intra-ASEAN conflicts and thereby strengthen existing social orders against 'subversion'. ASEAN states intervened unsuccessfully to prevent communist forces seizing power in Indochina, and also failed to induct these regimes into its sovereignty regime. ASEAN thus continued to intervene against these radical forces seen as aiding their own communist insurgencies.

Chapter 3 shows how, aided and abetted by ASEAN diplomatically and materially, Indonesia intervened in and eventually annexed East Timor in 1975 to prevent the emergence of another radical state in the region that could destabilise ASEAN's social orders. Chapter 4 explores ASEAN's response to Vietnam's 1978 invasion of Cambodia. ASEAN waged diplomatic and proxy war against Vietnam and Cambodia to contain what it saw as Vietnam's revolutionary expansion. This involved manipulating Cambodia's ousted regime and other guerrilla groups, and Cambodian refugees, to form a military 'buffer' against Vietnam, and an alliance with China whereby Beijing ceased supporting ASEAN's communist insurgencies.

Chapter 5 introduces Part II, delineating social conflict in ASEAN states and its consequences for (non)intervention after the Cold War. I explore this period at greater length, partly because it displays multiple and complex logics in comparison to the Cold War period and partly because it is more relevant to contemporary concerns. Chapter 5 argues that the containment of communism enabled powerful, illiberal business classes to arise and dominate ASEAN polities. Non-interference shifted meaning and focus to defend these opaque power structures from the West's new liberalisation agenda. Meanwhile the new oligarchs, resisted by elements of the old rich, used state power to wind down defunct anti-communist interventions to pursue their business interests in Burma and Indochina. ASEAN also staked a claim to manage its own regional affairs, safe from Western meddling. However, the preservation of this status required that ASEAN take interventionist action on areas of Western concern, like Burma's military regime. Pressure to do so has mounted since the profoundly debilitating 1997 Asian financial crisis. ASEAN states' attempts to recover from the crisis by embracing 'good governance' reforms has created powerful imperatives to intervene in member-states' internal affairs to avoid further damage to core states' domestic and international standing.

Chapter 6 considers the case of post-Cold War Cambodia. ASEAN's withdrawal from anti-communist intervention was repeatedly impaired by the actions of powerful politico-business and military elites who continued meddling in Cambodian politics for their own gain. This fuelled instability in Cambodia, contributing to the breakdown of the coalition government in 1997. ASEAN responded by imposing creeping conditionality for ASEAN membership on Cambodia, collaborating with Western aid donors to isolate Cambodia until the coalition was restored.

Chapter 7 considers ASEAN's intervention in East Timor. Until the Asian financial crisis, ASEAN's continued support for Indonesia's occupation of East Timor was secured through Indonesian coercion, often mediated through regional business networks. However, Jakarta decided to hold a referendum on East Timor's status to offset Western pressure after the financial crisis, resulting in a vote for independence. Resisted by powerful military-business elites, this precipitated a humanitarian crisis in the territory. The financial crisis had already emphasised the interdependence between ASEAN states' social, political and economic orders, and events in Timor only underlined this by raising the spectre of Indonesia's fragmentation and the contagion of unrest to the wider region. Core ASEAN states consequently promoted and joined a UN intervention force to contain the disorder emanating from Indonesia. Chapter 8 explores ASEAN's Burma policy. It shows how the policy of 'constructive engagement' sought to balance between the new rich's desire to gain access to Burmese markets and meet Western demands for ASEAN to help deliver political reform in Burma. Attempts to enhance ASEAN's interventionist posture by government of liberal, middle-class reformers in Thailand (1997–2000) were resisted by its domestic opponents and most other ASEAN states. The clear failure of constructive engagement by 2003, however, badly damaged ASEAN's international standing and economic relations with the West. ASEAN has since sought various ways to insert itself into Burma's democratisation process, becoming increasingly condemnatory and abandoning its conditional defence of Burma in international forums.

Part I
The Cold War

2
The Social Foundations of ASEAN and 'Non-Interference'

> It was the fact that there was a convergence in the political
> outlook of the five prospective member-nations... which pro-
> vided the main stimulus to join together in ASEAN.
> – *Adam Malik, Indonesian Foreign Minister* (Khong, 1997, p. 327)

ASEAN was founded in 1967, in the wake of war between Indonesia
and Malaysia, and amidst the wreckage of several failed regional cooperation initiatives. Since then, armed conflict among its member-states
has been relatively minimal, leading many observers to identify ASEAN
as the developing world's most successful regional organisation. Its
success is often attributed to the adoption of non-interference as a
cardinal principle of regional order, which underpinned a sub-regional
reconciliation mechanism, or even the creation of a regional identity.
This chapter offers an alternative reading of ASEAN's origins and evolution. The claim that non-interference successfully created a stable
international order is undermined by the fact of continued interventionist practices by ASEAN states throughout the Cold War. What
actually changed with ASEAN's foundation was that the forces controlling the member-states – which were, by 1967, all aligned in an
anti-communist direction for the first time – began collaborating
with each other to shore up rather than undermine their respective
domestic orders. This meant that intra-ASEAN interventions were
reoriented to help defeat insurgencies and other challenges, while extra-
ASEAN interventions continued against radical forces seen as linked to
these 'internal' rebellions.

'Non-interference' was thus not a neutral principle designed to further
some abstract desire for peace and international stability. It certainly
sought to transcend intra-ASEAN conflicts, but this was to permit ruling

elites to consolidate their own grip over society and achieve the economic growth necessary to undercut the appeal of communism, within an international context of waning Western guarantees to defend anti-communist regimes from opposition forces within their own societies. Their goal was to uphold and institutionalise a particular, capitalist social order which conferred disproportionate costs and benefits on different parts of society. This vision of political, social and economic order was often violently contested by other social forces. 'Non-interference' was strategically used to limit the scope of this contestation to a level where it could be managed and overcome by the forces dominating ASEAN states. Re-historicising the emergence of ASEAN and 'non-interference' and explaining what interests they were designed to serve is necessary to understand why non-interference was, in practice, always deployed very selectively. Interventions, which continued both within and outside ASEAN, against forces opposed to elites' preferred vision of social and political order, were an integral part of ASEAN's *de facto* sovereignty regime.

The chapter is divided into two sections. The first part traces the roots of ASEAN and non-interference in the social conflicts underpinning the Malaysia-Indonesian war and the victory of authoritarian, pro-capitalist forces in this conflict. It shows how both non-interference and intervention were used by these forces to help stabilise a particular socio-political order and defend it from 'subversion', through cooperation against insurgents and involvement in the violent conflicts raging in neighbouring countries. The second part turns directly to these conflicts in Indochina. It traces the growing emphasis on 'non-interference', and continued interventions alongside the US, as an attempt to insulate social order in non-communist Southeast Asia from the growing threat of communism.

From *Konfrontasi* to ASEAN

ASEAN was formed after the 1963–66 'confrontation' (*Konfrontasi*) between Malaysia and Indonesia. Rather than theorising ASEAN as a benign mechanism for post-conflict reconciliation, however, this section explores what *Konfrontasi* was actually about in order to grasp the interests involved in transcending it. The war expressed a transnational struggle over the form of social and political order that should prevail in post-colonial Southeast Asia. It was ended by the decisive defeat of the Indonesian left, which brought the Indonesian state into alignment with its anti-communist neighbours. ASEAN's formation – and its principle of non-interference – represented an international elite pact designed to stabilise their respective social, political and economic orders and prevent radical change.

Konfrontasi ultimately expressed the deep social and political conflicts that had swept East and Southeast Asia since World War II. Japan's seizure of European colonies during the war, and its promotion of nationalist forces during its occupation, shattered the myth of European invulnerability and radicalised significant sections of Asia's population. When the European powers tried to reoccupy their colonies, they faced resistance from nationalist forces in Indonesia, Burma and Indochina. The radical wings of such movements were seen as particularly problematic for imperialist interests, since they threatened not just political but social and economic revolution, involving the seizure of Western economic assets and the potential severing of vital strategic trading relationships.

The Cold War context exacerbated these concerns, since revolutionaries were often seen as linked to Moscow and particularly communist China. Many nationalists took inspiration from socialism, and organised communist parties also emerged across the region. Many of the latter recruited heavily from Southeast Asia's ethnic-Chinese population. Combined with the new People's Republic of China granting automatic citizenship to so-called 'overseas Chinese', this meant that ethnic-Chinese individuals were often viewed as having dubious political loyalties or even as a potential 'fifth column' throughout the Cold War. The imperial powers gradually recognised that they could not simply resume control of the region under such changed circumstances. Instead, they sought to create a post-colonial settlement that would preserve their basic interests and prevent communist advances in Southeast Asia by blocking the ascent to power of radical nationalist or communist elements.

This pattern was clearly displayed in Britain's post-war policy in Malaya. Here, the radical challenge came from mostly ethnically-Chinese labourers who had occupied agricultural plantations during the war and now resisted attempts to displace them, forming the Malaya Communist Party (MCP) to defend their interests. Britain fought a long colonial war, known as the 'Emergency', from 1948–1960 to defeat the MCP, pitching at its height 65,000 British and Commonwealth troops against 10,000 communist guerrillas. Through a combination of violence, forced displacement of rural populations, and political concessions, Britain managed to isolate the predominantly ethnically-Chinese MCP from the majority Malay population and then mobilise popular anti-Chinese sentiment against its remnants. In the meantime, a moderate nationalist force had emerged in the form of the United Malay National Organisation (UMNO), led by a group of anti-communist, ethnic-Malay aristocrats. UMNO's programme involved preserving propertied interests and ethnic-Malay domination, and was compatible with Britain's long-term interests in the region. Britain thus decolonised Malaya in 1953, handing control to an UMNO-led government in 1953 on the under-standing that it would continue to suppress communism. UMNO took power alongside smaller, subordinate coalition partners representing the non-communist elements of the ethnic Chinese and Indian populations.

UMNO's efforts to maintain a non-communist social order in Malaya involved attempts to control the scope of political conflict in ways that had important geostrategic implications. To defeat the MCP, it was necessary to insulate it from sources of external support. UMNO leaders believed that this was most likely to come from Singapore, where the political left was advanced, well-organised, and also predominantly ethnic-Chinese. In order to neutralise this threat and to 'pre-empt [the emergence of] a "Cuba" in the region', UMNO leaders and Britain agreed to incorporate Singapore into Malayan territory, where the left could be effectively policed by the Malayan state (Singh, 1994, p. 194). However, this would create an ethnic-Chinese majority in the country, under-mining UMNO's ability to retain Malay dominance democratically. Kuala Lumpur thus also sought to absorb Britain's territories in Borneo, where the population was overwhelmingly Malay.

This plan for a 'Malaysian Federation' was strenuously resisted by Singapore and Borneo's leftist forces, which rightly feared that Malaya's draconian internal security laws and military repression would be extended to crush them. While Singapore's communist party agitated against merger, the left-wing People's Party of Brunei (PRB), which had won all the seats in Brunei's first democratic elections in 1962, launched an armed uprising against the Federation, seeking to establish an independent north Borneo state. The revolt was crushed by British troops, the constitution suspended and the PRB banned. The plan for the Malaysian Federation continued apace, with its completion scheduled for 1965.

In neighbouring Indonesia, the path to independence had been markedly different, setting it on a collision course with Malaysia. The Netherlands had tried to reassert control over its empire in Southeast Asia after the war, but faced strong resistance from Indonesian nationalists, which eventually compelled it to depart. The Indonesian left played a sig-nificant role in this struggle and, unlike the MCP, consequently emerged from the 1945–50 war of independence as a political force that could not be marginalised or ignored. The left's influence was heavily expressed in

Indonesia's crusading, anti-imperialist foreign policy as Jakarta hosted the 1955 Bandung conference and helped to found the Non-Aligned Movement (NAM). However, the left also co-existed uneasily with contradictory social forces, notably traditional feudal elites, moderate nationalists, and Islamist forces.

The post-independence government headed by President Sukarno thus sought to balance between these elements, creating a syncretic ideology marrying nationalism, religion and communism (Leifer, 1983, ch. 1–4). The main beneficiary of this balancing act was the left. By 1965, the Indonesian Communist Party (PKI) was the largest outside the communist bloc, with over three million members – many of whom held political and bureaucratic office – and twelve million members in affiliated organisations (Cribb, 2001, p. 229; Alexander, 1999, p. 253). The country's gradual shift to the left severely alarmed right-wing elements in the army and other establishment groups, which collaborated in a series of secessionist revolts in the 1950s in order to preserve their privileges. Some of these rebellions attracted active US backing, and the Sukarno regime survived only by rallying moderate nationalists and the left around an anti-imperialist crusade, shifting the state even further leftwards. Indonesia's intensifying social conflict could no longer be contained within democratic institutions, which were limited and then suspended. By the early 1960s, Sukarno effectively depended on the PKI and the army to conduct the government's day-to-day business. When the plan for the Malaysian Federation was announced, in order to retain the PKI's support, Sukarno was forced to assist their allies in Singapore and Borneo by opposing the 'imperialist' scheme. He initially succeeded in persuading the Malayan government to hold a popular consultation in Borneo. However, when they reneged on this pledge, Sukarno had little option but to launch *Konfrontasi* and pledge to 'crush Malaysia' (Leifer, 1983, ch. 4).

What looks superficially like an *international* conflict, then, was actually very much about the management of *domestic* social order. *Konfrontasi* pitched the territorial requirements of the Malayan state's anti-communist struggle against Sukarno's attempts to manage the tensions between the rising PKI and right-wing nationalist forces in the army. Initially, the Philippine elite, combating their own communist insurgencies, also backed Sukarno's campaign, fearing the possible infiltration of Singaporean radicals into the Philippines via neighbouring Borneo if the Malaysian Federation was formed (Wurfel, 1990, p. 160). The conflict was about territorial sovereignty only insofar as it related to the attempt to scope and manage domestic social conflict in particular ways to uphold specific internal orders. The Malaysian foreign minister told the US that, if power was appropriately devolved, Malaysia would even be willing to enter a federation with Indonesia to resolve *Konfrontasi* as this 'would be the only way of keeping Communism out of the area'.[1]

With roots deep in the social conflicts animating the combatant states, *Konfrontasi* could only be terminated after radical socio-political change on one side or another. With British forces resolutely backing Malaysia, this meant Indonesia, where *Konfrontasi* dramatically intensified the struggle for power. Growing economic problems and military defeats pushed Sukarno into seeking aid from Beijing, withdrawing from the UN to found a 'conference of emerging powers' and declaring a 'Jakarta-Phnom Penh-Hanoi-Pyongyang axis'. He was also forced to promise the PKI a greater role in government, generating panic among the Indonesian establishment. The country's incipient bourgeoisie was too weak to resist, so the army acted on its behalf (Robison, 1986, p. 88). Senior generals had acquired a direct stake in capitalist property relations in the 1960s, having seized control of former Dutch enterprises that had been expropriated by striking workers. The profits from these businesses were vital in keeping the under-funded army afloat, but were now endangered by a rising red tide and the economic chaos accompanying *Konfrontasi*. Consequently, in October 1965, senior right-wing elements in the army leadership headed by General Suharto seized power, claiming to have pre-empted a communist coup. Supported by business leaders, the urban middle classes, students, and rural elites, and backed by the US, they initiated a bloody crackdown on suspected leftists, killing up to a million people and imprisoning a further 750,000 (Cribb, 2001, pp. 233–6). The PKI's power was decisively broken, with its shattered remnants fighting short-lived insurgencies or fleeing to Beijing. Suharto, who had been negotiating with Malaysia behind Sukarno's back (Anwar, 1994, pp. 29–30), quickly terminated *Konfrontasi*, and installed himself as president in 1967, declaring a 'New Order' in Indonesia.

This violent evisceration of the Indonesian left paved the way for the formation of ASEAN. The future member-states were now ruled by viscerally anti-communist regimes willing to cooperate to crush the growing class-based challenges to their domination. The absence of this condition had thwarted earlier attempts at regionalism. Thailand, Malaysia and the Philippines had tried to collaborate against communism through an Association of Southeast Asia (ASA), founded in 1961. According to Thailand's foreign minister, Thanat Khoman, ASA represented an effort to 'collaborate and strengthen [member-states] internally while the Vietnamese situation awaits political solution'. Its main goal was to foster the stability necessary to enable economic growth because, Thanat explained, 'to the extent that we achieve political, economic and social progress at home we strengthen our ability to withstand political subversion' (Pollard, 1970, pp. 251, 246). ASA was thus a pact designed to strengthen elites' struggles against communist insurrections in their own societies. It was essentially killed off, however, by *Konfrontasi*, which pitched Malaysia and the Philippines against each other, illustrating the Indonesian left's capacity to disrupt counter-revolution across the region.

With the Indonesian state now captured by anti-communist forces, however, a new inter-elite pact serving the now-shared goal of maintaining capitalist social order was possible. The need for such a pact was, if anything, even more pressing by 1967 than in 1961. The Malaysian state was still combating the MCP. In 1965, the Communist Party of Thailand (CPT) had launched armed struggle against the Thai state, a constitutional monarchy dominated by bureaucratic, military and business elites. By 1968 the CPT was launching significant attacks on the US bases used to launch bombing raids on Vietnam (Huxley, 1983, p. 4). By 1970, the CPT comprised 5,000 guerrillas and 25,000 supporters and was effectively governing hundreds of thousand of people (Alexander, 1999, p. 304). In the Philippines, a landlord-dominated government was combating a communist insurgency, which had begun before America decolonised the country in 1946. By 1967, the insurgency had achieved a mass base of nearly 30,000, seizing control of Central Luzon, site of the Clark US Air Force base. America's Central Intelligence Agency (CIA) predicted a 'major insurgent threat' and a 'vast social upheaval in the near future'.[2] Also keen to cooperate against the left was the government of newly-independent Singapore, where the People's Action Party (PAP) had ridden to power on the back of the left, only to destroy it through draconian security measures and usher in a developmentalist and fiercely anti-communist, one-party state.

Unsurprisingly, therefore, the new Association of Southeast Asian Nations, founded at Bangkok in 1967, 'expressed motivations and purposes strikingly similar to those of ASA' (Pollard, 1970, p. 256). The Bangkok Declaration articulated apparently unobjectionable goals like 'peace, progress and prosperity', 'cultural development' and 'peaceful community', but its fundamental aim was to preserve the prevailing social order – described as 'strengthening the economic and social stability of the region' (ASEAN, 1967). The Declaration indicated that this was primarily to be accomplished through economic cooperation. As Singapore's deputy prime minister argued, echoing Thanat's earlier remarks, 'the first defence is economic. Provide the masses not only with a decent living but also hope of continuing improvement in the future, and you have the best safeguard against Communist revolution' (Alexander, 1999, p. 304). Suharto now added his voice to such calls, urging cooperation to foster economic development in order to 'destroy the remnants of the Communist party' and 'resist subversion and aggression'.[3]

Although this anti-communist rationale was not made explicit, it nonetheless underpinned all that ASEAN did. Thanat stated that during the negotiations for the Bangkok Declaration, Indonesian foreign minister Adam Malik had insisted that this undeclared political logic must guide 'the development of anti-communist institutions and processes' (Sit, 1995, p. 45). As Singapore's prime minister, Lee Kuan Yew (2000, pp. 369–70), put it:

> The unspoken objective was to gain strength through solidarity ahead of the power vacuum that would come with an impending British and later a possible US withdrawal... We had a common enemy – the communist threat in guerrilla insurgencies, backed by North Vietnam, China and the Soviet Union. We needed stability and growth to counter and deny the communists the social and economic conditions for revolutions... While ASEAN's declared objectives were economic, social and cultural, all knew that progress in economic cooperation would be slow. We were banding together more for political objectives, stability and security.

Lee's foreign minister, S. Rajaratnam (2006c, p. 104), emphasised that 'the motivation behind ASEAN was not belief in the merits of regionalism as such, but it was more a response... to the Western abandonment of its role as a shield against communism'.

Commensurately, ASEAN's principle of non-interference, which was first articulated in the Bangkok Declaration, was also designed to help elites advance their preferred vision of social and political order. It expressed member-states' determination 'to ensure stability and security from external interference in any form or manifestation in order to preserve their national identities' (ASEAN, 1967). By asserting state managers' determination to 'preserve their national identities' it presented domestic socio-political arrangements as already fixed and pre-determined. As Rajaratnam (2006b, p. 102) claimed, their 'people have made it abundantly clear that communism is not for them'. In reality, as we have seen, ASEAN societies were in profound turmoil with various social groups violently contesting the meaning of 'national identity' or even struggling for a form of political organisation based not on nations at all but on transnational class solidarity. Declaring that communism had already been rejected by ASEAN's peoples deliberately externalised left-wing politics as an alien, illegitimate activity. It implied that leftist unrest could *only* be the result of 'external intervention' and foreign 'subversion'. In reality the region's insurgencies were 'rooted firmly in internal social, economic, and political contradictions'. Vast disparities in wealth and power were common to all ASEAN societies, yet were being defended by state power. By depicting challenges to these unequal social relations as alien and directed by foreign powers, the non-interference principle delegitimised any leftist – or even moderately liberal – attempts to influence domestic politics, while legitimising the use of violent suppression and the exclusion of opposition forces from state power. It also conveniently implied that 'those who benefited from... [the] economic, political and social status quo need not relinquish any of their privileges as part of a solution to the insurgency' (Huxley, 1983, pp. 7–8).

The non-interference principle also sought to prevent leftist forces from widening the scope of political conflict beyond 'national' borders where they could draw in aid and support from their allies. Because of the influence of Maoism and widespread suspicion of ethnic-Chinese populations' loyalties, China was particularly feared as an external supporter of 'subversion'. Regional communist parties did receive moral and political support and training from Beijing, plus limited material support like the provision of broadcast facilities in southern China (Halliday, 1999, pp. 111–15, 139–40, 204). 'Non-interference' declared such support illegitimate, while placing no such restrictions on the anti-communist forces controlling ASEAN states, which continued to receive vastly disproportionate external assistance from Western states throughout the Cold War.

The non-interference principle thus expressed the attempt of ASEAN state managers to restrict the scope of post-colonial socio-political conflict to a national level. Here, conflicts could be contained and managed in a way that suited *status quo* interests: geographically, within the artificial borders bequeathed by colonial powers, and institutionally, within nation-state structures which systematically excluded leftist forces. The goal here was not to 'preserve national identities' but to create space in order forcibly to manufacture them as part of an authoritarian, capitalist state-making project. This project was described by the head of Thailand's Internal Security Operations Command as a process by which 'we colonised our own people' (Girling, 1981, pp. 263–4). This was particularly true of social groups whose loyalty to the Thai state was dubious at best and among whom the CPT was heavily based: ethnic-Lao in the northeast, Malay Muslims in the south, and hill-tribes in the north. Likewise, for Singapore's foreign minister, S. Rajaratnam (2006a, p. 165), nation-building 'required that we perform some sort of collective lobotomy' on the population, to destroy transnational loyalties not oriented towards the PAP-dominated state. To insist on 'non-interference' in these violent and coercive processes was a highly partisan move designed to bolster the position of dominant social forces and their chance of preserving territorially-based, non-communist political orders.

ASEAN and its non-interference principle are therefore best understood not primarily as contributions to regional order or identity, as the mainstream IR literature suggests, but as a means by which ruling forces sought to impose their preferred vision of domestic order on their societies. Because there is nothing neutral about the state-making and territorialising processes they were engaged in, there is therefore nothing neutral about principles like non-interference which are designed to insulate them from political contestation. Having thus uncovered the social origins of ASEAN and non-interference, the chapter next shows how social conflict governed the evolution of non-interference and how it operated in practice both within ASEAN and externally.

Indochina: Non-interference and intervention

To get a better sense of how the non-interference principle was guided by the ultimate motive of defending capitalist social order, we need to examine its role in actual state practice. Doing so rapidly clarifies that non-interference did not uniformly constrain state behaviour but was selectively deployed. This selectivity was governed by the requirements of domestic social order: while destabilising intra-ASEAN interventions were abandoned, interventions continued to be used against forces regarded as a radical threat to the *status quo*, both within and outside ASEAN. This argument is very different to mainstream analyses. Many scholars recognise that non-interference initially sprang from concerns around what is loosely called 'regime security'. However, most then claim that the norm exercised a restraining effect on state behaviour independently of its origins, even 'redefining state interests and creating collective interests and identities' (Acharya, 2009a, pp. 71, 24). By contrast, this section argues that the operation of institutions like norms is powerfully shaped by the ongoing processes of social conflict that initially generated them.

'Non-interference' was starkly different in its internal and external applications, but nonetheless displayed a fundamental coherence. Internally, the principle was deployed to terminate the mutual interventions of the past to help create political stability, which was in turn required to achieve the economic development necessary to undercut the appeal of communism. This implied terminating support for each other's insurgencies, even where some narrow national benefit could be obtained, in order to avoid creating instability that the left could exploit. As Rajaratnam (2006d, p. 91) put it, 'we must think not only of our national interests but posit them against regional interests'.

Shortly after ASEAN's formation, for example, Malaysia discovered that guerrillas were being trained at a Philippine base to infiltrate Sabah, a province claimed by both countries. Malaysia retaliated by breaking diplomatic relations and sending arms to the Moro National Liberation Front (MNLF), an insurgent group operating in Mindanao, in the southern Philippines. Indonesia and Thailand sought to mediate the dispute, while Washington also pressed Manila to back down.[4] By 1968, the two governments had normalised their relations, promising to cease supporting each other's rebels 'because of the great value Malaysia and the Philippines placed on ASEAN' (Antolik, 1990, pp. 74–6). The dispute was shelved to maintain the inter-elite regional pact and to prevent destabilising conflict that might create opportunities for the left.

Nonetheless, this did not imply that ASEAN states disengaged entirely from each other's domestic affairs. Rather, they continued to intervene, but now to help shore up the political and economic *status quo*, rather than disrupt it. As Rajaratnam (2006f, p. 93) explains, this was necessary because the region's domestic orders were felt to be 'interdependent': 'what happens in one ASEAN country can affect the fate of the rest for better or worse. We are like passengers travelling in the same boat. We are separate entities but with a common interest – that the boat should not sink lest we all sink with it'. In line with the prevailing 'domino theory', the general elite perception was that a communist upsurge or victory in one ASEAN state would energise radical forces in the rest, while demoralising supporters of the *status quo*.

The forces occupying ASEAN states therefore collaborated against challenges to their domination, believing that enhancing each other's resilience would reinforce their own. Along the Malaysian-Indonesian border in Borneo, *Konfrontasi* gave way to coordinated, bilateral military campaigns against communist guerrillas. Over the next 15 years, Indonesian and Malaysian mediation in Mindanao helped sever Libya's support for the MNLF, defusing a major challenge to the Marcos dictatorship.

Malaysia and Thailand also cooperated militarily against MCP, CPT and Muslim separatist insurgents along their common border (Antolik, 1990, pp. 78–81, 54–60). By the mid-1970s, counterinsurgency cooperation agreements had been established between nearly all ASEAN governments. Indonesia also sought to stiffen the 'national resilience' of its non-communist allies by despatching military trainers and advisors to Malaysia, and advising Thailand's regime on ideology and development to help it resist communism.[5]

Although the non-interference principle thus involved a step-change in intra-ASEAN relations, it made very little difference to member-states' external conduct. ASEAN states continued intervening in their near abroad in order to weaken radical political forces and to disrupt actual or potential alliances between them and their own insurgent groups. Intervention abroad was seen as necessary to manage social order at home and was thus a crucial part of ASEAN's sovereignty regime.

Thailand's anti-communist government had begun intervening like this in the 1950s when, with the US, it had supported a Guomindang army that had retreated into Burma following the Chinese civil war. In exchange for cash and arms, which it paid for by trafficking opium through the CIA and the Thai army, the Guomindang battled the powerful Burmese Communist Party (BCP), keeping it at bay from Thailand's northeast, where the CPT was heavily based. Later, the Guomindang were partially resettled in Thailand, acting as an anti-communist *gendarmerie* along the border and within hill tribe villages targeted by the CPT. Until the late 1980s, Thailand also backed anti-communist ethnic insurgencies within Burma to create a buffer zone and prevent the CPT and BCP from linking up (Smith, 1991, pp. 120, 153, 172, 176–96, 213–16, 293–9).

ASEAN states also intervened in the Indochina War alongside the US to try to prevent communist forces coming to power. Thailand and the Philippines were members of the Southeast Asian Treaty Organisation (SEATO), sending troops and support units to South Vietnam and hosting US forces on their territory. Thailand took a particularly active role in covert operations in Indochina. Bangkok supported right-wing guerrilla movements fighting the neutral Cambodian and Laotian governments, hosting them on Thai soil (Huxley, 1983, p. 16; Chanda, 1986, p. 380). Thailand also sponsored repeated assassination attempts against Cambodia's ruler, Prince Sihanouk, who was considered too soft on communism (Chandler, 2000, p. 192). Malaysia also supported the South Vietnamese regime. It provided jungle warfare training to over 5,000 South Vietnamese officers and counter-insurgency training to US troops, transferred surplus military equipment left over from the 'Emergency' (including 641 Armoured Personnel Carriers and 56,000 rifles), and provided civil assistance, including transportation equipment, cholera vaccines and flood relief.[6]

The root of these interventions was the 'domino theory' belief that the fall of non-communist regimes in Indochina would inexorably lead to the communist overthrow of ASEAN regimes. In 1966, Lee Kuan Yew had told the American vice-president that if US forces failed in Vietnam, 'there would be fighting in Thailand within one-and-a-half to two years, in Malaysia shortly thereafter, and within three years, "I would be hanging in the public square"'.[7] These fears heightened as the US was increasingly worn down by the Viet Cong. Signalling America's desire to extract itself from the Vietnamese quagmire, the 1969 'Nixon doctrine' announced that US forces would no longer be used to prop up anti-communist regimes, and the following year Washington stopped bombing Indochina. The *de facto* US defeat electrified Southeast Asia's communist movements, prompting near panic in some ASEAN capitals. Malaysia had imposed emergency rule in 1969 after serious race riots following electoral gains for ethnic-Chinese parties. The government now faced a rapid upsurge in MCP activity (Stubbs, 1990, p. 115). In Thailand, a dramatic intensification of the CPT insurgency prompted the military to seize power in November 1971, claiming that the country's bourgeois parliamentarians were incapable of maintaining 'internal security' (Keefer, 2001, pp. 21, 86, 173, 242, 307–9, 315). Marcos declared martial law in the Philippines in 1972, stating that his government was 'imperilled by the danger of violent overthrow' by communists (Kessler, 1989, pp. 18, 41).

This intensified social conflict explains why ASEAN states' interventions accelerated rather than abating as the creation of the non-interference principle would superficially suggest. The intra-ASEAN counter-insurgency cooperation described above was largely a response to this upsurge in communist agitation. While maintaining a thin veneer of non-alignment, Suharto's New Order regime also intervened to contain communism in Indochina. Indonesian military intelligence encouraged a US-backed coup in Cambodia by General Lon Nol which overthrew Sihanouk (Leifer, 1983, p. 132). Jakarta sent covert arms shipments to the new regime and offered to act as an intermediary for further US aid which would 'otherwise compromise Cambodian neutrality'. Indonesia provided Cambodian troops with counter-insurgency training, hosted a conference in Jakarta to raise foreign aid for Lon Nol, and pushed for a 'peacekeeping' force to be deployed in Cambodia.[8] Indonesia also offered its own 'peacekeeping' troops to 'try to help South Vietnam develop the ability to resist a Communist takeover'.[9] Suharto stated that these efforts were necessary to prevent Indochina falling to communism and serving as a base to subvert ASEAN countries.[10]

Suharto had in fact wished to go even further, planning to 'despatch an expeditionary force to aid the Lon Nol government' (Leifer, 1983, p. 133), to which he unsuccessfully sought to recruit ASEAN forces. As Singaporean diplomat Barry Desker (2008) recalls, 'the Indonesians had been part of the intervention in Cambodia' and 'there was a conscious attempt by Indonesia to actually seek, in 1971, an ASEAN intervention in Cambodia at the Jakarta Conference'. This was rejected not on the grounds of 'non-interference' but for practical reasons. That year, Britain was withdrawing its forces 'east of Suez', leaving Singapore and Malaysia badly weakened, both economically and militarily. Especially given Malaysia's ongoing insurgency, they feared being drawn directly into the conflagration (Desker, 2008). ASEAN nonetheless admitted Saigon and Phnom Penh's anti-communist regimes as official observers at ASEAN meetings from 1971 onwards, making it quite clear which side it was backing. Thailand maintained its military approach, asking Nixon to bomb Laos from Thai bases and calling for full-scale SEATO intervention to support Lon Nol. Bangkok repeatedly deployed a covert artillery unit and 'special guerrilla units' comprising 20,000 soldiers in Laos to thwart the advances of the communist Pathet Laos, and also trained Cambodians to fight for Lon Nol.[11] A full-scale invasion of Cambodia and Laos was even contemplated (Girling, 1992, pp. 369–71).

ASEAN elites gradually recognised, however, that this confrontational approach to Indochina would be unsustainable after US withdrawal. Left-leaning regimes were likely to emerge and, as Thanat put it, ASEAN would be left with the 'stigma of having backed the wrong imperialist' (Sit, 1995, pp. 51, 64). Consequently, the non-interference principle was deployed to manage the coming transition with a minimum of disruption to ASEAN's social orders. ASEAN offered the Indochinese states an olive branch through the 1971 Declaration on a Zone of Peace, Freedom and Neutrality (ZOPFAN). ZOPFAN reiterated ASEAN's desire for 'stability and security from external interference... in order to preserve... national identities'. However, it also called for a 'relaxation of international tensions', a region 'free from any form or manner of interference by outside powers', with guarantees to be provided by the great powers, and the closure of foreign bases (ASEAN, 1971). Rather than expressing a genuine conversion to neutrality, ZOPFAN was clearly a pragmatic adjustment to the emerging balance of forces. With the US

already withdrawing from Southeast Asia, the only great-power involvement being rejected by ZOPFAN was that of Moscow and Beijing. ZOPFAN
sought to burnish ASEAN's tattered non-aligned credentials by position-
ing it equidistantly between the superpowers, in the hope that a leftist
Indochina might also distance themselves from the USSR and China, and
refrain from retaliating against ASEAN states.

ASEAN governments were, however, divided on how far to go in
achieving this goal. In the aftermath of the 1969 race riots, the Malaysian
government saw ZOPFAN as a way to demonstrate to its ethnic Chinese
citizens and 'the predominantly Chinese MCP' that its 'legitimacy... was
recognised and endorsed in Peking' (Leifer, 1983, p. 147). It also believed
that the Vietnamese revolution was sufficiently nationalist that Hanoi
might be willing to become a 'bulwark to contain the China threat',
as Prime Minister Hussein Onn put it (Sit, 1995, p. 55). ZOPFAN's offer
of neutrality and the removal of foreign (i.e., US) bases clearly sought to
tempt Vietnam into this role, and Hanoi was even invited to join ASEAN
in 1974. However, most of the other ASEAN states had little need to
appease their domestic Chinese population so urgently. They were wary
both of drawing too close to Beijing, which was still seen as the principal
external sponsor of their respective communist movements, and of rejecting the US presence altogether (Leifer, 1973). Indonesia's New Order, for
example, was pathologically suspicious of both China and its domestic
ethnic-Chinese population, and heavily dependent on Western support
for its survival, foreign aid comprising over 45 per cent of its development budget, for example (Booth, 1994, p. 15). Suharto's preferred response
to the Nixon Doctrine was to fill the 'power vacuum' by developing a
force capable of rushing to the aid of ASEAN regimes threatened by communist takeover.[12] Malik told the US that Indonesia accepted the closure
of its bases in the region only on the basis of 'a common understanding [that] it would not be significant whether you stay' because aid would
continue more covertly.[13]

ZOPFAN had little effect on Southeast Asia's social conflicts, which continued to intensify. In Thailand, unprecedented labour unrest helped
overthrow the military regime in 1973. A newly-elected democratic government struggled to mend fences with its neighbours, but the virulently
anti-communist military continued intervening across Thailand's borders.
This was insufficient to prevent, by 1975, the reunification of Vietnam
under communist rule, the overthrow of the Laotian monarchy by the
communist Pathet Laos, and the seizure of power in Cambodia by the
Khmer Rouge. Reporting the region's reaction to President Ford, Lee Kuan
Yew expressed his 'astonishment and alarm at the rapidity with which

the situation fell apart'. Marcos had rushed to ingratiate himself in Beijing, while the Thai elite were terrified of 'going through the Phnom Penh and Saigon mangling machine'.[14] Thailand's fearful establishment lashed out against leftists and liberals. The king unleashed fiery, anti-communist rhetoric, while the army recruited mercenaries to assassinate left-wing activists, launching campaigns like 'Right, Kill Left!' The military also massacred dozens of students at Thammasat University, claiming they were Vietnamese-backed communists bent on 'destroying the monarchy' as 'part of the communist scheme to take over Thailand' (Anderson, 1998, p. 171; Huxley, 1983, pp. 12–13). A viciously anti-communist military regime seized power in 1976, and thousands of urban intellectuals fled to join the CPT in the jungles.

This dramatic unrest in Thailand, which now appeared like a crucial domino poised to fall, was echoed elsewhere in ASEAN. 1975 saw a 'distinct upsurge' in MCP activity, including spectacular attacks on army and police personnel and bases, climaxing with the bombing of the national monument in Kuala Lumpur (Huxley, 1983, p. 23). Suharto told Ford that the insurgency in Thailand and Malaysia now constituted 'a greater danger than an overt physical threat' since it could 'bring the Communists right to our threshold'.[15] Suharto's New Order was itself at its most unstable since its inception, having recently been rocked by massive corruption scandals, the bankruptcy of the state oil company, and student riots which were apparently backed by some of Suharto's closest allies (Anderson, 1995, pp. 140–1). It was in this context that, when a leftist state threatened to emerge from the decolonisation of the Portuguese colony of East Timor, adjoining Indonesian territory, Suharto intervened to crush it, backed by the rest of ASEAN (see Chapter 3).

This context was also the backdrop for the signing of the Treaty of Amity and Cooperation (TAC) at ASEAN's 1976 summit. TAC is often seen as another touchstone of the 'ASEAN way' of regional order, enunciating a set of 'norms' to guide members' conduct, including, of course, 'the right of every State to lead its national existence free from external interference, subversion, or coercion'; and 'non-interference in the affairs of one another' (ASEAN, 1976b). However, as Singaporean diplomats told the British, the summit was less about developing regional norms or identity than 'impress[ing] the new victors of Indochina with a show of solidarity', with Lee Kuan Yew proposing to stage the summit in Bangkok in order to stiffen General Kukrit's shaky regime.[16] Indonesia likewise saw the summit as 'principally a symbol and expression of political will' designed to support Kukrit, and Malaysia's new prime minister.[17]

TAC was thus largely about projecting an image of non-communist stability and resilience, not expressing an abstract commitment to sovereignty and non-intervention. Indeed, when the summit was threatened with collapse by a renewed spat between the Philippines and Malaysia over Sabah, Suharto threatened to unleash Malaysian intervention in Mindanao unless President Marcos relented.[18]

To the extent that TAC proposed norms of regional conduct, its purposes were identical to ZOPFAN's: 'to conciliate the victorious communist regimes by announcing a self-denying regional ordinance' in order to 'appease these states and persuade them to join ASEAN in establishing a collaborative regional environment' (Jones and Smith, 1997, pp. 134–5). Like ZOPFAN, however, TAC had little effect on either side of the ideological divide. Indochina's communist forces refused to simply forget ASEAN's interventions against them. Vietnam issued broadsides against ASEAN, proclaiming its solidarity with 'the just, sure-to-win cause of the peoples of the countries of Southeast Asia' and 'all forces struggling for independence, democracy, peace and social progress', especially 'the Thai people's struggle for a really independent and democratic Thailand'. Bangkok also continued hosting right-wing Cambodian and Laotian guerrilla movements as a buffer against the new regimes, prompting Indochina's communist regimes to provide sanctuary and escalate material support for the CPT (Huxley, 1983, pp. 2–18). A secret report tabled at the 1977 ASEAN Ministerial Meeting (AMM) expressed the fear that this signalled the beginning of a full-scale revolutionary expansion. Despite acknowledging Vietnam's preoccupation with internal reconstruction, the report 'stressed Hanoi's strong ideological support for regional revolutionary movements, its huge weapons stocks, and the ease with which insurgency in the ASEAN countries could be supported from outside' (Huxley, 1983, p. 56).

However, ASEAN was granted a brief reprieve from the spectre of revolution by the internal divisions that quickly emerged within Indochina. After reunifying the country, the Vietnamese Communist Party (VCP) asserted its independence from Beijing and Moscow, which had aided its struggle. The virulently anti-Vietnamese leadership of the Khmer Rouge (KR), however, suspected that Hanoi planned to revive and dominate an 'Indochinese Federation', a concept first touted by Ho Chi Minh in the 1930s. This prospect also alarmed the Chinese leadership, whose increasingly all-consuming rivalry with the USSR led them to see Moscow's hand at work. China and the Maoist KR thus aligned against Vietnam, and KR forces were soon launching vicious raids into Vietnamese territory. Encouraged by China, in 1977 the KR launched diplomatic forays into ASEAN to gain support against Vietnam, reassuring its neighbours that it had no interest in promoting revolution outside Cambodia.

ASEAN governments were delighted to see these splits emerge, and hoped that they would intensify. Lee Kuan Yew had actually predicted the conflict in May 1976, suggesting that Cambodia might thereby become a 'buffer' against Vietnam to 'buy us considerable time' to defeat domestic communism (Huxley, 1983, p. 26). This initially seemed borne out as both sides sought improved relations with Bangkok. By 1978, Vietnam and its ally Laos had cut ties with the Chinese-backed CPT, with Laos even assisting the Thai army's counterinsurgency campaigns (Huxley, 1983, pp. 33–5). Vietnamese diplomats also toured ASEAN capitals, offering reassurances of Hanoi's good intent. Cambodia likewise cut its modest support for the CPT to appease Bangkok, with the Thai army engaging in 'grisly cooperation' with Pol Pot's genocidal regime by shooting anyone trying to flee into Thailand (Simon, 1982a, p. 106).

This conflict was not, however, sustainable. In response to growing Chinese hostility, Vietnam concluded a treaty of friendship with Moscow. After repeated provocations and massacres of Vietnamese citizens by Cambodian forces, Vietnam invaded Cambodia in December. Hanoi installed a new Cambodian government, destroying the buffer provided by the KR and reviving the prospect of revolution spreading from Indochina. Chapter 4 explores how ASEAN intervened in Cambodia to sustain a civil war designed to keep revolution at bay.

Concluding remarks

This chapter traced the evolution of social conflict and 'non-interference' from ASEAN's formation to the late 1970s. Rather than taking documents like the Bangkok Declaration, ZOPFAN and TAC at face value, as evidence of a principled commitment to non-interference, their emergence was re-historicised in relation to the strategies of competing social forces within a changing geopolitical context. In practice, 'non-interference' had both internal and external applications with a common purpose: to stabilise the prevailing domestic order in line with the interests underpinning specific state-making projects. Internally and externally, however, intervention also persisted, in pursuit of this same goal. Within ASEAN this involved military cooperation against insurgents and the provision of aid and policy advice; outside ASEAN this involved wide-ranging efforts to prevent leftist regimes from coming to power and to insulate ASEAN's own insurgencies from real or imagined sources of external support. Non-interference and intervention were combined in a sovereignty regime whose fundamental purpose was to assist the territorialising, capitalist state-making projects favoured by ASEAN elites after 1965. Rather than ASEAN norms acquiring a 'life of their own' and coming to exercise an independent influence on member-states' behaviour, the meaning and application of these norms continued to be determined by social conflict. The next two chapters develop this analysis further through detailed case studies of ASEAN states' interventions in East Timor and Cambodia.

3
East Timor: ASEAN and Third-World Colonialism

> Indonesia will give guarantees of not interfering in the determination of the future of Portuguese Timor.
> — *Adam Malik, Indonesian Foreign Minister, 1974*
> (*Sinar Harapan*, 17 June 1974)

> 50,000 people or perhaps 80,000 might have been killed during the war in Timor... what is the big fuss... It was war.
> — *Adam Malik, 1977* (Kohen and Taylor, 1979, p. 71)

> ASEAN turned the other way even though the same principle was at work [as in Cambodia] – a big state invading and occupying a small state.
> — *Singaporean Ambassador Krishnasamy Kesavapany* (2008)

In December 1975, after a concerted campaign of subversion and terrorisation, Indonesia invaded East Timor. It then brutally annexed the territory, which had declared its independence from Portugal the previous month, all the while backed by its ASEAN partners. Since critical scholarship has tended to emphasise Western complicity in Jakarta's actions, ASEAN's role has largely escaped scrutiny, such that the implications of the invasion for 'non-interference' have been left unexamined. Thus, for example, Leifer (1983, p. 167) claims shortly after noting the invasion that that '[n]on-violation of national sovereignty is regarded by Jakarta as a central precept of any system of regional order'. Constructivists tend to completely ignore East Timor. Yet as one rare critic observes, ASEAN's norms were 'systematically ignored' during the invasion, constituting a 'critical experiment' for the 'security community view' of regional politics (Cotton, 2004, pp. 84–5).

This chapter explains the gap between ASEAN states' stated principles and their actual practice. Building on the analysis developed in Chapter 2, it argues that Indonesia's invasion and ASEAN's support is best explained by the fear that a leftist state would emerge after Timor's decolonisation, providing a possible base for communist 'subversion'. Indonesian fears were conditioned by the conflicts that had given rise to the Suharto regime, the social order it was attempting to defend, and the likely effects of Timorese independence on that order. They were further exacerbated by the rise of communist regimes and insurgencies across Southeast Asia, and by the worst social unrest in Indonesia since Suharto had seized power. ASEAN largely shared these apprehensions and, with the brief and limited exception of Singapore, accepted the invasion as a contribution to regional 'stability', actively collaborating with Jakarta. The chapter focuses first on what Indonesia's intervention involved, considers competing explanations for its behaviour, and then explores the role of other ASEAN states.

Indonesian intervention in East Timor

Although Indonesia had quickly transformed into a pro-Western bulwark in Southeast Asia following Suharto's coup, it retained an image of non-alignment by keeping its interventions in Indochina covert and adopting apparently neutral positions on international issues. Consequently, in 1974, when Portugal began decolonising its five-hundred-year-old colony in East Timor, which adjoins Indonesian West Timor, Indonesia's studied assurances of non-interference and support for Timorese independence appeared genuine to many. In reality, Jakarta feared the emergence of an independent state alongside its borders as a possible base for communist subversion – a fear heightened by the emergence of a left-wing independence movement – and quickly prepared to impose Indonesian rule on the territory. Initially, Indonesia worked through a pro-integration party it created and financed, but its failure to win popular backing pushed Jakarta into more coercive measures, terrorising the population and arming guerrillas to seize the territory by force. When this also failed, Indonesia invaded instead.

Despite its pretensions to the contrary, the New Order was determined not to permit an independent East Timor to emerge from the very beginning. The decolonisation process began in April 1974, when Portugal's fascist regime was overthrown by a leftist military coup. The military, tired of fighting colonial wars, announced that the Portuguese empire would be swiftly disbanded. Publicly, Indonesia greeted this news positively. Adam Malik affirmed in June 1974 that 'independence' was 'the right of every nation with no exception for the people of Timor'. He emphasised that Indonesia had no territorial ambitions, and promised good relations with 'whoever will govern Timor... after independence' (Jolliffe, 1978, p. 66). The reality was quite different. Indonesia's state intelligence agency, BAKIN, had already assessed the implications of independence for East Timor in 1972–73, concluding that 'with the Americans withdrawing from Vietnam... even the continuation of Portuguese colonial rule was preferable to an independent state which could add a new dimension to Indonesia's security problems' (Dunn, 1983, p. 106).

What was the nature of the 'security problem' posed by Timor's decolonisation? As Leifer (1983, p. 155) argued, the territory was too small and impoverished to constitute a conventional security threat, still less an 'asset or a prize'; rather, the New Order was concerned about its 'uncertain utility to others'. However, this cannot be understood simply in realist, geostrategic terms. The New Order's 'security' outlook was determined by the violent social conflict that had brought it to power, and by the authoritarian, capitalist social order it was pledged to defend. The regime's consequent fear of communist 'subversion' led it to worry that East Timor, located amidst the sprawling Indonesian archipelago, might be used to funnel PKI remnants back into Indonesia, or support other rebel groups, such as the separatist movements resisting the army's brutal control and exploitation in outlying provinces. The fear, then, was what an independent East Timor would mean for socio-political and economic order within Indonesia.

This fear was even greater by the time of Portugal's announcement than in 1972–73. Domestically, Suharto's regime was facing its greatest period of instability since seizing power. In 1974, Jakarta had been rocked by a massive corruption scandal, the bankruptcy of the state oil company, and widespread rioting backed by some of Suharto's closest allies, which appeared to presage a violent succession struggle (Anderson, 1995, pp. 139–41). The regime feared that this unrest would be exploited by the 1,500,000 'undeclared communists' believed by military intelligence to still be at large in the country.[1] This paranoia was compounded by contemporaneous events in Indochina and rising insurgency in other ASEAN states, which had generated a 'general fear that the communists, or the leftists, were on the upper hand' (Alatas, 2008). With America's withdrawal from the region, it was also felt, according to Suharto's close ally General Murdani, who eventually led the invasion, that impoverished East Timor could only turn to 'Moscow, Beijing or Hanoi for help', thus potentially establishing a communist enclave – a Southeast Asian 'Cuba' – on Indonesia's borders (Singh, 1996, p. 61). Independence for East Timor in this context simply posed too much of a threat to social order in the region.

Consequently, while professing non-interference in East Timor's affairs, Jakarta moved quickly to gain control of the territory. Initially the New Order used covert means, in order to preserve good relations with non-aligned countries, and particularly the Western governments upon whom the regime relied heavily for economic and military aid. The plan was to recreate the 'act of free choice' staged in West Papua in 1969 – a 'popular consultation' rigged to ensure that this last vestige of Dutch colonialism was absorbed into Indonesia. The same generals who had manufactured this outcome were sent to negotiate with Portugal and believed that a *quid pro quo* along these lines had been agreed (Alatas, 2006, p. 3). To produce the required 'popular' support for this outcome, BAKIN agents created the *Associação Popular Democratica Timorense* (APODETI), a party to campaign for integration which openly admitted that it was funded by Jakarta (Jolliffe, 1978, p. 79; Hoadley, 1975, pp. 5–6, 1977, p. 134). However, APODETI attracted support from only about 5 per cent of the population. The remainder preferred the two pro-independence parties that had already emerged, the *União Democrática Timorense* (UDT) and the *Associação Social-Democrata Timorense* (ASDT). However, Indonesia initially believed that, with Portuguese connivance, time was on its side.

These plans were destabilised, however, by the radicalisation of the Portuguese revolution. In September 1974, amid severe turmoil in which the Portuguese Communist Party emerged as the only organised political force, Lisbon's interim government was replaced by a far more radical one. Left-wing military officers dissatisfied with the slow pace of decolonisation accelerated the timetable, despatching agents to East Timor to hasten the process. Portugal's social upheaval was also transmitted to Timor through left-wing Timorese activists returning from Portugal and Mozambique, who joined and radicalised the ASDT. The party was now rebranded as the *Frente Revolucionária de Timor-Leste Independente* (FRETILIN), in clear imitation of Mozambique's left-wing independence movement, *Frente de Libertação de Moçambique* (Liberation Front of Mozambique) (FRELIMO). A new manifesto pledged to 'revolutionise the social and economic structures of colonial inspiration' in a 'general struggle against poverty, illiteracy and economic and political oppression' (Capizzi *et al.*, 1976, pp. 388–94). FRETILIN subsequently established 'fraternal relations' with movements like FRELIMO,

Zimbabwe's African National Union, Namibia's South West Africa People's Organisation, the African National Congress, the POLISARIO Front, the communist New People's Army in the Philippines, and various separatist movements across Australasia (Ramos Horta, 1987, p. 104).

This apparent leftward lunge in the colony promoted a near-hysterical reaction from the Indonesian establishment. The tame Indonesian media relayed regime propaganda that Timor had been infiltrated by Chinese generals and weapons, Vietnamese communist cadres, troops and weapons, and Soviet submarines. Timor's ethnic Chinese were all said to be 'Maoist' and involved in a plot devised by Beijing (Dunn, 1983, p. 118). It was also reported that East Timor had already become a harbour for separatist rebels from the South Moluccas and a 'pivot for insurgent activity' that would 'pump Chinese leftists and Indonesian communist renegades into Indonesia' (Dawn, 1974; Observer Foreign News Service, 1974). Similar claims were broadcast via radio into East Timor in order to intimidate the population into supporting APODETI. UDT was branded 'neo-fascist' and FRETILIN 'communist' (Jolliffe, 1978, pp. 84, 96). FRETILIN was said to be 'riddled with Maoists and its headquarters plastered with posters of Mao', while pro-independence demonstrations were supposedly 'masterminded and financed by left-wing Chinese merchants'. Portuguese Maoist cadres and communist propaganda, four Chinese generals and large amounts of Chinese arms were all said to have arrived in the territory (Observer Foreign News Service, 1974).

Official Indonesian involvement in the territory's emerging political struggles quickly became apparent. The governor of West Timor, who had linked FRETILIN to an alleged Soviet-Chinese plot to 'stage a PKI "come-back"', hosted pro-integration leaders from September to November 1974, and publicly pledged to 'assist the struggle of APODETI'. Malik also warned that Jakarta would not tolerate the colony becoming a 'base for communist subversion', and gave APODETI his blessing (Roff, 1992, p. 62; Lawless, 1976, p. 953). APODETI began recruiting East Timorese youths for guerrilla warfare training in West Timor (Roff, 1992, p. 62; Lawless, 1976, p. 953). To further intimidate the population, Jakarta massed troops along the border in early 1975, warning that (in response to its own false propaganda about 'atrocities' being committed against APODETI), it would 'not tolerate it if the people of Portuguese Timor are terrorised' (Nichterlein, 1977, p. 489).

BAKIN also moved to recruit UDT into its schemes. Indonesian intimidation had prompted UDT and FRETILIN to form a coalition to defend the territory's future independence in January 1975. BAKIN now sought to disrupt this. The parties' leaders were invited to Jakarta in April 1975, shortly after the Khmer Rouge had seized control of Cambodia and Lon Nol had fled to Indonesia. The UDT leadership met with Generals Murtopo and Surono of BAKIN, who 'stressed the dangers of communism' and urged a UDT-APODETI alliance against 'communist subversion' (UN Department of Political Affairs, Trusteeship and Decolonization, 1976, pp. 48, 16). UDT subsequently terminated the coalition in May, stating that FRETILIN was threatening 'the political stability of the geopolitical context of Timor' (Nichterlein, 1977, p. 493). UDT leaders were again summoned to Jakarta in July to meet Suharto where, according to one of them, Murtopo 'talked at length about the dangers of communism in general and Indonesia's anxiety about it on Timor in particular', warning of an impending FRETILIN coup (Lawless, 1976, p. 951). However, instead of allying with APODETI, UDT staged a pre-emptive coup against the Timorese left on 11 August, in a last-ditch attempt to preserve the territory's future independence. Seizing key facilities in the capital, Dili, UDT demanded that FRETILIN moderates expel all leftists from the colony and work and with UDT to pursue independence, rejecting collaboration with APODETI and calling for US aid. FRETILIN refused to cooperate with UDT, recruiting the local garrison to strike back against the coup. Civil war quickly broke out.

Jakarta seized upon this unrest, which it had helped foment, as a pretext for further intervention. Covertly, the CIA reported, Indonesia infiltrated Timorese guerrillas trained in West Timor to 'provoke incidents that would provide the Indonesians with an excuse to invade should they decide to do so', supplementing them with 850 Indonesian 'irregulars' by mid-September (Dunn, 1983, pp. 174, 218–19; Taylor, 1991, pp. 58–60). Publicly, Suharto sought Lisbon's permission to despatch Indonesian 'peacekeepers' to East Timor, to be joined later by Portuguese troops which would establish a 'joint authority' over the territory. This scheme collapsed when Australia rejected Lisbon's subsequent request to participate. Disastrously for the New Order, by 28 September the civil war was over, with UDT routed and FRETILIN in full control.

Indonesia thus assembled a Timorese force to re-invade the colony, restart the civil war, and restore a pretext for Indonesian forces to invade. In exchange for sanctuary in West Timor, UDT's remnants were forced to sign a petition for the integration of East Timor. They were then made to join APODETI and two even smaller Timorese factions to form the *Movimento Anti-Communista* (MAC), which immediately demanded the colony's integration into Indonesia. Adam Malik pledged Indonesia's 'full support, quietly or openly', and later admitted that the military had provided training to MAC guerrillas (ST, 1975b). Meanwhile, the New Order broadcast propaganda falsely presenting East Timor as remaining locked in a violent civil conflict that was threatening Indonesia's 'stability' and 'security'. It claimed that 40,000 refugees had fled into West Timor and that FRETILIN was launching cross-border raids against Indonesian civilians. In reality, FRETILIN had restored order in the colony and was pressing Jakarta to settle tensions along the border peacefully. Indonesia responded by shelling Timorese territory and initiating a naval blockade, and by physically detaining Portuguese envoys sent to resolve the crisis (Jolliffe, 1978, pp. 124–5; Van Dijk, 1976, pp. 26–7; Republic of Indonesia, 1976, pp. 22, 17; Van der Kroef, 1976, pp. 22–3).

To seize East Timor, Jakarta ultimately had little choice but to invade in full force. MAC forces were unable to make any headway against FRETILIN, and had to be stiffened by covertly-deployed Indonesian commandoes from mid-September onwards. However, the CIA reported that by 26 September the clandestine operation had 'run into serious trouble' and Indonesia was forced to escalate its direct military involvement (Dunn, 1983, pp. 174, 218–19; Taylor, 1991, pp. 58–60). By late November, Indonesia was regularly shelling Timor from the air and sea, and its ground forces had advanced well into the territory, with FRETILIN issuing frantic appeals to the UN Security Council. On 28 November, with no aid in sight, FRETILIN declared the independence of the Democratic Republic of East Timor. According to General Murdani, this necessitated an immediate invasion 'before the newly declared republic was recognised by anyone. Otherwise Indonesia would be accused of invading an independent country' (Singh, 1996, p. 70). MAC was made to issue a 'declaration of integration', and with a final nod from US President Ford, Indonesia declared Portuguese sovereignty void and invaded in full force on 6 December.

Even with 20,000–30,000 troops on the ground, Jakarta still tried to claim that reports that it 'had committed military intervention were entirely unfounded'. Indonesian diplomats tried explaining away the invasion variously as the mere presence of 'volunteers' rushing to 'help their brethren free themselves from colonial suppression and FRETILIN terror', the accomplishment of MAC forces, or the result of a request by an APODETI-led 'provisional government' (Republic of Indonesia, 1975, 1976). Even the pro-Suharto Western powers on the UN Security Council rejected this interpretation, censuring Jakarta unanimously. A fact-finding mission was despatched by the Council but was rendered useless by Indonesian sabotage. Imposing a *fait accompli*, Jakarta staged a 'popular assembly' in Dili in February 1976 which duly petitioned

Indonesia for 'integration'. Although this was rejected by the UN, Jakarta stated that decolonisation had now been completed, and since East Timor was now part of Indonesia, any further discussion of the territory now constituted illegitimate interference in its internal affairs.[2]

This section argued that the Suharto regime was so terrified by the prospect of an independent East Timor being used to further destabilise Indonesia's social order that it orchestrated a concerted campaign to subvert the territory into placing itself under the New Order; when this failed, Indonesia accomplished its goal by force. Its attempts to avoid the appearance of blatantly violating the non-interference principle stemmed not from any genuine attachment to this 'cherished' norm, but from a desire to avoid straining its relations with Western donors and non-aligned nations. Jakarta's cynical deployment of non-interference to disguise its behaviour and silence its critics suggests a highly instrumental relationship to the norm. Before moving on to consider ASEAN's involvement in these events, however, we should pause to consider alternative explanations of Jakarta's behaviour.

A grab for territory and resources?

The 'social conflict' approach allows us to trace the intervention in East Timor to the specific forces in charge of the Indonesian state which wished to defend a capitalist social order when faced with revolutionary challenges in a situation of geopolitical flux. However, it might be objected that Indonesia merely cited a fear of communism to disguise other, perhaps more straightforward motives, such as territorial or economic gain. This section critically reviews the other existing interpretations of Indonesia's behaviour, ultimately rejecting them as less convincing.

Most of these explanations invoke standard 'realist' type motives like territorial or economic aggrandisement or geostrategic calculations; constructivists have entirely ignored these events. Some scholars argue that independent Indonesia had always been an 'expansionist dictatorship' and the invasion of Timor was merely the latest expression of 'Javan expansionism' (Dawson, 1995). Others suggest that the lure of petroleum deposits in Timor 'proved too much [to resist] for the oil oligarchs of Jakarta', and that Indonesia's 'entrepreneur-generals... were eager to create a new Bali to supplement the ones their hotels and concessions had already despoiled' (Nichterlein, 1977, p. 486). More frequent is that claim that Indonesia wished to secure the vital Ombar-Wetai straits off Timor, through which nuclear submarines could travel undetected from the Pacific to the Indian Ocean (e.g. Jolliffe, 1978, pp. 295–6), with some also claiming that Washington pushed a reluctant Suharto to do this (Singh, 1996, p. 207; Marker, 2003, p. 9; Severino, 2006, p. 122).

None of these suggestions are particularly convincing. First, it is false to posit an unbroken Indonesian 'expansionist dictatorship'. As Chapter 2 showed, Sukarno's apparently aggressive foreign policy was not about a quest for territory or resources *per se*, but was largely used to manage Indonesian social conflict. No territorial claim was made in Borneo, and although Sukarno initiated the campaign to integrate West Papua in Indonesia, this was because it was part of the Dutch territories promised to Indonesia at independence and thus important to nationalist and anti-imperialist forces. Sukarno repeatedly stated that Indonesia laid no claim to East Timor, and the only Indonesians involved in the colony prior to the 1970s were a handful of officers fleeing a failed regional uprising *against* Sukarno (Chamberlain, 2009). Given its dramatically different social underpinnings, Suharto's regime did not represent continuity from Sukarno. The reasons for Indonesia's invasion cannot be found in some timeless 'Javan expansionism'.

The economic incentives argument is also unconvincing, since Timor was widely seen as a basket case. Suharto had emphasised its *lack of viability* as a reason why it could not be allowed to attain independence (UN Department of Political Affairs, Trusteeship and Decolonization, 1976, p. 49). It was its very poverty that made it potentially dependent on 'subversive' foreign aid. Badly neglected, like all of Portugal's colonies, Timor had virtually no industry or infrastructure and was completely dependent on Lisbon. Australian companies prospecting for oil and minerals for over twenty years had found nothing (Evans, 1975, pp. 72–3). Given Indonesia's own profound poverty and the perceived need for rapid economic development to undercut communism, absorbing Timor was actually, as Suharto put it, a 'heavy burden' (Marker, 2003, p. 31). Timor was certainly exploited by Jakarta's 'entrepreneur-generals' during the long occupation, but to read this backwards as a motivation for invading is to ignore how Timor's economy was understood at the time.

The argument that Timor was strategically important is equally dubious. It appears to be based solely on a Canadian Defence Department paper that ranked Ombar-Wetai alongside Gibraltar as the 'most crucial deep-water straits in the world, in American defence planning' (Inbaraj, 1995, pp. 35–6). Americans themselves, however, disagreed. In 1972 the CIA stated that Timor was of 'little strategic significance' (Nairn, 1997, p. xiii). Admiral LaRocque of the Center for Defense Information told the UN that the straits were used only very rarely, and the main concern was for straits elsewhere in Indonesia.[3] Timor was actually of such little strategic value that Indonesia cited great-power indifference as a reason why it was 'forced' to intervene (Alatas, 2006, p. 238). A leaked Australian cable also revealed that Secretary of State Henry Kissinger had instructed the US ambassador 'not to involve himself on discussions on Timor... [because] the US is involved in enough problems of greater importance' (Dunn, 1977, p. 44). When Suharto and Malik discussed the issue with Ford and Kissinger, it was to seek their quiet approval, not to receive instructions.[4] The realist tendency to attribute all international events to great-power policies is extremely misleading, because it denies the agency and power of local states.

Realist-type explanations focused on geostrategy only make sense when they are married with the substantive content of politics provided by social conflict analysis. The New Order was concerned about East Timor's strategic value not because of its geographic position or physical attributes, but because it could potentially be used by its internal enemies, in league with external powers bent on 'subverting' Indonesia's social order. The invasion makes sense only when viewed from the perspective of elite fears of instability in their own authoritarian, capitalist domestic order when 'dominos' had begun falling in the region. The same essential logic also applied to Indonesia's ASEAN partners.

The other ASEAN states: Cooperation and complicity

Indonesian diplomats justified the invasion of East Timor by arguing that developments there endangered 'not only [Indonesia's] own peace and security, but also that of the region of Southeast Asia'.[5] Indonesia had therefore intervened 'not only in its own interest, but also in the interest of Southeast Asia as a whole'.[6] As one Singaporean diplomat recalls, on this basis, Jakarta 'literally demanded that other ASEAN countries support them' (Kesavapany, 2008). This section shows that, with the brief and limited exception of Singapore, ASEAN's anti-communist elites accepted Jakarta's claim to have acted on their behalf. This is because, as a Thai diplomat then stationed in Jakarta states, they shared a 'general feeling that FRETILIN was a communist front' (Bunnag, 2008). ASEAN states, particularly Malaysia, were complicit in the annexation of East Timor. 'Non-interference' was selectively applied to shield Jakarta and endorse its annexation of the territory.

Malaysia provided the most support for Indonesia. Having agreed to back Indonesia's quest to absorb East Timor in September 1974,

Malaysia hosted APODETI's leadership, and Malaysian media began disseminating Indonesia's anti-FRETILIN propaganda (Republic of Indonesia, 1976, p. 12; Van der Kroef, 1976, p. 20). To help Jakarta split the UDT-FRETILIN coalition, Malaysian diplomats reportedly met UDT leaders, 'warning them that ASEAN countries would not tolerate the emergence of an independent "left-wing state" in the region' (Inbaraj, 1995, p. 59). Malaysia's Prime Minister Razak also broadcast his fears about Timor becoming a 'base for communist subversion', and agreed to join Suharto's proposed 'joint authority' in Timor (Van Dijk, 1976, p. 17; ST, 1975a). When this scheme collapsed, Malaysia supported Indonesia's use of force. The CIA reported that Malaysia supplied Indonesian 'special force troops... with weapons that cannot be traced to Jakarta' in early October 1975 (Dunn, 1983, pp. 218–19, 228).

Malaysia also fully supported the eventual invasion. Razak publicly backed it, explaining that if Timor stood 'on its own and becomes a Communist stronghold, it will endanger the security in the Southeast Asian region' (Roff, 1992, p. 21). Malaysia echoed Jakarta's claims that 'volunteers' had been invited by 'moderate groups there to help restore law and order'. The foreign ministry stated that 'the situation in Timor had deteriorated into chaos which threatened the security of the region in general and Indonesia in particular', blaming Portugal and praising Indonesia's pursuit of a 'peaceful solution' (*Sunday Times*, 1975). Malaysia also funnelled arms to Jakarta to help it defeat FRETILIN's guerrilla resistance, including four Australian jets, thereby circumventing an arms boycott led by Australian unions. According to British diplomatic cables, Razak's 'only criticism of Indonesian action... was regret that they had not acted firmly earlier'.[7] Indeed, Indonesian diplomat Des Alwi recalls that Malaysia actively encouraged invasion since 'they believed communists would flock to an independent East Timor' (AP, 1999e).

Malaysia's policy stemmed from two distinct concerns. First, the recent upsurge in its domestic communist insurgency had terrorised the ruling elite, leading it to sympathise with Indonesia's judgements about Timor. Home Affairs Minister Ghazali Shafie claimed that 'China was experimenting with a new domino theory to isolate Indonesia, not hesitating to compare FRETILIN with the MCP in the post-Vietnam era' (Roff, 1992, p. 54). Second, Malaysia saw parallels between Timor and Brunei, which is adjacent to Malaysia's Borneo territories. As Chapter 2 noted, a leftist takeover of Brunei had only been suppressed by British intervention in 1962. Although Brunei remained an informal British protectorate, the withdrawal of Western forces from the region seemed to risk the re-emergence of 'instability' there unless it could be absorbed into

Malaysia. In November 1974, Ghazali had warned that 'vestigial colonial territories' were 'the foci of local discontent and foreign intrigue' and 'potential areas of instability'. The Malaysian press warned that delaying Brunei's formal independence would 'only give an opportunity to the Communists to look for a new base in the midst of the ASEAN nations'. Malaysia had consequently launched UN resolutions demanding Brunei's 'decolonisation', which were supported by Indonesia, Thailand and the Philippines. Meanwhile, it subverted the territory by hosting Bruneian rebels in Malaysia, some of whom were sent to Libya for 'instruction in terrorist techniques' (Leifer, 1978). Given this context, British diplomats concluded that Malaysia's cooperation with Indonesia had been exchanged for 'some future *quid pro quo* over Brunei'.[8]

Malaysia consequently led and organised ASEAN states' public support for Indonesian intervention, seeking to disguise and legitimise Indonesia's behaviour at the UN. On the eve of the invasion, Kuala Lumpur tabled a draft resolution in the Decolonisation Committee, backed by Thailand and the Philippines, calling for decolonisation to occur in 'an atmosphere of security and tranquillity' and urging all parties to cooperate with Portuguese efforts to restore order – which in reality Jakarta was deliberately blocking.[9] FRETILIN's supporters rightly identified this resolution as a 'smokescreen' for the invasion, forcing Thailand to withdraw the draft.[10] Subsequently, Malaysia, Thailand and the Philippines co-sponsored another resolution, which made no reference to the widely-reported invasion then underway, claiming instead that, since the Timorese were 'divided in their opinions in regard to their future political status', a fact-finding mission was required.[11] They then unsuccessfully tried to scuttle an Algerian counter-resolution condemning the invasion, and were conspicuous among the ten states voting against it – while 118 voted in favour.[12]

ASEAN diplomats' attempts to disguise and legitimise Indonesia's intervention in East Timor indicated their basic endorsement of Indonesian actions. The Philippine ambassador welcomed the invasion, warning that a 'power vacuum... would threaten peace in the region' and had threatened Indonesian security in particular, claiming that 'the people of Portuguese Timor had invited Indonesia to help them'.[13] Malaysia defended Indonesia not merely in the Decolonisation Committee but also the Security Council, where it echoed Jakarta's propaganda, blaming FRETILIN and Portugal for 'nearly four months of lawlessness and bloody fighting', while praising Indonesian 'restraint'. Like the Philippines, Malaysia clearly accepted Jakarta's claims to have acted on the region's behalf, claiming that 'the breakdown of law and order in Portuguese Timor… had in it the seeds of foreign intervention'. Decolonisation allegedly had to 'take into account the peace and security of the geographic region in which it was located' and required 'an atmosphere of peace and order', which Jakarta would provide.[14]

Singapore's position initially differed somewhat. Its diplomats did not defend Indonesia and merely abstained in votes on East Timor. This is generally ascribed to Singaporean concern for the 'territorial integrity of small [states]' or 'anxiety' at the violation of 'the norms of the non-use of force and non-intervention' (McDougall, 2001, p. 169; Haacke, 2003, p. 64). The evidence, however, suggests that Singapore's exceptionalism was very limited and brief. British cables show that Singaporean officials sympathised with Indonesian fears of a 'hostile regime' in East Timor serving as a potential entry-point for Sino-Soviet meddling and the return of 'overseas Chinese'.[15] The Singaporean press helped spread Jakarta's anti-FRETILIN propaganda, and Singapore was also reportedly mooted as a possible participant in Jakarta's 'joint authority'. Suharto also kept Singapore as well-briefed as Malaysia to assuage any fears of a revival of Sukarno-esque adventurism. Consequently, Singapore's ambassador to Jakarta told the British, Lee Kuan Yew had given Suharto '*carte blanche*' since 'the unity of ASEAN was worth a blind eye'.[16]

Singapore's concern was less about 'non-interference' than Indonesian strategy. Rajaratnam and Lee favoured an exclusively covert approach, fearing that other third-world states would perceive an overt military invasion as 'colonial'. Given the context of Sino-Soviet rivalry for third-world leadership, this would merely encourage the involvement of communist great powers in Southeast Asia.[17] Thus, while Rajaratnam accepted Indonesia's fear that Timor could end up 'like Cuba', he warned Suharto that overt military intervention would create a diplomatic 'albatross', counselling him to stick to covert subversion in the belief that 'if Indonesia had been patient, East Timor would have fallen into Indonesia's lap by assent' (Kesavapany, 2008). Given assurances by Indonesia, Singaporean officials 'did not think Indonesia would use force',[18] and were consequently dismayed by Jakarta's heavy-handed approach. Singapore's subsequent position on East Timor, therefore, was not dictated by a difference of principle, or by the city-state's size, but by a disagreement over the strategy used to annex the territory.

Singapore's abstention in the UN was nonetheless 'seen by the Indonesians as a major betrayal of ASEAN' (Desker, 2008). The CIA reported that Suharto planned to 'retaliate by postponing the appointment of a new ambassador, by suspending intelligence exchanges, and by closing Indonesian airspace to Singapore military aircraft' (Inbaraj, 1995, p. 51). Indonesia did indeed boycott Singaporean initiatives, and excluded Singaporeans from security and intelligence briefings (Desker, 2008). Even though the city-state's officials now concede that it was 'the same thing as [Vietnam] invading Cambodia' in 1978, by mid-1976, the government had nonetheless 'cut a deal with Suharto' because 'we had bigger issues at stake' (Kausikan, 2008). ASEAN's unity was still, apparently, worth a 'blind eye'. Singapore backed the invasion at the UN in 1977. If it had genuinely felt threatened by Indonesia's violation of territorial integrity or norms of sovereignty, we might have expected a slightly longer hold-out than one year. In practice, principles could always be sacrificed to preserve anti-communist regional cooperation.

All the ASEAN states thus supported Indonesian intervention in East Timor, and worked in relative international isolation to secure international recognition of the *fait accompli*. The July 1976 AMM claimed that Indonesian actions 'correspond[ed] with' UN decolonisation procedures, urging the UN to drop its opposition and endorse the outcome since 'the solution of the East Timor question would contribute positively to the maintenance of peace and stability in the Southeast Asian region' (ASEAN, 1976a). Thai, Malaysian and Philippine officials also joined a few other hand-picked observers invited to Jakarta's staged process of 'popular consultation'. Bangkok's delegate noted 'the absence of... consideration of any alternative other than integration with Indonesia' (Clark, 1980, pp. 16–17, n. 70). Nonetheless, Thai officials believed that in eliminating a 'communist front... the Indonesians did the right thing' (Bunnag, 2008). At the UN, ASEAN acted as an increasingly coherent bloc, with the Philippines joining Malaysia at Security Council debates in 1976 to claim that Timor's decolonisation had been 'scrupulously' implemented.[19] The Council again rejected Timor's annexation, but with Western powers unwilling to act against Jakarta, the issue was successfully pushed off the Council's agenda. It was thereafter discussed only in the Decolonisation Committee, where ASEAN states lobbied for the issue to be dropped altogether, claiming it now constituted 'interference' in Indonesia's 'internal' affairs.[20] Singapore and Malaysia reportedly also supported Indonesia in the NAM (Alatas, 2008).

This deployment of 'non-interference' is best understood as a highly partisan move to manipulate the scope of conflict over the settlement in East Timor. Severino (2006, pp. 129–30) suggests that ASEAN's stance was due to the fact that, since East Timor had been absorbed into Indonesia, it was now a domestic matter and to even discuss it would be to sanction 'separatism'. This ignores the selective application of such principles and why ASEAN was prepared to accept the conversion of an independent state into Jakarta's 'internal affair' in the first place. Initially, ASEAN raised no objection to Indonesia's violation of East Timorese sovereignty and self-determination; indeed, most actively supported it. Now, however, they suddenly demanded that non-intervention be respected. This was obviously designed to help Indonesia limit the scope of conflict in East Timor by insulating the Timorese resistance from any form of external support. Containing conflict to the national level would clearly favour Jakarta, given its military superiority over FRETILIN's guerrillas. ASEAN's efforts succeeded in 1982 when the issue was essentially erased from the international agenda, and Indonesia largely succeeded in quelling the resistance.

This partisan approach is underlined by the fact that, in stark contrast to ASEAN, other third-world states overwhelmingly rejected East Timor's annexation. New Order diplomats frequently claimed that Indonesia's 'heritage and record' as a founding father of non-alignment meant it could not possibly have behaved illegitimately.[21] But, led particularly by Cuba and African states, non-aligned governments overwhelmingly rejected this claim, denouncing the intervention in UN debates. Tanzania summed up their disillusionment:

> we had believed that Indonesia... an active member of the non-aligned group, one which itself emerged from the yoke of colonialism through a long and turbulent struggle, could not take measures which not only defy known principles of the Charter and of international law but also fly in the face of the very conduct that we ourselves, as non-aligned States, have consistently espoused and defended.[22]

Burundi similarly observed that 'Indonesia, which had contributed so decisively to the emergence of the NAM and struggled heroically to free itself from the Dutch colonial yoke, had now become an oppressor, thus betraying the spirit of Bandung, which had given rise to such hopes'.[23] Other third-world diplomats labelled Jakarta's defenders 'lackeys of imperialism' whose position 'had been determined by their countries' bilateral relations and economic interests, which should not overrule the principles of self-determination, freedom and independence'.[24]

Unlike most of their third-world counterparts, then, ASEAN states actively provided both material and diplomatic support for Indonesia's annexation of East Timor. Rather than upholding non-interference, they selectively applied the principle to aid Jakarta. Notwithstanding Singapore's brief demurral, ASEAN states backed the invasion because they shared Jakarta's concerns about the emergence of a radical state in the midst of the Indonesian archipelago. As one journalist killed in East Timor wrote before his death: 'visions of Chinese sampans, Hanoi dhows and Russian cruisers riding at anchor in Dili harbour [were] sufficient for ASEAN states, countering communist insurgencies, to see the threat as real and applaud its removal' (Aubrey, 2000, p. 141).

Concluding remarks

This chapter argued that 'non-interference' was violated and manipulated to disguise and defend its exact opposite: the subversion, invasion and annexation of one state by another. Fearing the possible impact of a radical state on domestic order in its own country and the wider region, in the context of waxing leftist power in Southeast Asia and domestic unrest in Indonesia, the New Order regime was determined to absorb East Timor. Notwithstanding some initial inter-elite frictions over strategy between Indonesia and Singapore, ASEAN supported the annexation, broadly accepting Jakarta's claim to have acted on behalf of regional 'stability'. Its defence of Jakarta became increasingly vociferous after Vietnam's 1978 invasion of Cambodia – an apparent *quid pro quo* for Indonesia joining the condemnation of Hanoi, despite the parallels with the Timor invasion (see Chapter 4).[25] ASEAN diplomacy helped Jakarta shift the issue from the UN to bilateral talks between Indonesia and Portugal from 1982 onwards. East Timor was not discussed again in international forums until the early 1990s. The scope of the ongoing conflict within the territory between Indonesian forces and the Timorese resistance was thereby dramatically contracted, bolstering the Indonesian side.

The impact on the East Timorese population was disastrous. An estimated 102,800 people were violently killed during Indonesia's bloody occupation (CAVR, 2005, p. 44). The army's brutal counterinsurgency campaigns forced the population into concentration camps and precipitated a famine described by the Red Cross as being 'as bad as Biafra and potentially as serious as Kampuchea' (Budiardjo and Liong, 1984, p. 78). An additional 84,200–182,000 people are estimated to have perished from illness and hunger under Indonesian rule, mostly during these campaigns (CAVR, 2005, p. 73). Village life was physically reorganised to assist with counterinsurgency. Indonesia's official language and ideology was imposed through schools, and feudal social relations were reinforced by Jakarta's use of local chiefs as its intermediaries. The only bene-ficiaries of Indonesian rule were Jakarta's 'entrepreneur-generals', who seized control of all the territory's significant assets, and a thin layer of Timorese collaborators (Aditjondro, 1994, pp. 44–5, 57–8; Saldanha, 1994, pp. 114–22). By the early 1990s, an Indonesian study found that the 'institutionalised tribute' system established by the army had per-petuated under-development and malnutrition, provoked widespread hatred of Indonesia, and constituted 'a new model of colonialism' (Mubyarto *et al.*, 1991, pp. 40–62). ASEAN had been directly complicit in this act of third-world imperialism.

4
Cambodia: Representation, Refugees and Rebels

> Without ASEAN there would have been no Cambodia issue. Because if we had not taken up the cause of Cambodia in early 1979, and steadfastly championed it, it would have disappeared.
> – *Singaporean ambassador Tommy Koh* (Acharya, 2009a, p. 115)

> What happened in East Timor was exactly the same thing, in principle, as what the Vietnamese did to Cambodia: a foreign-invaded, occupied Cambodia; a foreign-invaded, occupied East Timor.
> – *Thai ambassador Asda Jayanama* (2008)

While ASEAN scholars have largely ignored the invasion of East Timor, they have lavished attention on ASEAN's response to Vietnam's invasion of Cambodia in 1978. Indeed, it is principally through confronting Hanoi that ASEAN earned its reputation for fierce adherence to the principle of non-interference. The unchallenged consensus in the literature is that ASEAN reacted to the invasion because it was 'an evident breach of the ASEAN principle... of non-interference in the internal affairs of member-states as the sovereignty-reinforcing, unilateral-action-denying *sine qua non* of regional order' (D. M. Jones, 2009, p. 278). Despite the fact that neither Vietnam nor Cambodia were ASEAN members, ASEAN supposedly saw 'Vietnam's actions as a blatant violation of its norms', particularly 'ASEAN's doctrine of non-interference and non-use of force' (Acharya, 2009a, p. 99). ASEAN felt especially 'embarrassed' or 'betrayed' by the violation of its 'cardinal principle' given Vietnam's earlier assurances that it had no ambitions beyond its borders (Antolik, 1990, p. 116; Alagappa, 1993; Haacke, 2003, pp. 81, 83, 96; Caballero-Anthony, 2005, pp. 84, 86, 215–16, 259). ASEAN states are depicted as 'diplomatic gatekeeper[s]' concerned with 'the sanctity of national sovereignty... [their] most sacred corporate value' (Leifer, 1989, pp. 126, 14), whose strategic differences were set aside 'to defend [ASEAN's] primary principles' (Narine, 2005, p. 476). The literature is overwhelmingly concerned with how unity was maintained between ASEAN states despite the strains placed on the 'ASEAN way', with most authors concluding that 'ASEAN's response to the crisis was consistent with ASEAN's key norms' (Acharya, 2009a, p. 100).

This chapter argues that this overwhelming consensus confuses appearances with reality and, by focusing on problems of intra-ASEAN diplomatic coordination, ignores far more egregious violations of ASEAN norms *vis-à-vis* the Indochinese states. ASEAN certainly *claimed* to be defending Cambodia's sovereignty against Vietnamese aggression. However, it responded not to defend its non-interference principle, but rather to contain revolution in Indochina. To this end, far from merely being offended bystanders, ASEAN states engaged in counter-intervention, fomenting civil war inside Cambodia to keep Vietnamese forces pinned down and unable to support revolutionary movements outside Indochina. To pursue this proxy conflict, they helped rebuild the Khmer Rouge (KR) as a viable fighting force, and backed other, anti-communist guerrilla forces. ASEAN states diverted foreign aid and collaborated with China to rearm and supply these groups, gaining in exchange the cessation of Chinese support for their communist insurgencies. They also successfully championed the KR's retention of Cambodia's UN seat to deny Hanoi a *fait accompli*, and later assembled a new coalition government-in-exile to dilute the KR's influence and increase the chances of non-communists returning to power in Phnom Penh.

The chapter proceeds in four sections. The first explores ASEAN's immediate response to the invasion. The second details ASEAN's diplomatic championing of the KR, comparing it to their reaction to other foreign interventions. The third exposes ASEAN's aid to the Cambodian guerrilla movements. The fourth shows how ASEAN constructed the new coalition government-in-exile.

Understanding ASEAN's initial reaction

The ASEAN states' immediate response to the invasion was far more equivocal than a principled response to the violation of a 'cherished' norm would imply. In fact, ASEAN was significantly divided, since Indonesia was worried about the consequences of criticising actions that paralleled its own invasion of East Timor. Its relatively tepid initial response also suggests that the geopolitical implications of the invasion were unclear. The Association's response actually reflected a hard-fought consensus on the basis of a shared desire to resuscitate the buffer previously provided by Pol Pot's regime against the threat of Vietnamese 'subversion'.

Vietnam invaded Cambodia on 25 December 1978 with 100,000 troops, alongside the 20,000-strong Kampuchean Front for National Salvation, comprised mostly of KR cadres who had earlier attempted unsuccessfully to topple Pol Pot's genocidal regime. Hanoi justified its actions by claiming that its forces acted in self-defence, in response to Khmer Rouge raids into Vietnamese territory, while the task of overthrowing the government was carried out by the Front. In reality, of course, the 'two wars' were by no means distinct. The Khmer Rouge regime fell on 7 January 1979, and the state of 'Democratic Kampuchea' (DK) was replaced by the new People's Republic of Kampuchea (PRK), led by Vietnam's Cambodian allies. The PRK signed a Treaty of Cooperation and Friendship with Hanoi to legitimise the continued presence of Vietnamese troops in the country, which were engaged in mopping up KR remnants along the Thai-Cambodian border.

ASEAN's initial reaction to these events was surprisingly tepid. Indonesia's foreign minister, then chair of ASEAN's Standing Committee, issued a mild communiqué on 9 January expressing 'concern' at the invasion, citing not ASEAN norms but Bandung and UN Charter principles. On 13 January, an emergency AMM echoed this formulation, using opaque, non-condemnatory terms to call for the withdrawal of all foreign forces and respect for self-determination, and asking the UN Security Council to take up the matter. To reach this consensus, however, took a lengthy, 'heated debate', since there were significant intra-ASEAN differences: Indonesia in particular did not wish to 'internationalise' the issue and preferred, if possible, a low-key, negotiated solution (Alatas, 2008). Barry Desker (2008), a Singaporean diplomat present at the meeting, recalls that Indonesia 'favoured a very much lower-key ASEAN response, effectively condoning, acquiescence'. ASEAN was thus divided on the intervention from the start, which makes it difficult to argue that member-states acted on the basis of a strongly-shared commitment to the norm of non-intervention.

Intra-ASEAN divisions over Cambodia are generally noted by scholars only later, on issues of strategy in the 1980s. Typically, authors have argued that a concern for non-interference was universal, but 'threat perceptions' varied, accounting for differences of opinion. Realists have particularly emphasised the 'geopolitical reasons' behind states' reactions, arguing that ASEAN responded to a shift in the 'balance of power', and the 'direct threat' of Vietnam's army (Sukhumbhand, 1984, p. 32; Maisri-krod, 1992, pp. 294–5; Leifer, 1999, p. 30). Constructivists generally also admit that Thailand and Singapore favoured a 'hard line' response out of fear of Vietnam, while Malaysia and Indonesia favoured a softer stance since they saw Hanoi as a potential anti-Chinese bulwark. Several authors also claim that Indonesia's perceptions were coloured by a strong 'affinity' with Vietnam due to their common history of anti-colonial struggles (e.g. Caballero-Anthony, 2005, p. 91). Could these differences be read back to 1978, to explain the 'heated debate' on how to respond?

The difficulty with this realist-type explanation is that the 'threat' posed by Vietnam was *not* understood in conventional, military, balance-of-power terms. This is clear in considering statements from elites in Thailand, the state most directly affected by the invasion. Prime Minister Kriangsak accepted Hanoi's assurances that it had no intention to invade (ST, 1979). Foreign Minister Siddhi remarked that the Vietnamese 'know damned well they cannot conquer our country' (IHT, 1979). The Army's assistant chief-of-staff, General Chavalit, also insisted that 'no country which intends to invade another will deploy its forces in that way... Vietnam's intention to threaten us is not very clear' (Elliot, 1987, p. 89).

ASEAN's threat perceptions in fact turned on the likely consequences of the invasion for the balance of forces within their own societies. As Chapter 2 explained, ASEAN's ruling elites had welcomed the emergence of internal divisions within Indochina after 1975, because it distracted the victorious communist forces from assisting their fellow-travellers within ASEAN societies. The Indochinese states and China had all reduced their support for the CPT in order to ingratiate themselves with Thailand, and Cambodia under Pol Pot was seen as a useful 'buffer' against any Vietnamese plans to foment revolution abroad. The sudden removal of this buffer was, consequently, profoundly alarming.

Thailand, itself in a state of severe domestic upheaval, was now seen as the 'frontline state' against communism. Siddhi told the US secretary of state that 'Thailand's eastern boundary has become the frontier of the Free World in this part of the globe', requesting urgent assistance to prevent a 'further advance of what Vietnam has euphemistically called "Socialism's outpost" in Southeast Asia' (Sukhumbhand, 1985, p. 91). Singaporean elites linked events in Cambodia to the Soviet invasion of Afghanistan, positing the existence of a worldwide communist conspiracy to subvert the non-communist world (Rajaratnam, 1980). Lee Kuan Yew warned that the completion of Vietnam's mopping-up operations in Cambodia would inevitably be followed by 'increased communist insurgency in the ASEAN countries' (Huxley, 1983, p. 50). Rajaratnam (2006e, p. 52) noted with alarm that the Indochinese foreign ministers had declared their intention to change 'the balance of forces in Southeast Asia to bring about national independence and social progress'. Although, with its large and restive ethnic Chinese population, Malaysia was more concerned about China in the long run, Home Minister Ghazali Shafie had also warned that when Vietnam 'decided to pursue the creation of a Comecon in Southeast Asia' it 'would have no compunction in directing all her energies towards producing cadres who would be the creatures tasked to subvert the ASEAN states' (Huxley, 1983, p. 49). Malaysian elites also feared that the invasion would also distract the Thai army from policing the Thai-Malaysian border, allowing the MCP to re-establish its stronghold there. The Philippines' Marcos dictatorship also toed an anti-Vietnam and anti-Soviet line to maintain US support against a worsening communist insurgency. ASEAN state managers' threat perceptions thus converged not around geopolitics but around the spectre of communism.

Indonesia's leadership shared many of these concerns, as Chapter 2 showed; so why did Jakarta not wish to confront Vietnam internationally in the same way as its ASEAN partners? The explanation lies partly in divisions within the New Order. Like Thai and Singaporean leaders, Suharto believed it was only a matter of time before the Viet Cong resumed 'their communist missionary activities' against ASEAN.[1] This, and the New Order's record of counter-revolutionary intervention in Indochina, undermines sweeping statements about a historical 'affinity' with Vietnam that ignore Indonesia's socio-political transformation since the early 1960s. However, according to Adam Malik (1980, pp. 269–71), some nationalist forces, particularly in the army, still remained more sympathetic to the Vietnamese, believing they were essentially nationalists painted red who had been forced into a Soviet alliance to defend their country against China and its client regime in Cambodia. Many more in the army saw China as the major, long-term revolutionary threat, with their suspicion of the domestic ethnic-Chinese population and its imagined links to Beijing being a point of agreement with the Malay elite in Malaysia. Consequently, according to Admiral Sunardi, 'the need to avoid destabilising the New Order establishment' necessitated a 'dual track' approach whereby Jakarta supported Bangkok as the 'front-line' state against communism, but also promoted a conciliatory line towards Hanoi to achieve a negotiated solution (Sit, 1995, p. 129).

Perhaps more important, however, was the issue of East Timor. According to Desker (2008), Jakarta's 'underlying motive' in opposing a forceful response 'was Indonesia's search to win acquiescence for the incorporation of East Timor' to which a 'parallel' was drawn. This had two aspects. First, perceived parallels between the invasion and occupation of East Timor and Cambodia – both involving foreign powers using local forces to cover and legitimise the occupation – made it difficult for Indonesian diplomats to defend one while attacking the other. Secondly, Jakarta feared that confronting Vietnam might spur Hanoi to assist FRETILIN's guerrilla resistance against Indonesian forces in East Timor. FRETILIN representatives had sought aid from the Indochinese regimes after the invasion, but received only rhetorical support from Cambodia and China. Indonesia feared that antagonising Vietnam and the rest of the 'Cuban gang' now might prompt them to change their minds and provide material support to FRETILIN (Jasudasen, 2008). Because IR scholars have largely neglected the invasion of East Timor, they also overlook these explanatory factors for Indonesia's policy on Cambodia.

ASEAN's initial reaction to the invasion of Cambodia was therefore far from uniform. While Singapore and Thailand favoured a vociferous condemnation of Vietnam, Indonesia preferred to acquiesce in and condone the invasion. ASEAN's response did not, therefore, express shared revulsion at Vietnam's violation of their 'cherished' non-interference principle. However, geopolitical explanations of intra-ASEAN differences are also unpersuasive since even Thai elites apparently did not perceive the threat from Vietnam in conventional terms. Rather, state managers evaluated the threat in relation to the specific social conflicts animating their own polities. Despite a shared concern to maintain the capitalist social order that 'non-interference' was designed to preserve, variations in ruling socio-political coalitions, their domestic situations and their overall strategies also led to difficulties in coordinating a joint regional stance. 'Non-interference' did not motivate ASEAN's response, but merely became the trope through which it agreed to condemn the invasion, as the next section explores.

Representation: ASEAN as the Khmer Rouge's UN champion

The first, and perhaps most crucial, component of ASEAN's strategy was to prevent Vietnam achieving a *fait accompli* by blocking the necessary political victory required to cap its military success. The UN Security Council could not perform this task, since the Soviets vetoed resolutions calling on foreign forces to withdraw in January and February. Nor could Hanoi's military victory be undone, even by a punitive Chinese invasion of Vietnam in January. Had ASEAN not stepped in at this point, the issue would likely have vanished from the international agenda, effectively legitimising the new situation. However, ASEAN states managed to manipulate proceedings at the UN to acquire diplomatic leadership over the Cambodian conflict, which it used to frustrate Vietnam's designs, champion the deposed KR, and impose its preferred interpretation of events.

Which individuals get to represent states at the UN is usually determined entirely bureaucratically. Normally, governments dispatch diplomats to UN headquarters, where they are accredited by the Credentials Committee, whose reports are then rubber-stamped by the UN General Assembly (UNGA). In a historically unprecedented accomplishment, ASEAN politicised this process through successful annual campaigns for the KR to retain Cambodia's seat, despite it having been overthrown. The non-intervention principle was deployed to rally support from third-world states, while Western states also backed their non-communist ASEAN allies. ASEAN also sponsored critical annual UNGA resolutions on the 'Situation in Kampuchea' while hijacking Vietnam's counter-debates on 'Peace and Stability in Southeast Asia' to lambaste Hanoi.

Given the campaign's locus in the UN, the rhetoric ASEAN used to garner support against Vietnam understandably drew on UN Charter principles. This, rather than any specifically 'ASEAN' principle, largely explains the rhetorical emphasis ASEAN diplomats placed on non-interference. Appealing in particular to the third-world majority in the UNGA, ASEAN argued that the PRK was a 'puppet regime' established not by Cambodia's people but by Vietnamese intervention, whose seating would therefore violate basic Charter principles like non-interference, endangering the security of all weak states.[2] The Philippine ambassador, for instance, argued that seating the PRK would legitimise intervention and 'set in train a fatal sequence of events' whereby 'the small and weak nations of the world' would lose 'the right to exist except under conditions of bondage and servility'.[3] This rhetorical strategy allowed Singaporean ambassador Tommy Koh to claim that 'our opposition to Vietnam's action is based upon principle' and 'the right of DK to retain its seat in the UN has become coterminous with the defence of certain fundamental principles of the Charter of the UN'.[4] Such claims, taken entirely at face value, are the basis for the scholarly consensus that ASEAN opposed the invasion to defend the 'non-interference' principle.

The weakness of this argument can be further illustrated by comparing ASEAN's reaction to similar, earlier interventions. As Chapter 3 showed, ASEAN backed Indonesia's annexation of East Timor, which was similarly justified using a 'two-wars' explanation. Even more similar was Tanzania's invasion of Uganda in January 1979. Tanzania invaded alongside a very small indigenous liberation movement, using a 'two wars' justification to overthrow Idi Amin. Like Vietnamese forces in Cambodia, Tanzanian troops remained in Uganda for several years, policing the post-conflict settlement. Yet the new Ugandan regime was quickly recognised by over 80 states and was seated at the UN in 1980 with no hue and cry from ASEAN (Amer, 1992, pp. 207–9; Wheeler, 2000, pp. 119–20). Nor had ASEAN objected to French intervention to overthrow the Central African Empire's government in 1978: the replacement regime was seated without a formal vote.[5] Even the Soviet invasion of Afghanistan produced no comparable reaction from ASEAN states. Singapore, then a member of the Credentials Committee, even voted in favour of the new regime being seated – hardly a robust defence of 'principle'.[6]

ASEAN states' highly selective responses to interventions illustrates that they were motivated less by any 'cherished principle' than the specific implications of Vietnam's invasion for their own societies. The virtually non-existent international response to comparable interventions also underlines how important and unusual ASEAN's diplomatic campaign was. The campaign succeeded in its immediate goal of preventing a Vietnamese *fait accompli*. The withholding of international recognition for the PRK also created a crucial bargaining chip for the Association since, as Koh put it, there would otherwise be 'no incentive [for Hanoi] to negotiate a political settlement' favourable to ASEAN.[7] Moreover, it prevented the PRK from receiving the usual aid and development assistance afforded to poor countries by international agencies like the UN Children's Fund, the World Food Programme, the IMF and the World Bank. Consequently, the PRK was kept weak, poor and isolated, undermining the state's performance legitimacy. Vietnam was also isolated and sanctioned. Moreover, as the next section explores, these diplomatic manoeuvres were coupled with far more coercive moves on the ground.

Rebels and refugees: ASEAN's aid to anti-Vietnamese guerrillas

ASEAN states recognised that mere diplomatic victory at the UN would be insufficient to bring Vietnam to terms unless accompanied by favourable material conditions on the ground. They therefore moved to support anti-Vietnamese guerrilla movements, including the KR, to fight against Hanoi and the PRK. This in turn assisted ASEAN's annual campaigns at the UN since it allowed its diplomats to (falsely) claim that the deposed DK government still controlled large swathes of Cambodian territory and was effectively resisting 'foreign occupation'. In turn, these campaigns helped de-legitimise the PRK and stoke what would otherwise have been a doomed military struggle. This section shows how ASEAN kept the military resistance to the PRK alive, pinning down Hanoi's troops and resuscitating the buffer against revolutionary Vietnam previously provided by DK. This involved a *de facto* alliance with China, in exchange for a termination of Beijing's support for ASEAN's communist parties.

Using its longstanding experience of supporting Cambodian rebels, the Thai military began intervening even during Vietnam's invasion. Thai forces saved Pol Pot's deputy, Ieng Sary, from Vietnamese capture by airlifting him to safety. By January 1979, camps had been prepared on Thai soil where KR soldiers were fed, given medical treatment, re-armed and sent back over the border to fight Vietnamese forces. Having mined the border to exclude refugees, the army transported KR guerrillas safely across in their trucks. In just three days in April 1979, over 15,000 KR troops crossed the border in this way. Army spokesman General Som later confirmed that KR troops were being re-armed upon re-entering to Cambodia – a direct violation not only of 'non-interference' but the international law on neutrality (Jones, 2007, p. 528).

As it became clear that the KR had failed to resist the Vietnamese invasion, Thailand began collaborating with China, their main external patron, to provide more permanent support for the guerrillas on Thai soil. In January, Kriangsak met Chinese officials, agreeing 'to allow the use of Thai territory to supply the KR and provide transport and transit facilities for Cambodian personnel and materiel and also help KR leaders to make foreign trips through Thailand' (Chanda, 1986, p. 349). Thailand's Khemara Phumin island became a fortified entry-point for Chinese arms, and US intelligence reported that, during the 1980s, Bangkok funnelled $100m-worth of arms to the KR annually (Kiernan, 2002, p. 488). Thai artillery was also regularly used to cover KR forays into Cambodia, while Thai troops prevented Vietnam from pursuing KR forces retreating across the border. The tattered remnants of the KR were rebuilt into a 40,000-strong, well-armed fighting force. This fomented civil war inside Cambodia which both legitimised ASEAN's stance at the UN, and rebuilt a barrier against Vietnam's 'communist missionary activities'. As Thailand's supreme commander remarked, 'having lost Cambodia as [a] buffer, the best that Thailand could do was to sustain the fighting that in itself constituted a buffer' (Chanda, 1986, p. 381).

The fighting facilitated by Thai intervention displaced hundreds of thousands of Cambodian refugees, who tried to flee to safety across the border or the ocean. Initially, ASEAN elites saw the refugees as a threat to their domestic social orders, or even as fifth columnists sent to foment revolution. A senior Thai officer claimed that 'at least ten per cent' were 'Hanoi spies' sent to 'undermine the government' and Bangkok forcibly repatriated tens of thousands of them via minefields, killing many (Mysliwec, 1988, pp. 95–6). Singapore similarly referred to refugees as 'communist spies', 'human bombs', an 'invasion', and 'political warfare', refusing to accept any, while Malaysia deported 65,000 of them and adopted a shoot-on-sight policy, fearful that dealing with the refugees could distract its already-stretched security forces from anti-communist counterinsurgency operations (Sit 1995, p. 89; Rajaratnam, 2006c, p. 116; Richardson, 1982, pp. 10–107; Huxley, 1983: 49).

However, elite panic gave way to a more manipulative approach once 'the strategic value of the refugees as a buffer along the border and as a source for support for the re-emerging resistance movement' was recognised (Terry, 2002, p. 119). Bangkok refused to classify people fleeing the conflict as refugees, thereby denying them their rights under international law and enabling them to be manipulated to become a population base for the ASEAN-backed guerrillas along the border. Alongside the KR were two smaller, non-communist factions. The first, known as the Khmer People's National Liberation Front (KPNLF), was led by former prime minister Son Sann. The KPNLF began as the Khmer Serei, a right-wing group backed by Thailand since the 1950s. The second was Moulinaka, later renamed the *Front Uni National pour un Cambodge Indépendant, Neutre, Pacifique, et Coopératif* (FUNCINPEC), led by Prince Sihanouk, Cambodia's former head of state. Thailand's Task Force 80 rounded up Cambodian refugees and essentially kept them captive in these guerrillas' camps. By 1987, the UN Border Relief Organisation reported that anti-Vietnamese guerrillas were in control of all the refugee camps and over 260,000 refugees (Terry, 2002, p. 137; Mysliwec, 1988, p. 115).

The manipulation of Cambodian refugees supported ASEAN's intervention in Cambodia in three crucial ways. First, the camps were used by ASEAN diplomats to support their claims that the PRK lacked popular support and that the deposed DK regime still controlled 'liberated' parts of Cambodia's territory and population, even though they were mostly located on Thai soil. Michael Vickery (1987, pp. 309–10) argues that a United Nations High Commission for Refugees (UNHCR) facility was deliberately established at Khao-I-Dang to lure refugees across the border and discredit the PRK. Secondly, the refugees formed a useful human 'buffer', whose stated location varied with ASEAN's strategic requirements to protect their proxy forces. Whenever Vietnamese and PRK troops attacked the guerrillas' camps, ASEAN claimed that they were located in Thailand, and thus that Vietnam was 'invading' Thailand and 'slaughtering' Cambodian civilians. Such protests accompanied the 1979 and 1983 attacks on the KPNLF's headquarters (actually located just inside Cambodia), prompting such an international outcry that Hanoi was forced to terminate the offensives. In fact, Thailand had provoked both attacks by attempting to smuggle thousands of guerrillas into Cambodia under the guise of refugee repatriation (Vickery, 1987, p. 317; Van der Kroef, 1981, p. 519, 1983, p. 19). Thirdly, ASEAN used the refugees to campaign every year at the UN for international aid, which was used to sustain the conflict. Because the guerrillas controlled the camps, they were able to appropriate 50 to 90 per cent of all foreign aid sent to them. A top UN official admitted in 1987 that 'the border operation is a political operation. It's the UN system being used to keep the game going'. Another observed that 'if the UN stopped feeding the soldiers' wives and families, the resistance would stop' (Terry, 2002, pp. 73, 115, 130–1, 137–9; Vickery, 1987, pp. 318–20; Mysliwec, 1988, p. 99).

Without ASEAN states' support, the KR and the non-communist guerrillas would quickly have been destroyed by Vietnamese and PRK forces. Hanoi could then have withdrawn most of its troops, and the PRK regime's domestic stability and legitimacy would have been dramatically enhanced. ASEAN achieved the opposite outcome by aiding the guerrillas, recreating a buffer against Vietnam's revolutionary ambitions, tying down its troops and perpetuating an extremely costly conflict which exacerbated the Indochinese regimes' international isolation. In the final section, we will explore how ASEAN further intervened by creating a new Cambodian government-in-exile.

Representation II: ASEAN's construction of the 'Coalition Government of Democratic Kampuchea'

Since 1978, ASEAN and the US had repeatedly but unsuccessfully urged the anti-Vietnamese guerrilla movements to unite in their military struggle against Hanoi and the PRK. In 1981, the importance of getting the groups to work together was compounded when West European states hinted that they might stop backing the genocidal KR at the UN. ASEAN feared that this could trigger a wave of defections and lead to the widespread recognition of the PRK, rapidly unravelling its whole strategy. It therefore forced the factions together into a new Coalition Government of Democratic Kampuchea (CGDK). Despite having railed against the PRK as a 'regime not of the choosing of the Kampucheans themselves',[8] and defended DK on the grounds that 'we have no legal or moral right to change that people's representation in the UN',[9] ASEAN now went on to do precisely that. The goal, Lee Kuan Yew explained, was 'to preserve the DK seat in the UN and alter the leadership of the Government of DK' (ST, 1980). This section details this process, considering it as part of a raft of efforts – often the subject of significant intra-ASEAN disagreement – to resolve the conflict in a way favourable to ASEAN elites' own interests.

The task of assembling a new coalition government-in-exile involved direct ASEAN leadership, and a mixture of coercion and inducements. Initially, Thailand had taken the lead, hosting nine meetings between the faction leaders in Bangkok. Consistently frustrated, in April 1981 it handed the task to Singapore, which invited Son Sann for secret talks (ST, 1981; Tasker, 1982). The Singaporeans took a very bullish, 'carrot and stick' approach to the negotiations, which were led by diplomat Tony Siddique (Siddique, 2008). The non-communist groups were promised assistance 'in every possible way' if they united with the KR, but openly denounced when they stalled the negotiations (Japan Times, 1981). Lee Kuan Yew publicly warned the guerrilla movements that failing to unite would lead to 'the eventual legitimising of the Vietnamese puppet regime in Kampuchea' (ST, 1980). Bangkok followed suit, threatening to sever aid to the KPNLF if it did not compromise, while tempting Sihanouk to participate by promising to support his post-conflict plans for Cambodia (Quinn-Judge, 1981; Simon, 1982b, p. 204). In October 1981, Singapore brokered an outline agreement whereby Sihanouk, Son Sann and the KR's Khieu Samphan would serve respectively as president, prime minister, and deputy prime minister for foreign affairs. Malaysia now pledged aid to give 'beef and teeth' to the coalition if full agreement was reached (ST, 1982b). When the negotiations again faltered, ASEAN once more stoked speculation that DK would be ousted from its UN seat. The CGDK was finally announced in Kuala Lumpur in June 1982, after Malaysia had offered 'all out economic assistance' in addition to the food, clothes and arms already promised (ST, 1982a, 1982b).

The CGDK was thus very much a creature of ASEAN, and was immediately used to boost its diplomatic campaigns. The Thai foreign minister's claim that the coalition's formation was a 'domestic affair and the task of the Kampuchean people' and that 'neither Thailand nor ASEAN has interfered in this affair' is obviously false (Xinhua, 1982). ASEAN diplomacy was also repeatedly required throughout the 1980s to prevent Sihanouk from dissolving the coalition (Chanda, 1986, pp. 394–5). His participation, as a longstanding figurehead of nonalignment, was particularly crucial for ASEAN's strategy. Sihanouk put an acceptable face on an alliance still dominated by the KR, allowing more states to support ASEAN's campaigns in the UN from 1982 onwards. The dilution of the KR's diplomatic role also made it easier for ASEAN to present the conflict not simply as a defence of dry Charter principles but as an epic struggle for self-determination and a fight to save the Cambodian race and nation from extinction. ASEAN – backers of third-world colonialism in East Timor – even harnessed the Declaration on the Rights of People under Colonial or Alien Occupation to their cause.

ASEAN's long-term goal in creating the CGDK was to dilute the KR's influence and create an anti-communist alternative capable of returning to power in Phnom Penh if and when Vietnam was forced to withdraw from Cambodia (Siddique, 2008). The US was drawn directly into this project, which was particularly crucial after Vietnam's 1984–1985 offensive. The campaign virtually eliminated the CGDK's camps, and the Thai army was forced to suppress a revolt within and take effective command of the KPNLF (Chanda, 1986, p. 396). Despite earlier Indonesian disquiet over ASEAN being drawn into an overtly militarised confrontation with Vietnam, the offensive also spurred the Association to make a collective appeal for international aid 'for the Cambodian people "in their military and political struggle"' (Caballero-Anthony, 2005, pp. 89, 97). Washington supplied the CGDK with $20m of emergency aid, and provided between $17m and $32m a year thereafter (Kiernan, 1993, p. 199; Mysliwec, 1988, p. 83). A covert Singaporean-Malaysian-Thai-US group also convened regularly in Bangkok to coordinate assistance to the CGDK, sending arms, ammunition, communications equipment and food, providing military training and establishing a KPNLF radio station. The three ASEAN states dispensed around $70m and were critical in persuading Washington to participate (Lee, 2000, pp. 378–80). Although this aid never matched Chinese assistance to the KR, it was ultimately ASEAN's non-communist proxies who were levered into power when the conflict was finally settled (see Chapter 6).

This increasingly militarised intervention in Cambodia's affairs was not universally supported, however. As noted above, the Indonesian regime preferred a negotiated solution and usually rejected Singaporean suggestions of overt, collective ASEAN aid to the CGDK. For the New Order, this risked collaborating with Beijing's explicit desire to 'bleed Vietnam white' which, if accomplished, might allow China to return to its subversive activities within ASEAN countries. As an alternative, Suharto and Malaysian Prime Minister Hussein Onn issued the 'Kuantan Declaration' in March 1980. The declaration proposed a settlement that recognised

Hanoi's security concerns by proposing to create a neutralised, non-aligned Cambodia where Vietnam would exercise 'effective veto power over much of Cambodia's defence and foreign policy' (Peou, 2000, p. 140). Indonesia and Malaysia thus proposed permanently sacrificing Cambodian sovereignty to constrain what they perceived as the greater long-term revolutionary threat, Maoist China. Thailand and Singapore rejected this not because violating Cambodian sovereignty was wrong in principle, but because it would encourage rather than restrain Vietnam (Van der Kroef, 1981, p. 518).

Nonetheless, the 'Kuantan principle' – the idea that Cambodian sovereignty must be sacrificed in order to resolve the conflict – became a core element of the political settlements promoted by ASEAN's communiqués and UN resolutions from 1980 onwards. Other aspects included the withdrawal of foreign troops, measures to protect human rights and the rule of law (i.e., no recurrence of genocide by ASEAN's KR allies), national elections for a new government, and the repatriation of refugees (ASEAN, 1979, 1980, 1981).[10] Despite initial resistance from the US and China, which preferred all-out pressure on Vietnam, ASEAN's proposals became the basis for all future negotiations, and indeed the final settlement agreed in the early 1990s. Soon, the US, Japan, China and even Vietnam were all echoing ASEAN's calls for a neutralised Cambodia. ASEAN's remarkable capture of this international issue was reflected by the fact that since the early 1980s the major powers 'took their cues on the Indochina issue from ASEAN communiqués' (Simon, 1982a, p. 135).

This section showed how, in addition to creating the material conditions necessary to fuel conflict inside Cambodia, ASEAN also perpetuated the political conditions by assembling the CGDK to retain international support for its campaign against Vietnam. Most ASEAN states also sent material aid to the non-communist elements to increase their chances of returning to power in Phnom Penh. Indonesian unease over this military strategy, which ultimately flowed from the different strategies and interests within New Order factions described earlier, kept alive the possibility of a negotiated settlement. Yet this was scarcely more respectful of Cambodian sovereignty than armed intervention; indeed, peace apparently demanded its permanent sacrifice.

Concluding remarks

This chapter argued that, despite its protestations to the contrary, ASEAN was not a principled bystander in the Cambodian conflict, faithfully defending its norm of non-interference. Rather, was an active protagonist engaged in what was, at best, counter-intervention. Without this, the KR and its non-communist counterparts would likely have been destroyed while the PRK would have stabilised domestically and achieved international recognition. ASEAN states also campaigned diplomatically to isolate Vietnam and discredit the PRK, while manipulating rebel groups, refugees and aid, perpetuating the conflict until Hanoi agreed to a settlement that suited ASEAN. Difficulties in coordinating this strategy, stemming from intra-elite splits and differences in domestic social conflicts that led state managers to adopt varying strategic responses, meant that the extent and form of interventionist practices by ASEAN states varied. However, a shared determination to uphold capitalist social order in the region underpinned ASEAN's basic cohesion. ASEAN's preferred outcome involved the permanent diminution of Cambodian sovereignty in order to restore a buffer between ASEAN and revolutionary Vietnam. Ultimately, this settlement could not be imposed until the Cold War had ended, but in the meantime ASEAN's intervention successfully contained Vietnam's 'communist missionary activities'. As Singapore's Ambassador Kesavapany (2008) recalls, the dominoes had been poised to topple, 'but we managed to stop it at Laos-Cambodia'.

The KR's resuscitation, the alliance with China, and the manipulation of the refugees had highly significant consequences for social order in ASEAN countries, especially Thailand. China had already begun reducing its aid to foreign communist movements as the high tide of the Cultural Revolution subsided and the Deng Xiaoping regime became increasingly obsessed with counteracting Soviet initiatives. The *de facto* alliance with ASEAN over Cambodia rapidly accelerated this trend; indeed, China switched to supporting ASEAN's counter-revolutionary forces. After instructing the CPT's Maoist leadership to broadcast criticism of Vietnam's invasion, China closed the CPT's radio station, and other material aid essentially ceased in 1979. Beijing then pressed the CPT to enter a truce with the Bangkok regime and desist agitating in urban areas, declaring publicly in 1981 that it would not allow the CPT to sour Sino-Thai relations (Huxley, 1983, pp. 36–7, 43; Alexander, 1999, p. 316). The CPT leadership's decision to follow these instructions generated mass defections from the party.

Conversely, Chinese aid to the Thai government totalled $283m from 1985–1989 alone, and the Thai military gained preferential access to Chinese weapons, technology, and oil (Kiernan, 1993, p. 218; Shawcross, 1984, p. 126). Coupled with revived US aid – $100m in 1981–1982 and higher amounts thereafter – this allowed military spending to grow to a fifth of the national budget by 1982 (Sukhumbhand, 1984, pp. 36, 41). The Thai military also took a cut of all the materiel shipped to the KR and, along with allied business interests, profited hugely from black market cross-border trade mediated through its client guerrillas. By 1983, this value of this trade was estimated at $500,000 per day; by 1989, the KR was earning $2.4m per month from the territory it controlled with Thai assistance (Um, 1989, p. 101; Van der Kroef, 1983, p. 26; Chanda, 1986, p. 381). Even the UN's refugee agencies aided the struggle against communism, fuelling an economic boom and improving living standards by spending $350m in Thailand from 1979–1982, and over $32m annually thereafter (Rungswasdisab, 2006, p. 99).

The overall effect was to severely weaken the revolutionary forces of Southeast Asia while significantly strengthening their counter-revolutionary opponents. Before September 1978, the CPT had been growing at an estimated 6–10 per cent per year and had around 100,000 active sympathisers (Huxley, 1983, pp. 33, 38–9). By 1984, the Thai state had declared victory over the party. The rapid stabilisation of this vital 'domino', on which the social order of other ASEAN countries was seen to rest, boosted the cause of the *status quo* across the sub-region. There were also specific pay-offs for other non-communist regimes, such as Indonesia's New Order. China dropped its previously vocal support for FRETILIN, while DK quietly reversed its votes against Indonesia over East Timor at the UN. The ASEAN states' support for Jakarta's position on East Timor also became more vociferous – possibly to help assuage the New Order's reluctance to confront Vietnam. By the mid-1980s, the East Timor issue had essentially vanished from the international agenda while FRETILIN had been reduced to a tiny, rump force operating in remote, mountainous regions. ASEAN's intervention in Cambodia thus helped anti-communist forces across the region to stabilise their domestic social orders and further their territorialising, capitalist state-making projects.

Finally, the conflict also had important consequences for ASEAN as an international grouping. Like many, Ambassador Kesavapany (2008) identifies the Cambodian conflict as 'ASEAN's greatest success story in the political arena'. It forced ASEAN states not only to mediate their different positions into a common stance, but also to develop the most basic capacities required for regional cooperation, such as the training of officials in a common language. It 'put ASEAN on the map, substantively', and suddenly the Association was being consulted on all manner of diplomatic initiatives, not merely Cambodia (Siddique, 2008). ASEAN was thereby able to establish crucial 'dialogue partnerships' with Western powers. These yielded trade and investment cooperation, aiding economic development, and further enhanced ASEAN's internal stability. It is sobering to realise that all of this was accomplished through a decade of harmful intervention in a war-torn neighbouring country.

Part II
The Post-Cold War Period

5
ASEAN after the Cold War: Capital, Crisis, Conflict

> The common threat of communism... made for solidarity for ASEAN. After the collapse of communism, ASEAN needed a new common objective that could unite the group.
>
> – *Singaporean Prime Minister Lee Kuan Yew* (2000, p. 382)

> Before, it was the Communists who stirred up rebellion everywhere, including in Malaysia. Now we have the liberal democrats doing exactly the same in the same manner, complete with supplies of arms. Whether it is a communist or a liberal democratic insurrection, the people suffer not one bit less.
>
> – *Malaysian Prime Minister Mahathir Mohamad*[1]

Having feared for their very survival in the 1960s and 1970s, ASEAN's capitalist regimes stabilised and strengthened remarkably during the following decade. Thanks in part to their interventions in their near-abroad, the anti-communist military, bureaucratic, political and business elites which dominated ASEAN states defeated the threat of revolution. The sub-region's relative political stability and its suppression of labour unrest made it an attractive venue for foreign investment, which expanded rapidly following the de-regulation of global capital flows in the mid-1970s. This helped fuel the export-oriented, state-led development that ASEAN governments had prioritised to undercut the popular appeal of communism, generating rapid economic growth. By the 1990s, several ASEAN members had become second-tier 'tiger' economies. The region defied conventional wisdom by modernising economically while remaining politically undemocratic, which elites justified with reference to the so-called 'Asian values' of hierarchy, hard work and social harmony. In a sudden reversal, however, this impressive façade collapsed in the 1997 Asian financial crisis, which caused widespread social unrest and toppled governments. ASEAN was powerless to respond, and has emerged from the crisis enduringly weakened, its image tarnished and its relevance constantly questioned. This chapter traces the consequences of these developments for ASEAN's sovereignty regime.

The dominant view in the existing literature is that the norm may have been tested, but has fundamentally been maintained in the face of repeated challenges. Most scholars argue that non-interference remained static until the Asian financial crisis. Then, it endured some external and internal criticism, particularly in the form of Thailand's proposal for 'flexible engagement', but ASEAN 'stuck to a Westphalian view of sovereignty. It avoided any meaningful dilution of non-interference' (Acharya, 2009a, p. 242). However, after the crisis, particularly since around 2005, a few scholars have begun to identify some deviations from non-interference (Haacke, 2005; Caballero-Anthony, 2005). These are often seen as resulting from democratisation, particularly in Indonesia, and the rise of transnational security threats. Yet, as the introduction illustrated, the extent of these deviations from 'Westphalian' sovereignty is rarely fully recognised; more often, their significance is downplayed. Acharya's (2009a, p. 276) quite typical view of even the most recent developments is that 'ASEAN's norm of non-interference evolved somewhat but remained influential... There was no significant departure from this norm as demanded by reformist voices'.

This chapter takes a somewhat different approach. It agrees that ASEAN has not reached consensus on decisively and explicitly revising the non-interference principle. However, focusing predominantly on ASEAN's official corporate line on non-interference tends to give the misleading impression that Southeast Asia's sovereignty regime has been fairly static. The failure to shift ASEAN decisively into a 'post-Westphalian' mode stems less from an absence of interventionist practices than from ASEAN elites' inability to agree a way forward. This stems from divergences in processes of social conflict among ASEAN states, particularly since the Asian crisis. By tracing out these processes, and the interventions they have helped generate, this chapter suggests that ASEAN's sovereignty regime has been considerably more dynamic in practice than is commonly admitted. However, as ASEAN societies have become more diverse and differentiated, so the patterns of (non)-intervention related to them have also become less coherent and far more complex in comparison to those outlined in Chapter 2. These patterns are analysed here in three sections.

The first section explores how the defeat of communism in Southeast Asia paved the way for a dramatic transformation of ASEAN economies and polities, and for the meaning and application of (non)interference. As an illiberal 'new rich' emerged to dominate ASEAN states, ASEAN's Cold War-era interventions were terminated to facilitate trade and investment in neighbouring territories. 'Non-interference' was reconfigured to defend domestic power structures from external scrutiny and insulate new internal opponents from outside support. However, non-interference was circumscribed by ASEAN's need to prove its continued usefulness to external powers, leading to interventionist practices in Burma and Cambodia.

The second section considers the short-term impact of the Asian financial crisis on ASEAN societies and (non)intervention. The crisis propelled a liberalising government to power in Thailand, which sought to undermine non-interference to promote neoliberal reforms. This was generally resisted by embattled oligarchic forces elsewhere, which clung to non-interference as a way of managing domestic order. Nonetheless, intervention also served this same purpose during this period, particularly in the case of Indonesia. Following a humanitarian crisis in East Timor in 1999, Jakarta's immediate neighbours encouraged and joined a humanitarian intervention in order to limit the contagion of the social and economic chaos sweeping Indonesia.

The final section explores the long-term repercussions of the crisis. ASEAN states have tried to recover from their dramatic loss of investment and trade, domestic legitimacy, and international standing by announcing ambitious reform packages. The actual extent of reform is powerfully constrained by entrenched oligarchic interests within all member-states. However, ASEAN's post-crisis weakness compels it to address challenges to its reputation and image – if necessary, through intervention. Increasing tensions between the reformist impulse and the continued utility of non-interference in limiting the scope of socio-political conflict have prompted successive attempts to revise ASEAN's norms. While the process is marked by constant conflicts and setbacks, respect for sovereignty in Southeast Asia is openly being downgraded. As Malaysia's foreign minister put it in 2005, 'there is no such thing as absolute non-interference' (NST, 2005).

The rise of capital

One of the most important legacies of ASEAN's struggle against communism was the creation of powerful capitalist classes through processes of state-led development. While initially weak and reliant on the bureaucracy and military to defend their interests from revolutionary challenges in the 1960s and 1970s, by the late 1980s, Southeast Asia's capitalist elite had seized direct power for themselves. This section briefly describes this development, which has given rise to a particular form of state power, and analyses its impact on (non)interference. On the one hand, the strengthening of the capitalist class, and the demise of its revolutionary opponents, rendered Cold War-era interventions surplus to requirements, enabling them to be rolled back. This was, however, resisted by those bureaucratic, military and business interests that benefited from them. In practice, therefore, owing to the non-coherence of the state explored in Chapter 1, there was often a gap between official non-intervention and continued interventionist practices. On the other hand, non-interference remain an important tool to defend the power structures that had emerged from the Cold War from the West's 'new interventionism', which was seen as linked dangerously to domestic opposition groups. As such, the principle was retained, despite continued violations of it.

The rise of capital in Southeast Asia was intimately linked to the developmentalist policies pursued to defeat domestic communism, and broader transformations in the international political economy. Vast quantities of development spending by states lead to the creation of corrupt patronage networks between state officials and businesses seeking access to government contracts, permits and licences. Like most third-world states, ASEAN governments suffered a severe debt crisis in the 1980s and were forced to turn to the IMF for assistance, which imposed structural adjustment programmes on the region. However, with the exception of the Philippines, a massive influx of Japanese investment capital following the 1985 Plaza Accord uniquely allowed ASEAN governments to escape the debt crisis, preserving the region's developmental states. Neoliberal reforms were scaled back to suit the interests of corrupt state-business networks, which seized control of vast amounts of public wealth in highly-politicised privatisation processes. Buoyed by foreign investment as global capital flows were increasingly deregulated, the region experienced a massive economic boom and a new era of 'casino capitalism' which principally benefited the politically-linked 'new rich'. Increasingly wealthy and powerful business interests gradually reversed their dependence on government officials by capturing state institutions to obtain direct access to continued state largesse (Robison *et al.*, 1987). By the 1990s, 'one of the defining features of the political economy of Southeast Asia, with the exception of Singapore, [was] the highly instrumental nature of capitalist control of state power' (Rodan *et al.*, 2006, p. 25).

These developments took different forms across countries since their domestic political economies varied considerably. For our purposes, Thailand is crucial since it was the 'frontline state' from which many ASEAN interventions had been launched. During the Cold War, many businessmen and local 'godfathers' had sought elected office under the military regime to gain access to state resources. Many generals and bureaucrats also established their own business interests in similar ways. By the mid-1980s, with the CPT defeated, business interests began to outgrow the bureaucratic polity that had incubated it, particularly with an economic boom that generated a 'new rich' in areas like telecommunications and real estate. As their power grew and the Cold War ebbed, the state increasingly bowed to the interests of the new rich. In 1986, Foreign Minister Siddhi declared that Thailand's foreign policy would be directed by economic issues like trade, markets and investment, rather than 'politics' (Neher, 1990, p. 196). Two years later, the military prime minister was ousted in a parliamentary vote of no-confidence, necessitating elections. These were easily won by parties serving as vehicles for leading business oligarchs, through vote-buying and patronage politics. The first post-military government, led by general-turned-businessman Chatichai Choonhavan, was so corrupt that it was called the 'buffet cabinet', while a later successor, Banharn Silpa-archa, acquired the nick-name 'Mr ATM' for his habit of dispensing bribes in the parliament's toilets (Wingfield, 2002, p. 262; McCargo and Ukrist, 2005, p. 17). Since the mid-1980s, Thai politics has principally been animated by struggles among different factions of wealthy individuals to capture and use the state for their own purposes.

This process, albeit with significant national differences, was replicated in other ASEAN societies. Malaysia's ruling party, UMNO, had cultivated a class of Malay capitalists to counter ethnic Chinese domination of the economy in the wake of the 1969 race riots. These business elites gradually displaced UMNO's aristocratic leadership during the 1980s, and Malaysian politics quickly came to revolve around intra-party factional disputes over the spoils of the state (Gomez and Jomo, 1997). In Indonesia, bureaucratic and military officials had initially been the principal beneficiaries of state-led development under the New Order. They were increasingly eased out during the 1980s by a vast patronage network of Malay conglomerate owners, ethnic Chinese businessmen and other 'cronies' centred on President Suharto himself – with the Suharto family itself becoming exceedingly wealthy (Robison, 1986).

Singapore was a significant exception. The PAP had managed to destroy, disorganise or co-opt all alternative power-centres in Singaporean society. The rule of PAP's bureaucratic elites was legitimised through an elitist, depoliticising and meritocratic ideology which emphasised clean, pro-market, technocratic governance. Singapore's position as an international trading, services and financial centre also attuned the state to the interests of foreign capital rather than special pleading from domestic entrepreneurs. Thus, while PAP retained tight control of the commanding heights of Singapore's economy through government-linked corporations, the city-state avoided the sort of corrupt practices endemic across the rest of the region (Rodan, 1993).

The Philippines took a rather different trajectory. Unlike its ASEAN counterparts, the Marcos dictatorship proved unable to defeat the country's communist insurgency. Rather than stimulating economic growth and uniting the elite around Marcos, development spending was diverted to the president's own 'crony capitalists', alienating many of the landed, oligarchic families which have long dominated Philippine society. They successfully resisted Marcos's efforts to institute land reform to combat the socio-economic inequalities underpinning the insurgency. By the late 1970s, therefore, the Communist Party of the Philippines commanded large-scale mass backing and the possibility of revolution was openly discussed.[2] This unrest deterred foreign investment, precluding the Philippines' escape from the 1980s debt crisis. IMF-imposed austerity reforms exacerbated opposition to Marcos. He was gradually deserted by his core supporters among the capitalist and middle classes, within the Church, and in Washington as his ability to fend off revolution looked increasingly in doubt. Under US pressure, Marcos called snap elections in 1986, using widespread fraud to manufacture his re-election. A massive 'people power' protest erupted in Manila, forcing Marcos to resign and flee the country. Since the left had boycotted the elections, control passed to the new president, Corazon Aquino, a scion of the landed elite.

As usual when faced with the prospect of revolution, ASEAN had actually intervened to try to shore up the Philippines' counterrevolutionary forces. An ASEAN summit was deliberately held in Manila in 1983 to help bolster Marcos (Antolik, 1990, pp. 82–3). In the middle of the 'people power' protests, Suharto loaned military aircraft to the Marcos regime, and ASEAN issued a joint statement calling for the 'peaceful resolution' of the crisis, calling on 'all parties to restore national unity and solidarity' and exercise 'restraint' (Anwar, 1994, p. 148; ASEAN, 1986). After Marcos fell, ASEAN also sought to bolster the new Aquino government against more radical alternatives by staging another summit in Manila in 1987, with an Indonesian warship stationed in Manila Bay to 'scare off' those plotting against Aquino (Dwipayana and Ramadhan, 1991, p. 443; Lee, 2000, p. 340).

The net effect of these developments was the 'return of elite democracy' to the Philippines (Hutchison, 2006, p. 57). Aquino successfully stabilised the post-Marcos state by promising land reform and pledging to bring popular organisations into local governance. In practice, social, economic and political reforms were stalled and diluted by the 'traditional politicians' (*trapos*) drawn from the old landed families and the ranks of the industrial, banking and real estate oligarchies. The *trapos* have been able to use 'guns, goons and gold' to maintain their effective domination of the Philippine state, which is interrupted only periodically by mass protests provoked by grinding poverty and gross inequality. The state's internal and external priorities are thus not dissimilar from the rest of ASEAN's. However, the country's relatively well-organised nongovernmental and popular organisations, and the state's heavy reliance on the US, means that oligarchic domination occasionally requires that lip-service to be paid to liberal-democratic principles.

These socio-economic developments have generated state forms that systematically favour business interests while weakening and disorganising other classes. Contrary to the expectations of modernisation theory, Southeast Asian capitalists are 'contingent democrats', favouring democracy only to the extent that it facilitates their continued access to state power and largesse (Bellin, 2000). The region's democracies are thus often described as 'pseudo-', 'semi-', 'defective', and 'quasi-authoritarian' democracies. The surface appearance of democratic rule conceals to varying degrees electoral gerrymandering, strict media controls, violence, coercion, corruption, patronage politics and vote-buying, which principally serves dominant, state-linked business interests. Other forces have been systematically undermined. ASEAN's communist parties had all been defeated by the 1990s, depriving the left of its vanguard political force. The unleashing of global capital flows and local anti-labour measures also profoundly weakened organised labour. Labourers were forced into state-run unions, strikes were violently suppressed, and workers became dependent on state-provided benefits such as food and fuel subsidies and public housing (Hadiz, 2004; Deyo, 2006). The middle classes formed by rapid economic development were also dependent on the state to generate further growth, continued employment and security from the lower orders. They largely imbibed the illiberal political culture of the region's capitalist elites and supported its authoritarian, developmentalist regimes (Bell *et al.*, 1995;

Rodan, 1996a; Jones, 1998). These flows of material resources to sub-ordinated groups – the byproduct of rapid economic growth – coupled with tight political and ideological controls, ensured the hegemony of the new rich. Only small, radical social groups, including some middle-class non-governmental organisations (NGOs) and popular organisations representing the poor, openly opposed the *status quo*. They were often suppressed and marginalised while their more moderate counterparts were co-opted.

The consequences of these developments for ASEAN's sovereignty regime can now be traced out. First, the post-Cold War geostrategic and ideological context meant that non-interference would continue to be an important strategic tool for state managers to limit the scope of political conflict. 'Non-interference' was initially developed to insulate communist insurgents from sources of external support, and this threat to dominant interests had now been defeated. However, the geopolitical and ideological shifts associated with the end of the Cold War implied new dangers for ASEAN's ruling classes. Western powers shifted quickly from providing unconditional geostrategic and economic support for anti-communist regimes to promoting a 'new world order' and 'democratic enlargement'. Interventions were launched against developing countries from Panama to the Persian Gulf, promoted by liberals who dreamt of sweeping away the authoritarian regimes made 'necessary' by the Cold War.

This 'new interventionism' was seen in Southeast Asia as risking the socio-political stability and potentially undermining the authoritarian, developmentalist state projects which overwhelmingly benefited the new rich and their allies. Just as communist states like China had been perceived as directing insurgencies within ASEAN countries, so Southeast Asian elites now saw the West's new interventionism as linked to their contemporary domestic oppositions. Renewed unrest in East Timor, for example, which explicitly sought to attract UN intervention to the territory, was seen as directly inspired by Western meddling. Reformist opposition parties were similarly branded lackeys of the West. As Malaysia's prime minister put it,

> Before, it was the Communists who stirred up rebellion everywhere, including in Malaysia. Now we have the liberal democrats doing exactly the same in the same manner, complete with supplies of arms. Whether it is a communist or a liberal democratic insurrection, the people suffer not one bit less.[3]

Reflecting their capture by highly illiberal and often predatory oligarchic interests, ASEAN states argued that granting genuine democratic rights would, as Singapore's UN spokesman put it, only sow 'confusion and discord', exacerbate 'the risk of instability posed by ethnic and other tensions' and undermine the social 'discipline' required for economic development. Regional governments rejected calls for liberalisation, 'placing political stability above all else'.[4] Some ASEAN states also argued that human rights and liberal democracy clashed with 'Asian values' and the 'right to development'. Local advocates of liberalism were branded as Western-inspired saboteurs whose politics were alien to accepted cultural values (Rodan, 1996b; Robison, 1996).

ASEAN states' reaction was principally about insulating these opponents from external support, rather than any principled attachment to sovereignty *per se*, or even a total rejection of human rights. Malaysia, for example, had played a leading role in the anti-*apartheid* movement and, due to the growing role played by Islam in UMNO's legitimation strategies, repeatedly called for Western intervention to protect Muslims in Yugoslavia, which ASEAN often echoed. Domestically, some ASEAN states were also adapting to the new *Zeitgeist* by ratifying some UN human rights conventions and creating tame national human rights bodies, which helped dilute Western criticism and co-opt domestic opponents. As parts of their territories became tightly integrated into the global economy, ASEAN states' domestic sovereignty was also becoming increasingly 'graduated'. While *de facto* authority was ceded to multinational companies in export-processing zones, coercive state control was reinforced in other areas, particularly in relation to the lower social orders (Ong, 2000). ASEAN's sovereignty regime was thus far from uniformly rigid but was shaped to benefit the dominant forces within ASEAN societies. 'Non-interference' was maintained as a strategic measure, to insulate domestic opponents from sources of external support and thus control the scope of social and political conflict to a level at which dominant interests would prevail.

However, in the post-Cold War geopolitical context, the non-interference principle faced powerful contradictory pressures arising from the economic and geopolitical strategies adopted by ASEAN's ruling classes. First, ASEAN states' adoption of a capital-intensive, export-driven economic growth strategy makes their economies reliant on access to US, European and Japanese investment and export markets. The sustenance of growth – and the resultant flows of resources to both powerful and subordinated social groups that preserve stable domestic power relations – therefore depends on politically-mediated relations with these foreign markets. Secondly, and relatedly, ASEAN foreign ministries have consistently pursued a geopolitical strategy of omni-directionality that maximises the political and economic benefits it can extract from relations with all the major powers. They have been particularly concerned to entrench the US presence in the region. This is partly due to post-Cold War strategic uncertainties, particularly *vis-à-vis* China. However, it is also to maintain and expand access to markets for investment and trade, development assistance, aid, the financing of regional cooperation initiatives, and so on. Again, these flows are vital to the maintenance of the economic growth and political stability that underpin the strategies of domestic rule pursued in ASEAN states.

However, this engagement with external powers and markets is always asymmetric and carries significant risks. External powers often raise issues like human rights or democracy or demand that ASEAN manage regional problems in ways that often threaten the interests underpinning state power in the region. ASEAN has tried to generalise 'non-interference' in institutions like the ASEAN Regional Forum, founded in 1993, in order to moderate these pressures. It thereby retains the ability to invoke the principle to keep threatening issues off the regional agenda and to prevent the scope of domestic conflicts being widened by external forces. As Chapter 7 shows, this was crucial in containing the scope of conflict in East Timor, preventing it from becoming internationalised for many years.

However, ASEAN must still provide reasons to maintain external powers' interest and engagement. In the early 1990s, ASEAN succeeded in channelling Western engagement away from politics to economics thanks to the region's rapid economic growth, which attracted over a third of foreign investment in Asia by 1997 (UNCTAD, 2009). However, ASEAN states still had to make strategic concessions on political issues. In particular, it had to intervene in Burma to promote liberalising political and economic reforms in order to assuage Western concerns (see Chapter 8). The price of maintaining 'non-interference' in relation to external powers – in order to insulate domestic orders from significant external challenge – is a pressure to suspend it internally, within ASEAN, in order to substantiate the Association's corollary claim to be primarily responsible for managing regional order in Southeast Asia. This dynamic was particularly clear in 1997 when Cambodia's ruling coalition broke down. ASEAN's prior intervention in Cambodia meant that its credibility as a regional organisation was heavily premised upon its diplomatic 'ownership' of the situation there. Consequently it felt little alternative but to intervene to restore order (see Chapter 6). As we shall see, this imperative to intervene to safeguard ASEAN's capacity to shape the regional agenda – to control the scope of socio-political conflicts – has been significantly strengthened since the Asian financial crisis.

In the meantime, just as the practical meaning of non-interference shifted to suit the interests of the 'new rich' in extra-regional relations, so it was also transformed within the region itself. ASEAN's anti-communist interventions had become defunct by the late 1980s. Indeed, they now actively impeded business interests wanting to invest in and trade with neighbouring countries. This was particularly the case in Thailand, where the 1980s boom had generated large capital surpluses but depleted domestic commodity supplies. As we shall see in Chapters 6 and 8, therefore, the new oligarch-dominated government of Thailand led the way in winding down Cold War-era interventions in order to turn 'battlefields into marketplaces', in Prime Minister Chatichai's catchphrase. The other ASEAN states, despite some initial misgivings, quickly followed suit. This scramble for new markets partly underpinned ASEAN's plans to integrate its former erstwhile enemies into the Association and its Free Trade Area (AFTA).

Expanding economic ties and the widening umbrella of ASEAN's non-interference principle were attractive to the forces governing Burma and Indochina, which were presiding over their own internal transformations. The Indochinese states had been quickly abandoned by their Soviet patron from the mid-1980s, and to avoid collapse they had each launched domestic 'restructuring' programmes designed to create a form of state-managed capitalism. The gradual dismantling of Indochina's revolutions and the collapse of ideological contestation between the two blocs in Southeast Asia meant that the developmentalist state projects pursued by the Vietnamese, Cambodian and Laotian states were increasingly aligned with those of ASEAN. Ruling elites were keen to insulate the significant domestic strains emanating from domestic reforms from external influences in order to manage them on their terms. For example, Vietnam's *doi moi* reforms created serious tensions between pro-market reformers and anti-reform hardliners within the Vietnamese Communist Party (VCP), which were linked respectively to business groups with an interest in expanding international trade and investment, and patronage networks in the state-owned sector of the economy (Beresford, 1993; Dixon, 2004). This struggle has provoked waves of rural unrest and featured hard-liners linking reformers to the USA, which they accuse of trying to destroy 'communism' in Vietnam (Thayer, 1999). The VCP regime has strongly emphasised Vietnam's sovereignty, partly as a sop to conservative forces and partly to contain these conflicts in the domestic sphere. Therefore, once ASEAN's non-interference principle shifted from being a weapon with which to beat the Indochinese regimes to one which they could benefit from, membership became a very attractive option.

However, ASEAN's *rapprochement* with the 'CLMV' states (Cambodia, Laos, Myanmar and Vietnam) changed the nature of intervention in neighbouring countries rather than terminating it altogether. Firstly, the policy demanded that support for insurgencies in neighbouring socialist states be ceased. This was resisted by domestic groups that profited directly from these interventions, particularly the entrenched bureaucratic, military and business interests which dominated the cross-border black-market trade with the aid of guerrilla movements like the Khmer Rouge. Their refusal to sever these relationships continued to generate destabilising interventions in neighbouring countries well into the 1990s. This stemmed directly from the non-coherence of state power discussed in Chapter 1, whereby different elements of the state apparatus, linked to forces beyond the state, may pursue divergent policies in practice, with complex consequences for the *de facto* sovereignty regime.

Secondly, the attempt to integrate the new member-states politically and economically into ASEAN could itself involve interventionist measures. ASEAN leaders tried to persuade the Burmese government to adopt economic reforms and ASEAN-style governance to assist their allied business interests, fend off Western criticism and preclude the country becoming too dependent upon China. The transition from battlefield to marketplace in Cambodia required an unprecedented United Nations intervention, which ASEAN states welcomed and participated in. The settlement this intervention produced was, however, rather tenuous, and was further destabilised by influxes of state-linked ASEAN capital. When the ruling coalition collapsed in 1997, ASEAN again intervened in Cambodia to restore the *status quo ante* (see Chapter 6). The case for these interventions was strengthened by the need to demonstrate to external powers ASEAN's capacity to manage its own region, discussed above. Reflecting the transformation of the region's societies and the shifting geopolitical context, then, while ASEAN interventions continued, their purpose shifted from counter-revolution to serving the requirements of ASEAN's developmentalist agenda: opportunities for trade and investment, political stability, and maintaining favourable relations with external powers and markets.

The rise of capital thus had significant consequences for ASEAN's sovereignty regime. The non-interference principle persisted but was reconfigured to defend the region's illiberal domestic power structures from the 'new interventionism' and to maintain the stability of a socioeconomic and political order which overwhelmingly benefited elite groups. The defeat of communism in the region rendered obsolete ASEAN's anti-communist interventions in its near abroad. The new rich pushed for their replacement by policies more conductive to their interests, though this was resisted by those forces benefiting from their relationships with foreign insurgent forces, leading to continued intervention. Interventions also persisted in order to maintain the region's engagement with external powers and to substantiate ASEAN's claim to manage regional order. For several years, ASEAN state managers performed a remarkable balancing act, presiding over a massive economic boom while resisting domestic and foreign pressures to liberalise their polities. This was not to last.

Southeast Asia in crisis

The 1997 Asian financial crisis was the worst economic catastrophe to hit Southeast Asia since World War II. The crisis devastated the region's economies, provoked widespread social unrest and demands for political reform, led to the fall of the Thai and Indonesian governments, almost followed by Malaysia's, and profoundly damaged ASEAN's international standing. In Thailand, the liberalising Democrat party came to power and launched a direct attack on the non-interference principle, urging the use of 'flexible engagement' to legitimise intra-ASEAN intervention as part of their campaign to reform Thailand and the region. This was staunchly resisted by most other ASEAN states, where oligarchic forces were struggling to contain the challenges to their political and economic domination within territorial boundaries. The principle consequently survived, but, in practice, the imperatives of restoring domestic social order and the conditions necessary for economic growth in the region generated further interventions.

The crisis stemmed from the interface between international financial speculation and the 'crony capitalism' described above. The weak regulation produced by politicised liberalisation processes had created severe weaknesses in Southeast Asia's apparently healthy financial sectors. Domestic financial institutions were often bilked for loans by their oligarch owners, such that by the early 1990s regional banks were massively exposed to 'bad', non-performing loans. Along with speculative foreign investment attracted by high economic growth rates, bank loans were pumped into speculative bubbles in areas like real estate and stocks. This toxic mixture prevailed until 1996, when domestic banks started to collapse. Initially, they were bailed out by their patrons in government, but Thailand's inability to rescue a major bank in 1997 prompted foreign investors to panic and flee from the entire region. Stock markets collapsed, prompting more banks to fail, and a widespread financial crisis quickly ensued.

This had a devastating effect on ASEAN's investment-dependent economies. Malaysia's Gross Domestic Product (GDP) contracted by 7.4 per cent in 1998, Thailand's by 11 per cent and Indonesia's by 13 per cent. The value of Philippine, Malaysian, Thai and Indonesian currencies fell by between 40 and 86 per cent (UNCTAD, 2008, 2009). Indonesia, the worst-hit economy, saw generations of development undone as the percentage of the population in absolute poverty rose to 70 per cent and unemployment increased by five million (Thakur, 2000, pp. 243–4). ASEAN's paper-thin regional institutions could do nothing to stem the tide. To keep their states afloat and prevent the total collapse of their banking systems, Jakarta and Bangkok were forced to turn to the IMF for aid, which imposed fiscal austerity measures on the region. This severely exacerbated the financial crisis and, by slashing domestic subsidies that were a key ingredient of social peace, escalated violent social unrest. State-dependent oligarchs, too, faced their sources of wealth and power being switched off.

The crisis had dramatic effects on social conflict in the region and thus significant political consequences. In Thailand, the oligarchic Chavalit government fell because it was unwilling to move against its allies in the financial sector. The neoliberal Democrat Party, based predominantly in Bangkok's middle-classes, had previously only been able to govern in coalition with oligarchic parties, but now came to power alone in a deal brokered by the palace. Thai liberals saw the crisis as an indictment of Thailand's entire political and economic system, and the Democrats eagerly embraced IMF-imposed reforms as a means to destroy the power of the 'new rich' and usher in 'good governance' (Hewison, 2000, pp. 206–7). The crisis also strengthened the hand of reformers in the Philippines somewhat. We will explore the consequences of these changes for 'non-interference' momentarily.

Elsewhere in the region, liberalising social forces were energised but beaten back. Indonesia's New Order regime resisted fully implementing the IMF's prescriptions since they 'struck at the heart of politico-business and conglomerate power' (Robison and Rosser, 2000, pp. 179, 182). However, Suharto's transparent efforts to safeguard his cronies' interests merely exacerbated the crisis. Separatist and communal conflicts escalated, including in East Timor, Aceh, West Papua and the Moluccas. The military was also accused of fomenting unrest, including by inciting anti-Chinese pogroms to divert blame for the crisis away from the state. Middle-class protests movements emerged to demand *reformasi* (reform) to end 'corruption, collusion and nepotism', but they were far too weak to seize power, instead urging the IMF to impose democracy on Indonesia. However, in May 1998, cuts in fuel subsidies provoked widespread riots, Washington withdrew its backing for the regime, and Suharto was forced to step down. Vice-President Jusuf Habibie took over and, with the state entirely dependent on Western aid for survival, was forced to announce a programme of political liberalisation. The Indonesian state staggered on, unable to avoid implementing externally-imposed neo-liberal reforms altogether but buffeted by oligarchic interests struggling to salvage their corporate empires and reorganise themselves in the country's emerging democratic institutions (Robison and Hadiz, 2004).

Despite significant unrest in Malaysia, the Mahathir regime managed to survive. Initially Mahathir allowed his deputy, Anwar Ibrahim, to promote IMF-style reforms in response to the crisis. However, when these reforms began striking at the interests of Mahathir's patronage networks within UMNO, Anwar was deposed and Mahathir instead imposed capital controls, blaming a foreign conspiracy of Jewish speculators for the crisis (Gomez, 2002, pp. 104–8). Anwar subsequently became the figurehead of Malaysia's own *reformasi* protests, which attracted urban middle-class and Islamist adherents tired of oligarchic corruption. While the government managed to suppress the protests, mass disillusionment and economic hardship generated heavy losses for UMNO in the 1999 elections. A nationalistic and reactionary foreign policy ensued as Mahathir strove to maintain the *status quo* against these challenges.

ASEAN's newer member-states were much less affected by the crisis. Because of their underdevelopment, lack of significant financial sectors, heavy capital market regulation, and their relative non-integration with the core ASEAN economies, the 'CLMV' economies (Cambodia, Laos, Myanmar, and Vietnam) were far less exposed. Indeed, they continued to prosper, averaging a rate of 5.1 per cent GDP growth in 1998 (UNCTAD, 2008). Correspondingly, social unrest linked to the crisis was relatively limited. As Chapter 6 explores in detail, Cambodia had already been plunged into political crisis by the collapse of its ruling coalition and was being subjected to ASEAN intervention, but the financial crisis played little role in these events. Burma suffered no unusual upheaval. A spate of peasant uprisings occurred in Vietnam in 1997, prompting leadership changes in the VCP, but this was apparently a reaction to internal reforms rather than the Asian crisis (Bolton, 1999, pp. 189–90). If anything, the crisis reinforced those entrenched, conservative forces in CLMV states whose anti-liberalisation posture seemed to have vindicated.

The crisis thus had extremely uneven and contradictory impacts on Southeast Asian societies and thus on ASEAN's sovereignty regime. Two main outcomes need to be highlighted. The first is that Thailand's new

Democrat government seized on the crisis to demand neoliberal reforms, not only in Thailand but across the whole region. Foreign Minister Surin Pitsuwan (1998a) argued that in the age of globalisation, Southeast Asia faced 'formidable impersonal forces that heed no borders'. ASEAN faced a stark choice: 'we either reform ourselves to meet international standards, or we can resist and be overwhelmed in the end, with no control over the pace or direction of change'. Crucially, Thailand could not 'meet the challenge alone; the region as a whole must rise to the occasion', Surin argued, since 'the credibility of the region's institutions has [also] been cast into doubt by the crisis'. This allegedly required 'reform of our economic, social and... political institutions to meet international standards and expectations... the region, if it is to maintain its dynamism, has no choice but to move in the direction of greater openness'. Southeast Asia's economies could thus only recover from the crisis by collectively conforming to neoliberal standards of 'good governance'.

Relatedly, Surin argued that the challenges of 'globalisation' also necessitated drastic revision of ASEAN's non-interference principle. First, Surin argued, since the region was viewed *en bloc* by investors, the effectiveness of any single reform effort would depend on complementary reforms being adopted throughout ASEAN. The non-interference principle would consequently have to be weakened to permit 'peer pressure' to be exercised to on governments which resisted implementing appropriate policies (Surin, 1998a). Secondly, Surin and his deputy, Sukhumbhand Paribatra (2004), also argued that the transnational contagion of the Asian crisis, plus problems like environmental degradation and transnational crime, showed how 'dividing lines between what is domestic and what is external have become very indistinct'. Since 'instability in our neighbouring countries is bound to affect the region and ourselves' and 'delays and setbacks in one country can affect the region as a whole', Surin (1998a) insisted that on 'domestic issues with regional implications', non-interference had to be relaxed to enable these issues to be governed regionally. Sovereignty, he therefore insisted, 'cannot and should not be absolute' (Surin, 1998b). What the Democrats envisaged, Sukhumbhand (2004) explained, was a 'shift from a culture of sovereign impunity to acceptance of the principle and practice of sovereign accountability... to the region and to the international community'.

From this perspective, the crisis had exacerbated the contradiction between ASEAN's tightening integration into a liberalising global political economy and the attempt of state managers to uphold fundamentally illiberal domestic political and economic arrangements.

This tension had been increasingly apparent in ASEAN's external relations since the Cold War, which ASEAN states had attempted to manage using 'non-interference'. ASEAN had always been required to reckon with powerful external interests, but the Democrats now proposed to concede far more than ever before. Essentially, they were exploiting the crisis to try to entrench greater respect for liberal values and embed 'good governance' domestically and regionally. This was an ideological class project which had hitherto been thwarted by the power of the new rich and the use of 'non-interference' to fend off external neoliberal agendas and preserve the corrupt structures of the developmental state. Now, the Democrats urged that ASEAN's sovereignty regime be altered to permit 'international standards' to be enforced and allow certain domestic issues to be governed at the regional level.

As many authors note, however, the demand for 'flexible engagement' attracted little support from other ASEAN states. This is often explained by reference to the normative grip of non-interference over ASEAN. Acharya (2009b, p. 131), for instance, argues that Surin's proposal failed 'because it was not backed by any prior regional tradition'. Other scholars have emphasised the domestic political situations in the region. Philippine reformers who shared the Democrats' goals and ideals were alone in backing the proposal. Singapore's government favoured pro-market reforms and clean, technocratic governance, but not liberal values, and thus demurred. The other ASEAN states were openly hostile. The newer member-states had been attracted to ASEAN partly because of the utility of non-interference in maintaining domestic power relations. As Haacke (2003, p. 181) notes, states like Vietnam were struggling to maintain domestic order and legitimacy amidst their strained transitions to capitalism. They also had a wary eye on ASEAN's ongoing intervention in Cambodia and wished to avoid this being turned into a generalised precedent. For older ASEAN states like Indonesia and Malaysia, non-interference remained immediately useful in controlling the scope of political conflict given the intensity of their domestic crises. State managers struggling to protect patronage networks and contain demands for political reform were obviously disinterested in implementing 'international standards'. They preferred to retain non-interference in order to insulate their opponents, who were seeking this goal, from sources of external support.

Indeed, embattled state managers in these countries had already reacted fiercely to attempts to widen the scope of their internal conflicts, even those with external repercussions. The Singaporean government, desperate to restore market stability in the region, had publicly urged Suharto to implement IMF reforms, making its own loans to Indonesia conditional upon him doing so, and criticised the appointment of Habibie, a notorious *dirigiste*, as Suharto's presumptive successor. Habibie reacted ferociously, menacingly reminding the city-state that it was a mere 'red dot' surrounded by Indonesian territory. The Malaysian government joined in, threatening to sever Singapore's water supply. Similarly, when Mahathir's heavy-handed treatment of Anwar Ibrahim drew criticism from the Indonesian and Philippine presidents, Malaysia sharply protested, threatening to support the Philippines' Muslim rebels in Mindanao (Henderson, 1999, p. 53; Lee 2000, pp. 310–19, 386). Incidents like this underlined the risks of formally diluting non-interference, and the principle's strategic utility in maintaining political stability. Surin's timing was also particularly unfortunate, as 'flexible engagement' was proposed just two weeks after Suharto's fall from power.

Consequently, the 1998 AMM agreed only to sanction 'enhanced interaction' on matters of regional concern, balanced by the official retention of the non-interference principle. This is typically interpreted as the total defeat of this attempt to revise ASEAN's sovereignty regime. Acharya (2009a, pp. 154, 242) argues that ASEAN 'stuck to a Westphalian view of sovereignty', avoiding 'any meaningful dilution of non-interference'. 'Flexible engagement failed to produce any meaningful institutional change... ASEAN did not depart from its non-intervention doctrine in any significant way'. Similarly, Caballero-Anthony (2005, p. 213) states, 'flexible engagement did not have any significant impact on the ASEAN way of non-interference'.

However, we cannot assume that a lack of inter-elite consensus on explicitly revising non-interference translated automatically into ASEAN states continuing to abide by the norm, as is too often implied. As Haacke (2003, pp. 175–7) observes, 'flexible engagement' partly reflected the Thai foreign ministry's desire to liberate Thailand from the constraints of non-intervention in dealing with Burma, and to grab back control of foreign policy from the country's entrepreneur-generals. The Democrats, moreover, had long been ideologically hostile to Burma's military regime and had opposed its entry to ASEAN. As Chapter 8 shows, far from sticking to 'Westphalian' sovereignty, Thailand pursued a far more aggressive, interventionist policy culminating in military clashes with the Burmese army by mid-2000.

Moreover, the societal interdependence underlined in Surin's proposal also generated imperatives to intervene in Indonesia (see Chapter 7). Ongoing social and political upheaval in Indonesia had serious effects on the wider region's attempt to recover from the crisis as separatist insurgencies escalated, refugees fled, regional markets fell, and the possibility of the country's disintegration was openly discussed. Amid this unrest, in 1999 the Habibie government decided to offer East Timor a vote on independence to alleviate Western pressure. However, when the Timorese voted for independence, the Indonesian military razed the territory, creating a major humanitarian crisis. In order to contain the violent unrest sweeping Indonesia, which threatened the social stability and economic recovery of neighbouring countries, core ASEAN states encouraged and joined a humanitarian intervention in East Timor. 'Non-interference' and intervention were both used to contain political conflicts.

The Asian financial crisis thus had highly uneven effects on Southeast Asian societies and ASEAN's principle and practice of (non)intervention. Most countries whose economies were most exposed to foreign capital suffered severe socio-economic and political crises. Serious opposition to authoritarian-developmentalist regimes erupted in several countries. Liberalising, middle-class forces severely destabilised UMNO rule in Malaysia, contributed to Suharto's downfall, and seized power in Thailand. This led to a direct assault on non-interference to support the cause of liberalising reform. Yet the region's entrenched state-business networks were not about to give up without a fight. ASEAN's newer member-states had also been insulated from the worst of the crisis and saw little imperative to reform. The attempt to explicitly weaken the non-interference principle was therefore defeated, with the restoration of social, political and economic stability being prioritised by most regional states. However, despite a lack of formal 'institutional' change, these priorities also helped to generate continued interventions during the crisis, particularly in Cambodia and Indonesia. We now need to explore the long-term repercussions of the crisis for ASEAN and non-interference.

ASEAN in the long shadow of crisis

Although the worst of the economic chaos and social unrest afflicting Southeast Asia has passed, the political consequences of the Asian crisis are still playing out today. The crisis has left the region's states, and in many cases their dominant forces, severely weakened in relation both to external powers and to their domestic opponents. As one typical observer suggested, after the crisis, when

> Southeast Asia is compared to the Balkans, it is not to draw a contrast but a parallel. Most regional economies are in disarray. They

have emerged from the Asian economic crisis of 1997–98 not improved but enduringly impaired. The collective Southeast Asian economy is smaller today than it was before the crisis. Many dormant ethnic and religious resentments have exploded into violence. Democratic systems are under tremendous stress and a stinking tide of corruption is on the rise... ASEAN... has lost the power of action and degenerated to the brink of meaninglessness (quoted in Beeson, 2004, p. 138).

This section explores how ASEAN states have tried to recover from the crisis, and traces out the consequences for ASEAN's sovereignty regime. To regain its lost standing, ASEAN has embarked on an ambitious programme of reform and renewal, including an apparent embrace of 'good governance', democracy and human rights. This 'liberal turn' reflects not just a rhetorical effort to curry favour with Western powers, but the challenge of re-establishing domestic political and social order in the wake of the crisis. The imperatives behind this reformist trajectory have also generated increasing pressure on non-interference and repeated attempts to intervene in Burma, the region's pariah state, to defend the group's image and credibility. However, despite some significant changes, the region's entrenched political economy relationships severely constrain this 'liberal turn'. Thus, despite continued interventions and explicit efforts to dilute sovereignty within ASEAN, 'non-interference' officially persists contradictorily alongside growing emphasis on liberal-democratic values.

ASEAN states' core priorities were not significantly changed by the Asian crisis, but their ability to realise them had drastically altered. Their first priority was to 'regain business confidence, enhance economic recovery and produce growth' (ASEAN, 1998). This unoriginal agenda was now a major challenge. The region remained fundamentally dependent on foreign investment and export markets for economic growth, but the crisis had deeply discredited Southeast Asian markets and institutions and prompted a major relocation of capital to China. From 1997–2002, foreign investment in ASEAN halved; its share of investment in Asia slumped from 36 to 20 per cent, while China's rose from 48 to 60 per cent (UNCTAD, 2009). While China's continued growth helped ASEAN to eventually export its way out of recession, there is growing fear that Chinese competition and outsourcing is hollowing out Southeast Asia's economies. ASEAN has consequently made an escalating series of concessions to lure investors back to the region. These include repeated accelerations in the implementation of AFTA, the granting of equal market access to foreign investors, and the 2003 launch of the ASEAN Economic

Community, which aims to turn ASEAN into an integrated production base by 2015. ASEAN has also drawn closer to China, Korea and Japan through its 'ASEAN Plus Three' initiative and regular East Asia Summits. Free trade agreements with major economic partners have also proliferated. Having largely resisted neoliberal reforms at the peak of the crisis, ASEAN states thus found it necessary to implement some of them in its long shadow.

The second, clearly related, priority was to resume engaging external powers on terms favourable to the region's weakened states. This remained vital to support the economic accumulation and hegemonic political strategies adopted by ASEAN state managers. Since the Cold War, ASEAN's capacity to successfully engage external powers had largely been premised on its economic dynamism, combined with its willingness to take some Western concerns into consideration when managing regional order. As ASEAN Secretary-General Ong Keng Yong observed, 'only with economic clout can we continue to draw the big powers and our key trading partners, like the US, China, Japan and the EU, to engage with us in the equally important political and security areas' (AFP, 2003c).

However, the crisis had not only profoundly damaged the regional economy, but had also exposed the severe political limitations of ASEAN as an organisation and a manager of regional order. ASEAN's secretary-general at the time of the crisis later reflected that 'ASEAN's image had been irreversibly altered' (Severino, 2006, p. 97). In a soul-searching review of ASEAN's weaknesses, Singapore's foreign minister quoted journalistic and academic critiques of ASEAN as a 'feeble vehicle' that was 'drifting apart'. ASEAN was perceived as an 'ineffective... sunset organisation', and perceptions, he warned, were 'political facts. Perceptions can define political reality – if we continue to be perceived as ineffective, we can be marginalised as our Dialogue Partners and international investors relegate us to the sidelines' (Jayakumar, 2000). The continued rise of China and India while ASEAN was divided and distressed was a particular concern. ASEAN feared that it could be 'torn apart' by centrifugal pressures, or that the two giants might 'occupy all political, economic and diplomatic space, squeezing ASEAN into irrelevance'. Embarking on ambitious reforms was thus necessary not simply for economic purposes but also to avoid 'political suicide' (Kausikan, 2007).

Consequently, to re-engage disillusioned Western states and investors, ASEAN state managers offered not only economic inducements but also increasingly dramatic political and ideological concessions. The discourse of 'Asian values' suddenly disappeared from regional discourse and was replaced with neoliberal jargon promoted by institutions like the World

Bank. Terms like 'good governance', 'transparency', 'partnership', 'stake-holders', 'capacity-building', 'social risks', 'participation', and even refer-ences to human rights began appearing in ASEAN documents (ASEAN, 2004). The ASEAN Economic Community was supplemented by two other 'pillars' of regionalism, the ASEAN Security Community and ASEAN Socio-Cultural Community, which involved pledges to address transnational security challenges, enhance the well-being of ASEAN citizens, and create a 'caring, sharing' and 'people-centred' ASEAN. In 2000, the ASEAN People's Assembly was launched to co-opt civil society organisations into this com-munity-building agenda and from 2008, ASEAN Civil Society Summits have taken place alongside annual ASEAN leaders' summits. In 2009, an ASEAN Charter was ratified, committing member-states, among other things, to 'strengthen democracy, enhance good governance and the rule of law, and to promote human rights and fundamental freedoms' (ASEAN, 2008b). An ASEAN Intergovernmental Commission on Human Rights was also established in 2010.

Although ASEAN's apparent (neo)liberal turn is extremely striking in comparison with the earlier reactionary discourse of 'Asian values', its transformation must not be overstated. To appreciate fully why these reforms were adopted, their limits, and the consequences for (non)inter-ference, we need to return to the social, political and economic dynamics of ASEAN societies. The reforms are *not* simply a cosmetic exercise designed by foreign ministry bureaucracies to appease foreigners. In several key ASEAN states, dominant social forces needed to adopt new forms of governance and ideology in order to retain or regain their hegemony. However, to a degree which varies with individual cases, the scope of these reforms remains highly constrained by entrenched oligarchic power and neo-patrimonial rule, which survived the crisis in various ways. Con-sequently there is a large disjuncture between ASEAN's stated ambi-tions to embrace democracy, good governance and human rights and the reality of regional politics. This is particularly obvious in Burma, where serious human rights abuses make a persistent mockery of ASEAN reforms, but it is also true of governance in most ASEAN states. In the last few years alone we have seen corruption scandals engulf the Indonesian and Philippine presidents, counter-insurgency campaigns and/or asso-ciated human rights abuses in southern Thailand, Mindanao, and West Papua, the brutal suppression of anti-government demonstrations in Thailand and less violent suppressions in Malaysia, Singapore, and several other states.

It is this contradiction between the reality of ASEAN state govern-ance and the group's stated reformist ambitions that has significant consequences for ASEAN's sovereignty regime. When reformist domestic forces and key external powers take an interest in a particular domestic, international or transnational problem in Southeast Asia, attention is drawn to the gap between ASEAN's rhetoric and reality. Because the imperatives driving reform in the region are very real, stemming from both domestic counter-hegemonic challenges and the difficulty of favourably re-engaging foreign powers and markets, this sort of scrutiny is now hard to ignore. It is experienced and described by regional state managers as a threat to the 'credibility', 'image' and 'reputation' of ASEAN and its member-states. In turn, this creates powerful imperatives to act on the highlighted problem, if necessary by weakening or bypassing 'non-interference'. Yet, entrenched anti-reform elements exist in all ASEAN states and frequently resist attempts to broaden the scope of conflicts in which their interests are directly implicated.

The net result is a highly uneven and complex, even incoherent sovereignty regime. Whether intervention occurs or not in a given scenario now depends on two main factors. First, how a specific issue (domestic or regional problem) relates to the interests of powerful social forces in key regional states determines states' basic attitudes. If no powerful interests are at stake, but inaction will compromise a 'reformist' image, states will tend to support an interventionist approach, attempting to widen the scope of conflict over the issue to govern it regionally. If powerful interests are at stake, however, they may use the state to invoke non-intervention to constrain the scope of conflict. Secondly, how forceful an interventionist approach emerges in practice depends on the degree of inter-elite coordination and consensus. The post-crisis divergence of social conflict processes has made it harder than ever for ASEAN states to reach consensus on important issues. Increasingly, core member-states act singly or in concert to defend their domestic and/or international legitimacy, even without corporate agreement. However, they are obviously able to achieve less as individual states than a united bloc of ten.

A more concrete sense of how these dynamics play out in practice requires analysis of the conflicts underpinning key ASEAN states. Here it is crucial to avoid the simplistic distinctions between 'democratic'/'liberal'/'open' and 'undemocratic'/'illiberal'/'closed' states that often prevails in the literature. As we have seen, 'democratic' states can often harbour highly illiberal practices and defend narrow, predatory interests. The key is to identify what social forces are at work and how their interests are expressed in state policy.

Indonesia's post-Suharto transformation is critical to understanding ASEAN's contemporary sovereignty regime. On the one hand, this transformation has been dramatic, involving the creation of democratic institutions, the liberalisation of the media, and the enlivenment of 'civil society'. IMF reforms and continued international dependency have strengthened the hand of reformers demanding 'good governance', particularly under the presidency of Susilo Bambang Yudhoyono. The human rights situation has improved for many Indonesians. After 2003, representatives of middle-class, liberal NGOs were also elected to parliament and have exercised some influence on policy through legislative committees (L. Jones, 2009, pp. 398–400; Rüland, 2009). For some, this illustrates how democratisation produces liberalisation in foreign policy (Dosch, 2006). However, Indonesia's transformation should not be overstated. Many of the oligarchic forces that dominated the New Order survived the crisis, rescuing their corporate empires and entrenching themselves within the country's new 'democratic' institutions (Robison and Hadiz, 2004). The new political parties are so financially dependent on these interests that they have described as ideologically-indistinct 'trojan horses' for the oligarchs (Tan, 2006). If anything, corruption has worsened as a result of decentralisation and the rise of money politics. Reformers still confront entrenched resistance and are often able to deliver only 'mock compliance' with international standards (Walter, 2008).

This mixed picture means that, contrary to those who see democratisation as automatically producing liberalisation in foreign policy, Indonesia's position is often complex. Jakarta's attempt to recover its post-crisis international status has often assumed an apparently liberal content due to the country's post-crisis dependency, the delegitimisation of authoritarianism, and the strengthening of reformists. Thus, Indonesia's bid to recover ASEAN leadership has been expressed through the promotion of a 'democracy agenda', which has involved significant shifts in Indonesia's relationship to 'non-interference'. Jakarta proposed the creation of an ASEAN peacekeeping force in 2003, has been at the forefront of recent attempts to intervene in Burma (see Chapter 8), and championed the creation of a regional human rights body. Moreover, the Yudhoyono government has selectively relaxed Indonesian sovereignty to help resolve internal conflicts, most notably in Aceh, where an ASEAN-EU Monitoring Mission was deployed to oversee the implementation of a peace deal with separatist forces in 2005.[5] The EU's involvement helped reassure the separatists and domestic liberals, while ASEAN forces were necessary to maintain the military's cooperation (Kausikan, 2008).

However, this liberal turn remains constrained by powerful illiberal interests. As Rüland (2009) argues, this bid for regional leadership primarily expresses a nationalistic, chauvinistic sense of entitlement from Indonesian politicians, rather than a commitment to liberalism. This expressed itself in gunboat diplomacy in a territorial dispute with Malaysia in 2005. Moreover, powerful elements within the Indonesian state still deploy 'non-interference' to limit the scope of conflicts where their own interests are at stake. Parliament persistently refuses to ratify an ASEAN agreement to combat pollution arising from Indonesian forest fires because agri-businesses, corrupt politicians and state officials are the principal beneficiaries of the fires, which are used illegally to clear land (Tay, 2009). Similarly, Indonesian legislators have been at the forefront of the ASEAN Inter-Parliamentary Myanmar Caucus (AIPMC), which campaigns for intervention in Burma, but refuse to support a similar caucus on 'good governance' since it would strike at their own interests (L. Jones, 2009, p. 400). Indonesian elites' commitment to liberal reforms is consequent partial and uneven, producing a selective position on 'non-interference'.

The situation is similar in the Philippines. Philippine politics remains characterised by formal democracy and liberal values on the one hand, and the entrenched domination of *trapos* and oligarchic clans on the other, punctuated by sporadic mass protests against venal elites. In 2000, President Estrada faced a massive, middle-class 'people power' protest following a serious corruption scandal. The unrest prompted the military to switch its allegiance to Vice-President Gloria Arroyo, who was sworn in as Estrada's successor on a 'good governance' platform. Arroyo immediately suppressed another 'people power' revolt by Estrada's supporters among the urban poor, and despite her neoliberal pledges of technocratic reform, proved to be a *trapo* extraordinaire. She presided over large-scale corruption, electoral fraud, political violence, the suppression of dissent, the manipulation of democratic institutions, rising human rights violations, and resumed counter-insurgency operations in Mindanao alongside US troops as part of the 'war on terror' (Abinales and Amoroso, 2005, ch. 10). A 'liberal' foreign policy is largely used to burnish the state's standing in Washington and as a concession to middle-class voters and civil society groups, but as in Indonesia its scope is determined by oligarchic interests. Like Arroyo, the Philippine congress has happily flaunted its liberal credentials by criticising Burma, but has refused to commit itself to 'good governance' campaigns (L. Jones, 2009, p. 401).

'Good governance' has played a more significant role in efforts to re-legitimise oligarchic rule in Malaysia. Despite surviving *reformasi*,

UMNO suffered heavy losses to reformist and Islamist parties in the 1999 elections. State managers therefore adopted a reformist, liberalising posture to regain both international investor confidence and popular support. Mahathir launched a drive for 'good governance', cancelling major *dirigiste* projects, purging leading cronies, and establishing a national human rights body, which initially displayed surprising independence in criticising the government. Abdullah Badawi succeeded Mahathir in 2003, intensifying the 'good governance' campaign by attacking 'tycoons' and 'wealthy tax-dodgers' to 'restore [UMNO's] credibility and image' (Case, 2005, pp. 299–303). This stance was directly expressed in foreign policy, too, as Malaysia took a leading role in promoting liberalising reforms in Burma, deployed peace monitors in Mindanao, and called for adjustments to non-interference to entrench regional 'good governance' (Abdullah, 2006b).

Yet, as elsewhere, powerfully entrenched interests have resisted the reform process. Malay tycoons within and linked to UMNO have compelled policy reversals and forcefully defended their privileges. Even the famously clean Abdullah was drawn into their corrupt practices, destroying his reformist credentials (Case, 2005, pp. 298–304). Institutions like the national human rights watchdog have also been muzzled. Abdullah's second term was marked by growing popular disillusionment and social unrest. Middle-class Malays increasingly turned from UMNO to the reformist opposition, while Malaysia's ethnic minorities increasingly protested for equal rights, with the state suppressing demonstrations by reformist NGOs like *Bersih* and the Hindu Action Rights Force. In 2008, a multi-ethnic grand alliance of opposition parties inflicted serious losses on the UMNO-led coalition, precipitating Abdullah's resignation. His successor, Najib Razak, has tried to boost his reformist credentials at home and abroad, but hard-liners continue to resist change, using racist and religious language to mobilise Malay support and thereby retain their privileges. The tension ASEAN faces between reform and reaction is clearly expressed in Malaysia's ongoing crisis.

Thailand's social conflict has been even more intense yet its character differs substantially, generating very different consequences for ASEAN's sovereignty regime. After the Asian crisis, the Democrats sought to impose neoliberal reforms on Thailand. These reforms severely depressed wages and employment and also struck so hard at corporate interests and so exposed the economy to foreign control that powerful tycoons feared that 'the demise of their class was possible' (Hewison, 2006, pp. 97–8). An anti-Democrat alliance of workers, farmers, pro-poor intellectuals and NGOs, politicians and big businessmen emerged, coalescing into the *Thai*

Rak Thai (TRT) party, led by telecommunications tycoon Thaksin Shina-watra. TRT won the backing of the rural poor through populist policies like universal healthcare and swept to power in the 2001 elections. Thaksin's cabinet, a *Who's Who* of Thai oligarchs, signalled the recapture of state power by the 'new rich'. TRT repaid IMF loans early, celebrating 'national independence day', and scaled back reforms to a level consistent with big business interests (Hewison, 2006, pp. 98–101). While keeping his populist promises to the poor, Thaksin also rode roughshod over the constitution, engaging in serious human rights abuses in a 'war on drugs' and initiating counter-insurgency in the restive southern provinces, while ruthlessly promoting the business interests of his family and allies (Pasuk and Baker, 2004, pp. 138–66).

This power shift back to the new rich had significant consequences for Thailand's attitude towards 'non-interference'. Thaksin's foreign policy of 'forward engagement' essentially revived Chatichai Choon-havan's plans to put Thailand at the centre of a mainland Southeast Asian trade and investment network. To smooth the way, the government retreated from the Democrat policy of confronting neighbours like Burma, instead promoting 'non-intervention in the internal affairs of each other' (Surakiart, 2003, p. 42). 'Non-interference' was also invoked to fend off criticism of Thaksin's counter-insurgency warfare in the south. Contrary to generalisations about 'democratic' states, therefore, under Thaksin, Thailand impeded regional liberalisation andreinforced the salience of 'non-interference' in pursuit of dominant societal interests.

Since 2006, however, the situation has been far more fluid, reflecting an escalation of social conflict. Thaksin's corrupt self-aggrandisement, and the TRT's growing electoral dominance, provoked an alliance of convenience between the politically-excluded and ideologically-affronted urban middle classes and the network of businessmen, politicians and generals clustered around the palace, generating a military coup in 2006. Thaksin flew into exile and was prosecuted in absentia for corruption, and the TRT was disbanded. However, the alliance between pro-Thaksin oligarchs and the urban and rural poor remained intact, reconstituting itself as the People Power Party (PPP), which won the first post-coup elections in January 2008. Unwilling to accept this outcome, the anti-Thaksin coalition staged street protests – the so-called 'yellow-shirt' movement – and launched politically-motivated lawsuits against the PPP and its leaders, resulting in the PPP's dissolution. The Democrats, in league with army generals, also tempted an ex-TRT faction to defect, allowing them to form a coalition government in December 2008. The new government was repeatedly besieged by pro-Thaksin 'red-shirt' protests, finally resorting to a bloody crackdown in spring 2010.

This violent social conflict has expressed itself forcefully in Thailand's external relations and its attitude towards state sovereignty. When the TRT/PPP faction has controlled state power, a pro-sovereignty, pro-business outlook has dominated. By contrast, the Democrat-fronted, anti-TRT/PPP alliance has struck a more liberal-reformist posture to reassure Western allies and compensate for its lack of domestic democratic legitimacy (Chachavalpongpun, 2009). This includes a far more critical stance on Burma. However, the illiberal and nationalist content of yellow-shirt ideology has further complicated the picture. One of the ways in which the PPP government was toppled was through the politicisation of Cambodia's bid for United Nations Educational, Social and Cultural Organisation (UNESCO) recognition for Preah Vihear temple as a world heritage site, which the PPP supported. The Democrats and their supporters – particularly the People's Alliance for Democracy – claimed this unconstitutionally alienated national territory, since the temple adjoins a small, disputed area of scrubland along the Thai-Cambodian border. A similarly-politicised court ruling forced the foreign minister to resign and compelled the government to dispatch politically-unreliable troops to the border. The People's Alliance for Democracy has kept up the pressure on this issue, and Cambodian and Thai forces have since clashed on several occasions, killing at least 16 people. Cambodia's prime minister has retaliated by appointing Thaksin as a government advisor, prompting shrill denunciations of 'interference' in Thailand's internal affairs. While meddling in Cambodian territory and criticising Burma, the Democrat government has repeatedly invoked 'non-interference' to try to limit the scope of its own political conflicts – to prevent ASEAN discussing, for example, the violent suppression of the red-shirts in 2010 or the conflict with Cambodia. Thailand's socio-political conflict since 1997 has therefore generated a rather schizophrenic attitude to state sovereignty.

By stark contrast, the remaining ASEAN societies have experienced little upheaval since 1997. Relatively insulated from the crisis and/or generally lacking well-organised opposition movements, dominant forces have maintained their hegemony without significant reforms.

In Singapore, the PAP's hegemony has survived largely unscathed. In the absence of a *reformasi* movement willing to contest the meaning of 'good governance', the state was able to hijack the concept to refresh its technocratic-developmentalist performance legitimacy (Surain, 2001). The PAP's hegemony gave it wide latitude to implement neoliberal reforms and restore the economic growth on which socio-political stability in the city-state depends. The government has liberalised the state's more draconian features, with new 'participatory' institutions safely directing opposition into unthreatening channels (Rodan and Jayasuriya, 2007). The PAP regime remains principally attuned to the interests of international capital and strongly committed to Western engagement in Southeast Asia. Because it sees Singapore's fate as bound up with the region's stability and prosperity, and ASEAN's corporate standing, it has strongly pushed ASEAN's economic reform agenda (less so its political one). Despite its fundamentally illiberal outlook, therefore, Singaporean elites have been willing to bypass and weaken 'non-interference' to safeguard their broader economic and (geo)political strategies.

In Indochina, illiberal, neo-patrimonial rule remains deeply entrenched. In Cambodia, the CPP has intensified its grip on rural areas and the state apparatus. Its highly corrupt, coercive domination is only moderated by the need to appease external donors, upon whose funds the formal state apparatus relies quite heavily. This has generated some concessions to the liberal-nationalist opposition, the Sam Rainsy Party (SRP), enabling occasional critical commentary on Burma (L. Jones, 2009, pp. 393–4). However, the CPP's patronage networks are largely funded by off-budget activities like the pillaging of Cambodia's natural resources, granting it significant autonomy from donor influence. The Cambodian state therefore largely supports ASEAN's non-interference principle so that the CPP can control the scope of domestic conflict and insulate its weaker opponents from sources of external support. Vietnam and Laos generally maintain a similar posture to help manage the tensions arising from their strained transition to state capitalism. As in Singapore, the VCP has sought to co-opt domestic opponents and enhance its legitimacy via carefully controlled 'participatory' mechanisms (Rodan and Jayasuriya, 2007). Indochina's ruling forces have thus accepted only a very limited case for reform, with their domestic opponents too weak to compel greater concessions. For incumbent forces, 'non-interference' remains useful in perpetuating this situation.

Burma's profound ethnic and political fragmentation makes the military regime there even more reliant on 'non-interference' to contain the scope of the country's long-running conflicts and prevent territorial disintegration. As Chapter 8 details, some concessions were made to the democratic opposition in 2000–2003 in order to improve relations with the West. However, a hard-line faction resumed control thereafter and has rigidly emphasised the country's sovereignty to buy time to impose its goal of 'disciplined-flourishing democracy' on the population.

Processes of social conflict in ASEAN states have therefore diverged considerably since the Asian financial crisis, with significant consequences for ASEAN's sovereignty regime. In several ASEAN states, socio-political tensions have compelled significant reforms – though they are everywhere constrained by entrenched oligarchic forces. These constraints are heaviest in the CLMV states, where relative crude and coercive governance styles prevail, along with sour memories of ASEAN states' interventions. However, as Haacke (2003, p. 225) rightly cautions, 'it is a misconception to suggest that the "ASEAN way" is first and foremost hostage to the concerns of the leaderships of the new members... even among the old members several have been reluctant to endorse major conceptual or practical revisions'. Analysing the conflicts animating these states is crucial to explaining the extent of reforms and relaxation of 'non-interference' that they are willing to accept. These limitations clearly do not correspond to a crude democratic/non-democratic dichotomy.

As a result of the uneven and contradictory nature of socio-political change in the region, ASEAN's sovereignty regime is increasingly complex. One the one hand, there are powerful imperatives, both domestic and international, to pursue a reformist trajectory and demonstrate ASEAN's 'relevance' by intervening in domestic issues. Malaysian mediation in Mindanao to help terminate the insurgency there, the ASEAN-EU Aceh Monitoring Mission, disaster relief efforts, and other ventures involving domestic issues are now regularly cited in order to boost ASEAN's 'credibility' (ASEAN, 2005a; Abdullah, 2006b). On the other hand, however, these imperatives are contradicted by entrenched illiberal, oligarchic forces present in all ASEAN states, which resist the rescaling of their domestic and/or bilateral conflicts to the regional level in order to maintain control over them and defend their particular interests. As Chapter 8 explores, this resistance has been particular fierce in Burma. In response to domestic liberals' campaigns and Western powers' threats to boycott ASEAN, key member-states have repeatedly tried to expand the scope of Burma's domestic politics and insert themselves into its democratisation process. This has been staunchly resisted by the military regime. As noted earlier, however, the junta is far from alone in continuing to instrumentalise 'non-interference' to constrain the scope of socio-political conflicts in which powerful interests are implicated.

Repeated confrontations like this have prompted attempts to decisively revise the non-interference principle to enable some domestic issues to be governed at the regional level. Malaysia's Prime Minister Abdullah (2006a) argued that ASEAN needed a formula whereby 'community interests would prevail over national interests on issues affecting the community'. Non-interference required 'refinement' to help enforce 'adherence... to a common set of community values', which would be topped by 'good governance in our respective countries and societies'. This directly echoed Surin's (2000) earlier analysis that 'each member nation has to be responsible... to the grouping as a whole... ASEAN will not be able to withstand the pressures from outside if each country cannot manage its own problems'. This initially controversial idea has apparently found growing acceptance. The chair of the group which drafted the ASEAN Charter argued that there was now a 'consensus' that when a problem 'within the borders of a sovereign nation is perceived to have any negative effect on the collective interest of the community... it would be, and should be, made a concern of this community' (Kyodo, 2005). However, as Chapter 8 explores, the Charter failed to resolve the contradiction between the reformist and reactionary impulses in ASEAN, restating 'non-interference' alongside contradictory principles like the promotion of human rights and democracy.

Because both of these contradictory impulses persist, ASEAN's sovereignty regime remains extremely conflict-ridden, evolving through *ad hoc* responses to crises. Whenever a socio-political conflict brings ASEAN or its member-states into disrepute, a struggle now occurs over whether its scope should be expanded to the regional level. When the Thai-Cambodian border conflict broke out in 2008, both Malaysia and Indonesia intervened, pushing both parties to resolve the conflict by invoking the threat to ASEAN's reputation as a manager of regional order (ASEAN-Affairs.com, 2008; AP, 2008). The Cambodian government sought to widen the conflict by involving ASEAN and the UN Security Council, with Thailand vociferously resisting. ASEAN states successfully constrained the issue's scope by persuading the Security Council to ignore Cambodia's appeals, but insisted on expanding it to the regional level, discussing it at an ASEAN summit despite Thai protests (Kyodo, 2008). Bangkok was thereby forced into bilateral talks with Cambodia. Similarly, Singapore has invoked ASEAN's image in trying to pressure Indonesia to suppress forest fires generating transboundary pollution (Acharya, 2009a, p. 253). ASEAN states also called for restraint in response to Bangkok's suppression of red-shirt protestors in spring 2010, with Indonesia pushing for an emergency summit (BP, 2010). This led to a statement on the crisis being issued by the ASEAN chair, Vietnam. In all these cases, powerful forces resisted the socio-political conflicts regionalisation, precluding deep ASEAN involvement. Yet what is striking is ASEAN states' determination to regionalise these conflicts in spite of the 'non-interference' principle.

In the long shadow of the Asian crisis, ASEAN states are thus increasingly torn between the interventionist imperatives arising from a need to restore their domestic and international legitimacy and the contrary pressures of entrenched domestic interests. Because the strategies of the region's ruling forces have diverged considerably in response to domestic social and political conditions, ASEAN states increasingly struggle to achieve meaningful consensus on regional issues. The net effect is a highly uneven, contradictory and conflict-ridden sovereignty regime which evolves in response to crises. The norm of non-interference technically persists, but is increasingly articulated alongside incompatible aspirations of community-building and the promotion of democracy and human rights. Which prevails in any given situation is determined in quite an *ad hoc* fashion by the specific forces at play and their relationship to the issue at hand.

Concluding remarks

The patterns identified in this chapter are very complex, reflecting how the increasingly complicated and divergent nature of ASEAN's social conflicts has made inter-elite coordination evermore difficult (see box, below, for a summary). The intensifying demands for national interests to be subordinated to a collective, 'regional interest' are not entirely new. They were first articulated in the Cold War, when it was proposed that ASEAN states should forego opportunities for disruptive, short-run gains in order to stabilise social order across the entire region. During the Cold War, such inter-elite agreement was possible because a clear division existed between *status quo* and revolutionary forces, and the former held sway in all ASEAN states. Now, a range of different groups are contesting state power, pursuing divergent and contradictory strategies. Consequently, ASEAN is increasingly unable to achieve meaningful consensus on what the 'regional interest' involves. Despite this growing incoherence, ASEAN nonetheless seems to be moving towards a sovereignty regime in which 'non-interference' is permanently downgraded, and where domestic issues with important ramifications for the region are subjected to an emerging form of regional governance.

ASEAN and (non)interference after the Cold War

From the Cold War to the Asian crisis

The defeat of communism and the rise of a new business class in ASEAN states gives rise to a withdrawal from Cold War, anti-communist interventions towards policies, sometimes interventionist, designed to promote the interests of capital. Resistance to these policies, or rivalry over the spoils of peace within ASEAN states, generates continued interventions in neighbouring states. Non-interference is reconfigured to shield the domestic power relations established during the Cold War from the West's 'new interventionism'. The norm is part of ASEAN elites' attempts to manage economic and political engagement with external powers on their own terms. Thanks to the region's economic boom, this strategy is relatively successful.

ASEAN in crisis

Along with other aspects of the region's political and economic order, non-interference comes under direct attack from liberalising forces, which are temporarily ascendant in Thailand. However, ASEAN states' internal unrest produces a hypersensitivity to external meddling, defeating the attempt to revise the principle. Nonetheless, widespread social, economic and political upheaval gives rise to intervention in some states in order to restore their domestic stability and contain negative consequences for neighbouring states.

ASEAN in the long shadow of crisis

Internal and external imperatives for reform generate an apparent 'liberal turn' in ASEAN, designed to re-engage external powers and stabilise domestic governance arrangements without radical revision of political economy relations. The necessity to prove that ASEAN states are committed to reform and can offer regional solutions to regional problems creates strong imperatives to intervene or accept intervention in conflict-ridden areas, such as Mindanao, Aceh and Burma. Non-interference consequently comes under severe pressure. However, ASEAN's 'liberal turn', and thus the revision of non-interference, is limited by the interests, alliances and strategies of powerful, illiberal social forces.

6
Cambodia: From Cold War to Conditionality

In the case of Cambodia, we were very much involved. We actually interfered... we set up the state, the rules and the conditions, and we built Cambodia... We were quite strict, stern, on making our demands when there was a coup [in 1997]... we felt that Cambodia was 'our baby', you know – we took a lot of trouble to set up the international conference on Cambodia, we fought many years against Vietnamese, 10, 11 or 12 years of resolutions. So it was our special interest.
– *Asda Jayanama, Thailand's UN Ambassador, 1996–2001* (2008)

[Cambodian Prime Minister] Hun Sen was livid with rage... he gave a half-an-hour criticism of me when I first met him... He said, 'this is foreign interference! This is against ASEAN's own principles! What are you doing here? You have nothing to do with what is happening to Cambodia! I don't want to become a member of ASEAN, not with that kind of organization!'
– *Ali Alatas, Indonesian Foreign Minister, 1988–98* (2008)

The change wrought by the defeat of communism and the rise of a new business class on ASEAN's practice of (non)interference is very clear in the case of Cambodia. To insulate their own societies from Indochina's communist forces, ASEAN had fuelled a bitter proxy war in Cambodia for over a decade. However, when communism was defeated in ASEAN countries – partly through this intervention – the war became obsolete. Powerful business groups began demanding that the conflict be terminated to permit them to exploit lucrative opportunities in neighbouring markets. Combined with Vietnam's decreasing capacity and willingness to continue fighting, and the end of the Cold War, this led to a serious push to settle the conflict. This required an unprecedented UN intervention, encouraged and participated in by ASEAN, which organised elections that generated a power-sharing coalition between parties representing the former communist regime and the anti-communist FUNCINPEC. This transition to peace was by no means smooth. Reflecting the non-coherence of states, discussed in Chapter 1, bureaucratic, military and business elites who benefited from the conflict resisted and undermined its settlement, continuing to meddle in and destabilise Cambodia well into the 1990s. Moreover, ASEAN states' efforts to promote their allied business interests in Cambodia had a destabilising effect. This foreign involvement contributed to the breakdown of the coalition government in 1997, despite ASEAN governments' belated palliative efforts. To restore the settlement that ASEAN had laboured to produce, the Association responded by imposing a series of conditions on Cambodia's pending membership, which lasted until 1999.

The chapter proceeds in four sections. Section one shows how the rise of the business class in Thailand created demands for an exit strategy from Indochina, and how this was resisted by other interests. Section two surveys the UN-imposed settlement from ASEAN's perspective. Section three shows how fractions of ASEAN capital undermined political stability in Cambodia after the UN intervention. The last section details ASEAN's response to the collapse of the ruling coalition, the imposition of creeping conditionality for membership.

The rise of capital and the 'new look'

As with many regional conflicts, superpower involvement in Cambodia meant that peace was not possible until the Cold War had ended. Although ASEAN had identified the basic elements of the eventual peace settlement by the early 1980s, whilst Beijing and Moscow were willing to support their clients, Vietnam and the Khmer Rouge respectively, stalemate persisted. Realists have consequently emphasised the role of great powers in settling the conflict, branding any talk of an 'ASEAN peace process' as a 'category mistake' (Leifer, 1999). While this geostrategic view is important, it ignores the agency of smaller, local states, particularly Thailand which, as Chapter 4 showed, was crucial in fuelling the conflict. It also overlooks important movements towards conflict resolution emanating from those states. This section shows how powerful new business groups pushed for the Thai state to turn 'battlefields into marketplaces'. This push was undermined not by great-power strategy but conflicts between local military, bureaucratic and business elites.

As explored in Chapter 5, by 1988, Thailand's 'new rich' had seized power directly in Thailand, with a newly-elected government headed by general-turned-businessman Chatichai Choonhavan. As Chatichai's son Kraisak (2008) recalls, the Thai government was now 'full of undisciplined and quite greedy politicians', looking to expand their own interests and also highly receptive to business lobbying:

> the private sector way ahead of the state in Thailand. It was going into Burma, it was going into... Cambodia... [to make] investments in tourism, in services, consumer goods... the private sector were feeding back to the Thai politicians, including Chatichai: 'they are quite appreciative of Thai investments, and there is room to make profits and interests for Thai expansion, as far as business is concerned'.

Consequently, on coming to power, Chatichai dramatically reversed Thailand's foreign policy. His 'new look' aimed to 'turn the Indochina battlefield into a trading market', transforming Thailand's business sector into the 'nucleus of an Asia-Pacific [economic] zone' (Um, 1991, pp. 246–8). In 1989, Chatichai expressed his willingness to abandon the Cambodian guerrilla movements that ASEAN had sponsored for a decade in order to achieve this vision.

This policy shift was resisted by other powerful interests at home and abroad. Many bureaucrats, military officers and businessmen had grown wealthy and powerful through the high defence spending, Chinese aid and lucrative smuggling networks associated with the Cambodian conflict. Chatichai faced immediate resistance from these interests, including efforts by the foreign ministry to undermine the 'new look' (Rungswasdisab, 2006, p. 101). He therefore bypassed the state apparatus, assigning the task of *rapprochement* with Thailand's neighbours to a network of liberal academics led by Kraisak, and General Chavalit, another soldier with a 'business mind, rather than a security mind' seeking 'business opportunities for his friends, for himself' in neighbouring countries (Kraisak, 2008).

Other ASEAN states were also alarmed by this sudden departure from their agreed line. Kraisak ascribes this to their desire to continue monopolising 'the shares of investments [in Indochina] while we held up this ideological fence of capitalism, defending it'. Jakarta was particularly irritated since it had led the negotiations for a settlement favourable to ASEAN's corporate interests, hosting laborious discussions between ASEAN, Vietnam and the Cambodian factions, known as the Jakarta Informal Meetings

(JIMs). Indonesian elites complained that Chatichai had dealt a 'rude blow' to 'ASEAN cohesion and political solidarity' and 'seriously undermined ASEAN credibility' (Maisrikrod, 1992, p. 296). Moreover, they wondered just how long Chatichai's profoundly corrupt administration would last (Alatas, 2008). Beijing was also hostile to the idea of simply dumping the KR, hoping they might still return to power in some post-conflict settlement. Chatichai forged on regardless, and was foiled only by internal resistance. Instead of seeking agreement from all parties, like Indonesia, Bangkok proposed to simply bounce everyone into a settlement. Kraisak's team persuaded the PRK Prime Minister, Hun Sen, to agree to sign a ceasefire with the non-communist guerrillas, form an interim coalition with FUNCINPEC, and stage UN-monitored elections that would exclude the KR. In return, Bangkok would stop backing the KR, allowing Cambodian government forces to finally crush them (Kraisak, 2008). That this bold plan was thinkable reflected Thailand's crucial role in perpetuating Cambodia's civil war. However, the Chatichai government's overreaching against powerful domestic groups ultimately foiled the plan. In addition to antagonising many entrenched military, bureaucratic and business interests with the 'new look', rampant government corruption had also upset the Bangkok stock market, alienating the middle classes and damaging the business interests of the monarchy and the old rich. In 1991, Chatichai was overthrown in a military coup supported by these groups (Ukrist, 2008). The coup leader, General Suchinda, clearly indicated where his sympathies lay, calling Pol Pot a 'nice guy' (Kiernan, 2002, p. 94). This recapture of state power by groups allied to the interests profiting from the Cambodian conflict temporarily ended the 'new look'.

The 'new look' illustrates the critical role of social conflict in generating foreign policy and determining the meaning of (non)interference in Southeast Asia. The rise of by powerful new business interests led to a dramatic reversal in Thai policy. Yet, because elements of the Thai state were interpenetrated with forces with divergent interests, the Chatichai government struggled to enforce its policy and faced serious resistance. The policy was ultimately undone not by great-power policies or opposition from ASEAN, but by wider struggles for state power.

UNTAC: Welcoming the 'new interventionism'

The initiative for resolving the Cambodian conflict now passed back to Jakarta and the UN. Negotiations eventually generated an ambitious and wide-ranging peace agreement whose implementation required resources well beyond ASEAN's capabilities. These resources were unavailable until the thawing of the Cold War released the UN Security Council from paralysis, enabling the deployment of the UN Transitional Administration of Cambodia (UNTAC) in 1992. In contrast to those who emphasise only the great powers' role in bringing this about, however, this section illustrates that the fundamentals of the UNTAC settlement were essentially those proposed by ASEAN in the early 1980s, including the permanent diminution of Cambodian sovereignty. This helps explain why ASEAN states set aside their concerns about the West's 'new interventionism' to encourage and participate in UNTAC.

The groundwork for a comprehensive political settlement of the Cambodian conflict was laid in the early 1980s. As Chapter 4 noted, ASEAN had identified the major elements of the settlement in successive communiqués. It institutionalised them via the 1981 International Conference on Kampuchea, which became the basis for all subsequent negotiations. Indonesia, as ASEAN's principal interlocutor with Vietnam, sought to persuade Hanoi, the PRK and the ASEAN-backed guerrillas to accept the idea of a 'non-aligned Cambodia' from which Vietnamese troops would be withdrawn and wherein the KR would be 'controlled' (Alatas, 2008). The eventual Paris Peace Agreements (PPA), signed in 1991, essentially reflected the priorities ASEAN had identified a decade earlier.

Core Elements of the Paris Peace Agreements

- UN-verified withdrawal of foreign forces;
- Respect for self-determination through free and fair elections under UN auspices, to be held in a politically neutral environment, facilitated by the UN;
- Measures to protect human rights;
- Repatriation rights for all Cambodian refugees and displaced persons;
- International guarantees to preserve the sovereignty, independence, territorial integrity, neutrality and national unity of Cambodia (UN, 1991b).

The last point particularly reflects ASEAN's lack of fundamental respect for Cambodian sovereignty. The PPA technically endorsed the official

ASEAN line that 'non-interference and non-intervention in the internal and external affairs of States is of the greatest importance for the maintenance of international peace and security'. However, in line with ASEAN's 'Kuantan principle', the Agreements permanently impaired the Cambodian state's sovereign authority. They specified that 'the perpetual neutrality of Cambodia shall be proclaimed and enshrined in the [new] Cambodian constitution', banning Cambodia from forming alliances or hosting military bases. The PPA's signatories, including ASEAN, committed themselves to joint action through the UN should these restrictions be violated (UN, 1991b, pp. 46–51; 1991a). The Agreements also committed Cambodia to adopting capitalism, respecting 'private property rights' and using the 'private sector' for post-conflict reconstruction. Other limitations placed on Cambodia's sovereignty reflected the values underpinning the West's 'new interventionism'. The PPA imposed a 'system of liberal democracy, on the basis of pluralism', banned political parties opposed to the PPA from participating in elections, prohibited independent candidates, thus favouring the existing factions, and committed Cambodia to 'adher[ing] to all relevant international human rights declarations', adding it would be 'closely monitored' by the UN Commission on Human Rights (UNCHR) thereafter (UN, 1991b, annex 3, part 3, annex 5; 1991a, 1991c).

The inclusion of these liberal elements reflected ASEAN's decision to rely on the UN to terminate the conflict, rather than the Chatichai solution of abandoning the guerrillas. Whatever uneasiness ASEAN had were set aside, since member-states were 'relieved' that the UN was supplying resources that they could not (Jasudasen, 2008). UNTAC eventually deployed 22,000 personnel from February 1992 to September 1993, and cost over $1.5bn. Moreover, the liberal elements actually served ASEAN's particular interests by restricting the KR and paving the way for ASEAN's non-communist clients to return to power in Phnom Penh. The commitment to free markets also opened Cambodia up to ASEAN capital. Ultimately, UNTAC allowed ASEAN to terminate an intervention that had become obsolete. ASEAN's satisfaction was reflected in member-states constituting about one-quarter of UNTAC's total force strength, with Malaysia and Indonesia both commanding a sector and Indonesia co-commanding Phnom Penh (Boutros-Ghali, 1995, p. 23; Findlay, 1995, p. 8).

From UNTAC to the 1997 'coup'

Despite setbacks in Thailand, in the longer run, the interests behind the 'new look' prevailed. With the settling of the Cambodian conflict, the 'new rich' across the region could freely exploit lucrative opportunities across Indochina. However, rather than simply terminating intervention in Cambodia, the formal settling of the conflict instead changed its character. First, continued resistance from the politico-military-business networks that profited from relationships with the KR seriously undermined the peace process, reigniting the civil war. Second, fractions of state-linked ASEAN capital, and ASEAN diplomats themselves, meddled in Cambodia to promote political conditions favourable to their own interests. This continued intervention contributed to the destabilisation and eventual collapse of Cambodia's ruling coalition by 1997, despite belated efforts by ASEAN to prevent it.

While many ASEAN business interests had a basic interest in the peace process succeeding, others did not. This applied particularly to the networks of generals, politicians, bureaucrats and business elites who profited from the illegal cross-border trade mediated through the KR. Estimated at $120m a year by 1989, this trade had expanded markedly by 1992, with private businesses signing new deals to export timber and gems from areas under KR control. This included firms owned by government ministers and even Thailand's state timber company (Rungswasdisab, 2006, pp. 105–6). Benny Widyono, an Indonesian serving as a provincial administrator for UNTAC, and later the UN secretary-general's special representative in Cambodia, visited the KR headquarters at Pailin in late 1992. He found their leaders living in luxury, thanks to their control of mines and timber leases 'operated by unscrupulous Thai companies and controlled ostensibly by Thai regional military commanders' (Widyono, 2008, p. 87). The peace settlement threatened both partners in this lucrative arrangement because disarming and demobilising the KR's forces would terminate their physical control over the resource-rich territory they held with Thai assistance. Ultimately both sides proved unwilling to allow this to happen.

Thus, reflecting the non-coherence of the state, while one socio-political coalition tried to turn 'battlefields into marketplaces', another struggled to maintain their monopoly control of the marketplaces provided by battlefields. Citing UNTAC's failure to expel all Vietnamese from Cambodia, the KR refused to canton and disarm as specified in the PPA. The UN Security Council therefore moved to isolate the KR by banning petroleum exports to Cambodia and the export of logs and gems from the country. However, the Thai politicians, local governors, business groups and military officials involved in the border trade put enormous pressure on Thailand's new government, headed by the Democrats' Chuan Leekpai, to ignore the embargo. Officially, Bangkok pledged to respect UN sanctions, but this was simply ignored by the powerfully entrenched state-business networks along the border. Just a few days later, Thai police and military units were observed helping to transport petroleum to KR-held areas (Rungswasdisab, 2006, pp. 107–11). The trade in gems and timber also continued. As late as 1995, the KR were still earning $10m a month from the logging trade alone (Curtis, 1998, p. 38).

Thus emboldened and resourced, the KR re-launched the Cambodian civil war. While 50,000 other Cambodian troops, including government forces, had been demobilised by UNTAC, KR forces remained intact and supported elements in the Thai state. Thai soldiers were accused of supplying the KR with 30 tanks and anti-aircraft weapons, hosting the KR on Thai soil, and assisting them to capture UN personnel (Buszynski, 1994, p. 731). Thai soldiers also reportedly helped the KR seize the historic Preah Vihear temple and to attack the country's only operative railway line (Findlay, 1995, p. 94). In December 1993, Thai soldiers were caught red-handed delivering arms to a KR base, while 12 warehouses of arms were uncovered in Thailand (Heinberger, 1994, p. 2). Thanks to such assistance, by 1994, the KR controlled or threatened half of Cambodia's territory. This renewed civil war eventually cost the Cambodian government $185m, a third of its annual budget (Peou, 2000, p. 240). The interpenetration of particular social groups with parts of the state apparatus thus continued to generate destructive interventions by the Thai state, contrary to official government policy.

Official ASEAN government policy during the transitional period was scarcely any less meddlesome, however, systematically favouring its erstwhile clients, apparently to help them return to power in Phnom Penh. In January 1993, ASEAN backed Sihanouk's demand for presidential elections prior to the constituent assembly elections being organised by UNTAC, and endorsed his candidature (Peou, 2000, pp. 263–4). This demand failed, however, and general elections went ahead as planned in May 1993. The Cambodian People's Party (CPP), the vehicle of the former PRK regime, won 51 seats in the constituent assembly, FUNC-INPEC won 58 seats, and the Buddhist Liberal Democratic Party, the KPNLF's political vehicle, won ten seats. Since the PPA had specified a two-thirds majority requirement, a coalition government was now necessary. Initially, however, the CPP accused UNTAC of electoral fraud, and leading CPP figures even launched a secession bid in eastern Cambodia, apparently to frighten FUNCINPEC into agreeing to share power. Amid the chaos, ASEAN backed another power bid by Sihanouk, who declared himself Cambodia's president, commander-in-chief, and prime

minister of a FUNCINPEC-CPP coalition, without even consulting
FUNCINPEC (Peou, 2000, pp. 263–5). This was, however, flatly rejected
by the US and UNTAC, and a formal power-sharing agreement was
reached on 20 June, which included all three parties.

This outcome was, however, inherently unstable, pitching together
erstwhile enemies in an uneven compromise. FUNCINPEC's leader,
Sihanouk's son, Prince Ranariddh, was installed as 'first prime minister'
ahead of the CPP's Hun Sen as 'second prime minister', and both parties
appointed either ministers or vice-ministers to every government department. However, the CPP's *de facto* dominance was overwhelming (Hughes,
2003). The dismantling of communism in the 1980s had involved highly
politicised privatisation processes, generating patronage networks that
tied PRK state officials to emerging, powerful conglomerates. This alliance
formed the basis of the CPP. The party thus dominated both the economy and state apparatus, and had massive patronage resources at its dis-
posal. FUNCINPEC, comprised of foreign-educated former exiles with
extremely weak roots in Cambodian society, was not well-placed to challenge the CPP's domination, especially in rural areas. CPP networks adapted
quickly to the arrival of a few thousand FUNCINPEC officials in the state
apparatus, resulting in little transfer of effective power. FUNCINPEC leaders
quickly began trying to build their own patronage networks through dispensing development assistance in the provinces. Ultimately, this rivalry
within the state apparatus itself was unsustainable, particularly since the
constitution permitted only one prime minister to emerge from the next
elections in 1998.

In this context, how ASEAN states engaged with the new Cambodian
government would clearly shape the country's internal power relations. ASEAN states primarily promoted the interests of the 'new rich',
seeking special concessions for state-linked businesses and encouraging
them to invest in Cambodia. Widyono recalls that Malaysia 'led the
pack'. Kuala Lumpur's ambassador played 'a major role in attracting
Malaysian investments', and Mahathir 'took a personal interest in persuading top Malaysian companies to invest in Cambodia'. Malaysian
investment flooded into areas like logging, tourism, entertainment and
services (Widyono, 2008, p. 199). Singaporean interests also rushed to
invest in tourism (Frost, 1991, p. 124). By 1996, 59 per cent of all foreign
investment in Cambodia came from ASEAN (UNCTAD, 2003a, p. 13).
ASEAN statesmen also promoted reforms in Cambodia that would favour their business interests. Mahathir proposed ASEAN-style governance
arrangements on his frequent visits to Cambodia, suggesting ways to
'manage' democracy to maintain social stability and enhance economic

growth. The CPP leader, Hun Sen, seemed particularly keen to embrace such advice, modelling the CPP on UMNO and Suharto's GOLKAR party. ASEAN ambassadors also pressed the Cambodian government to expel the UNCHR's field office in 1995 (Widyono, 2008, pp. 203, 207). ASEAN investment played directly into the CPP-FUNCINPEC rivalry. The parties were competing for popular support by dispensing patronage resources and initiating development projects. ASEAN capitalists happily agreed to help the protagonists since 'they were used to benefiting from special relationships and deals struck with the powers that be in their own countries' (Widyono, 2008, p. 203). They consequently became heavily involved, 'with the support of their governments', in financing various development projects. Singapore ploughed $35m into 18 projects; Malaysia, $20m into 23; and Thailand, $47m into seven. Crucially, ASEAN firms 'generally favoured Hun Sen over Ranariddh because the former was stronger – and thus a more stable investment' (Peou, 2000, p. 373). This was true even during the transitional period, when Malaysia bypassed both UNTAC and the Supreme National Council (SNC) – the temporary embodiment of Cambodian sovereignty – to sign an aviation deal with the CPP-controlled foreign ministry (Findlay, 1995, p. 62). Ranariddh's desperate attempts to catch up included closing domestic businesses to smooth the way for a $1.3bn investment from Malaysian firm Ariston – which never materialised, much to the anger of his domestic constituents (Widyono, 2008, pp. 200–1). Ranariddh's corruption also alienated many of his allies. When FUNCINPEC Finance Minister Sam Rainsy accused Ranariddh and Hun Sen of accepting $108m in bribes from Ariston, they purged him from the government. Rainsy took a large part of FUNCINPEC with him, forming his own party and leaving Ranariddh even more isolated (Hughes, 2003, p. 43).

This growing political instability in Cambodia was not simply an unfortunate by-product of trade and investment, but reflected the nature of state power in the region. While some ASEAN foreign ministry apparatchiks obviously sought stability and peace, entrenched state-business compacts were often more interested in short-term gains. The interests involved were often so predatory that they knowingly destabilised Cambodia simply to line their own pockets. Because Cambodia's military comprised former PRK soldiers and former FUNCINPEC guerrillas, the army was highly factionalised, with units principally being loyal to their respective political parties, rather than 'the state'. Suharto's son-in-law, General Prabowo, used his command of Indonesian special forces to provide training and illicit weaponry for Hun Sen's enormous 'bodyguard' in exchange for lucrative forestry concessions

(Widyono, 2008, pp. 200–1). This significantly destabilised the military balance between the two factions. Divisions within the parties were also exploited. In 1994, a CPP faction led by General Sin and Prince Chakrapong attempted to overthrow Hun Sen. Kraisak Choonhavan was summoned to Cambodia, where Hun Sen told him that the plot had been masterminded by Thai telecommunications tycoon Thaksin Shinawatra. Thaksin's company, ShinCorp, had allegedly recruited several dozen Thais to help the plotters by cutting power and communications lines in Phnom Penh. Four officers from Thailand's National Security Council were also arrested in Cambodia in connection with the coup, one of whom was a close ally of General Chavalit, then Thailand's interior minister. General Sin also fled to Chavalit's safe house in Bangkok. Thaksin had allegedly moved against Hun Sen because he had curtailed ShinCorp's expansion into Cambodia. The plot also involved a Thai-Cambodian businessman-gangster, Teng Bun Ma, who apparently hoped to force his way into Cambodia's banking sector in partnership with Thaksin and Chavalit (Kraisak, 2008; see also Phnom Penh Post, 2007).

The civil war restarted by the KR with Thai assistance also had significant consequences for the CPP-FUNCINPEC coalition. The Cambodian government's response had combined military counter-offensives with offers of amnesties to KR leaders willing to surrender. In August 1996, a major KR faction headed by Ieng Sary decided to take this opportunity so as to enjoy its ill-gotten wealth in peace. Negotiations with the government began, which also involved Teng Bun Ma and Malaysian tycoon Andrew Yo seeking lucrative concessions in the area around Pailin (Widyono, 2008, p. 235). Ranariddh, however, was now struggling to prevent FUNCINPEC disintegrating and had pledged to 'strive for military balance with the CPP'. Short on options, he tried to form an alliance with Ieng Sary against the CPP. When this was rejected, he turned instead to the remaining KR hard-liners at Anlong Veng, led by Pol Pot, Khieu Samphan and Ta Mok (Widyono, 2008, pp. 235–48, 214–17; Curtis, 1998, pp. 46–8). Cambodia's governing coalition began to collapse, with FUNCINPEC and CPP military units clashing by February 1997.

ASEAN did not observe non-interference and stand idly by while the coalition broke down. As early as May 1996, ASEAN had despatched Malaysia's foreign minister to counsel 'against any escalation of violence' between the factions, warning that 'open hostilities would force ASEAN to leave Cambodia alone'. This was a serious threat given Cambodia's dependence on ASEAN capital and markets, and Cambodia's pending admission to ASEAN in July 1997. In December 1996, Mahathir also wrote to the co-prime ministers, 'urging them to settle their differences and to ensure political stability in the country'. Singapore's prime minister likewise stressed the importance of stability for sustaining foreign investment. Suharto led a large Indonesian delegation to Cambodia in February 1997, reiterating ASEAN's demands for stability, while the Philippines publicly voiced fears about Cambodia's readiness for ASEAN membership following a grenade attack on a Sam Rainsy Party (SRP) rally in March 1997 (Peou, 2000, pp. 373–5).

None of these interventions could stave off the inevitable. When Ranariddh finally moved against Hun Sen in early July 1997 by smuggling arms and KR soldiers into the capital, CPP forces struck back, swiftly defeating him. Ranariddh flew into exile, claiming that a 'coup' had been launched against him, and immediately sought external support in Western capitals. The Western media accepted these claims, raging against Hun Sen. Meanwhile, FUNCINPEC-affiliated army units quickly joined the hard-line KR forces, apparently seeking to capture and hold Pochtenpong airport long enough for a hoped-for UN intervention force to arrive (Kevin, 2000).

Remarkably, the dominant critique of ASEAN in this period is that it did not interfere enough in Cambodia. In May 1997, a Malaysian Institute for Policy Research (1997) 'study mission' of liberal Southeast Asian scholars criticised ASEAN's 'reluctance to "assist" Cambodia in addressing her domestic problems for fear of violating the principle of non-intervention'. ASEAN was urged to intervene in Cambodia to help ensure free and fair elections, advise on and assist Cambodia's institutional development and legal reforms, train state officials, and help develop the economy. After the 'coup', this position was echoed by the Institute's political patron, Malaysia's deputy prime minister, Anwar Ibrahim (1997):

> We need to 'intervene' before simmering problems erupt into full-blow crises... our non-involvement in the reconstruction of Cambodia actually contributed to the deterioration and final collapse of national reconciliation. We should have nursed the baby, at least through its teething period. That's why we need to consider the idea of 'constructive intervention'.

Clearly, however, it is simply inaccurate to talk about ASEAN states' 'non-involvement' in Cambodia's internal affairs. Some ASEAN states had long been promoting policy advice and business involvement in Cambodia. That this advice and involvement was probably not what liberal scholars intended reflects the region's entrenched political economy relationships, which govern how state power is actually used in practice. Unsurprisingly, given the socio-political constellations underpinning them, ASEAN states preferred to export managed 'democracy' rather than genuinely supporting electoral mechanisms and civil society development. Many within ASEAN states doubtless desired political stability in Cambodia, both to gain kudos for ASEAN's diplomacy in ending the Cambodian conflict, and to realise returns on the vast sums of capital ASEAN capitalist had invested there. However, the influence of predatory, state-linked business interests instead contributed to factional rivalry, the renewal of the civil war, and the collapse of the ruling coalition in 1997.

Creeping conditionality for ASEAN membership

ASEAN's reaction to the breakdown of Cambodia's ruling coalition was not to practice non-interference, but to postpone the country's admission to the Association and impose a creeping set of conditions to be met before it would be admitted. In so doing, ASEAN aligned itself with the Western powers' response, which was to withhold foreign aid, demand free and fair elections, and suspend Cambodia's UN membership. ASEAN collaborated closely with Western donors and essentially became the gate-keeper for Cambodia's re-entry to the 'international community'. This section explores ASEAN's reaction and considers potential explanations for this renewed intervention. It argues that ASEAN's principal concern was not for democracy, but to restore the peace settlement it had laboured for, and to safeguard its closely-related diplomatic standing. Its reaction is thus incomprehensible without considering the long history of ASEAN intervention in Cambodia, which gave ASEAN countries a sense of 'ownership' over its internal affairs.

ASEAN's immediate response was to defer Cambodia's admission to the Association, which had been due to take place just a few days later, and to offer to mediate a solution. Indonesia summoned an emergency AMM, which combined a restatement of non-interference coupled with a declaration of intervention:

> While reaffirming the commitment to the principle of non-interference in the internal affairs of other states, [ASEAN] decided that, in the light of unfortunate circumstances which have resulted from the use of force, the wisest course of action is to delay the admission of Cambodia into ASEAN until a later date... The ASEAN countries

stand ready to contribute their efforts to the peaceful resolution of the situation in Cambodia (ASEAN, 1997b).

The foreign ministers of Thailand, the Philippines and Indonesia were then appointed as ASEAN's 'Troika', tasked with intervening in Cambodia to resolve the crisis. Unlike earlier ASEAN interventions in Cambodia, this decision to intervene was so overt that it has not gone unnoticed by other scholars. Let us therefore consider the explanations they offer. Those most wedded to proving the normative determination of state behaviour understandably seek to minimise the extent of deviation from non-interference. Thus, Acharya (2009a, p. 136) argues that events in Cambodia were 'not strictly an "internal" matter', since the PPA had been broken; consequently, ASEAN, as a guarantor of the Accords, did not violate the non-interference principle by reacting. This is, however, inaccurate. The PPA made no mention of any international response to a breakdown of the Cambodian government. In fact, it committed signatories to 'refrain from interference in any form whatsoever, whether direct or indirect, in the internal affairs of Cambodia'. The PPA only obliged signatories to consult through the UN in the event that Cambodia's sovereignty, neutrality or territorial integrity was compromised. No independent role for ASEAN was authorised (UN, 1991a). Unsurprisingly, ASEAN leaders hardly even mentioned the PPA to explain or justify their response.[1]

Scholars who do accept that ASEAN's response clashed with its norms offer a variety of *ad hoc* explanations, mostly based on the predilections of individual ASEAN leaders. Moller (1998, p. 1099) claims that ASEAN was concerned for human rights and democracy in Cambodia, particularly Thai Prime Minister Chuan who was 'committed to promoting democracy in the region' due to his belief in democratic peace theory. However, Chuan was not yet prime minister at this point. Moreover, Chuan's foreign minister rejects Moller's suggestion (Surin, 2008b). ASEAN leaders' public statements also lack any references to liberal-democratic values. Constructivist scholar Jürgen Haacke (1999, p. 590) argues that ASEAN's response stemmed from a 'moral grammar of outrage which sprang from the embarrassment suffered by ASEAN governments generally and President Suharto in particular', but this could 'not, for obvious reasons, be translated into official explanations' (see also Henderson, 1999, p. 39). Unfortunately, however, he provides no explanation of what 'moral grammar' means, or what the 'obvious reasons' were.

These rather unpersuasive explanations reflect the general treatment of non-interference in ASEAN scholarship. Since they overwhelmingly believe that intervention is profoundly rare, scholars have not developed theoretical frameworks capable of explaining the selectivity of non-interference. Thus, when discrepant evidence *is* noticed, scholars can only resort to *ad hoc* explanations for these apparently one-off instances. Yet a full understanding of this episode is impossible without reflecting on the *long-standing* nature of ASEAN's involvement in Cambodia's internal affairs, and the interests bound up in this. This generated two powerful, related impulses to intervene in 1997.

The first impulse stemmed from the importance of ASEAN's prior intervention in Cambodia for its international standing. The intervention cohered ASEAN, forcing it to develop new capacities for cooperation, and established it as a significant international presence. As Surin Pitsuwan (2008b) states, ASEAN 'had invested quite a bit of energy and resources and emotion into helping Cambodia return to national reconciliation... we thought that was a success story, that we could quote it'. ASEAN's intervention in Cambodia constituted the main basis for ASEAN's claim to manage regional order in the post-Cold War period. It had enabled ASEAN to engage external powers in ways that complemented their domestic economic and political strategies. Uniquely in the developing world, ASEAN had established itself as the hub of regional institution-building and thereby retained significant control of the regional agenda, allowing member-states to curtail discussion of human rights, democracy and other domestic issues. This enabled them to control the scope of conflicts in their own societies, preventing their expansion to the international level and precluding subordinated social groups gaining external support.

However, as Chapter 5 explored, the credibility of ASEAN's regional role always rested on its willingness to at least partially respond to the concerns of key dialogue partners, particularly Western states. ASEAN's standing in Western capitals had recently been badly damaged by its decision to admit Burma, despite vociferous protests from the US and EU. In this context, and particularly given that ASEAN's role rested largely on its supposed achievements *vis-à-vis* Cambodia, the collapse of the ruling coalition could not be ignored. As Singapore's foreign minister put it, the 'purpose and credibility of ASEAN was at stake' (AFP, 1997). A senior Singaporean diplomat (2008) elaborates: 'it makes us look a bit stupid if someone pulls a coup and then you let them in immediately... that looks like you have no standards whatsoever, not even minimal... Myanmar was a mistake... why go and compound your mistakes?'

The second, related impulse was that ASEAN states, particularly their foreign ministries, felt a strong sense of ownership over Cambodia's internal affairs as a result of their earlier interventions. As Thailand's then-UN ambassador explains, 'we felt that Cambodia was "our baby"... we took a lot of trouble to set up the international conference on Cambodia, we fought many years against the Vietnamese, 10, 11 or 12 years of resolutions. So it was our special interest' (Asda, 2008). A sense that ASEAN was entitled to intervene, stemming from the group's long-term meddling in Cambodia, overrode any consideration of non-interference. Ali Alatas (2008), Indonesia's foreign minister and the head of ASEAN's Troika mission, explained: 'I felt the least danger of interference... Indonesia felt that... it was entitled to pick up the broken pieces and try to get it [back together]'.

Furthermore, ASEAN businesses had invested over $2bn in Cambodia by 1997 (UNCTAD, 2003a, p. 13). The resumption of full-scale civil war would have destroyed the stability necessary for these investments to bear fruit. Powerful sections of ASEAN's business classes also had an interest, therefore, in their governments mediating a settlement. Contrary to the situation in the Cold War, then, ASEAN states had every incentive to curtail rather than fuel the re-emerging civil war.

The decision to intervene, and thus widen the scope of Cambodia's internal conflict to the regional level, was not uncontroversial, however. The conflict pitched the erstwhile clients of the older ASEAN members, FUNCINPEC, against the longstanding allies of ASEAN's newest member, Vietnam, which had joined the Association in 1995. FUNCINPEC, the weaker party in the conflict, naturally sought to broaden its scope by appealing to outsiders. Alatas (2008) recalls that 'we were under pressure, by Sihanouk, by Ranariddh... we were erstwhile supporters of Sihanouk and the CGDK, and here was Hun Sen again getting [them] into these kinds of problems'. Conversely, the CPP had every incentive to limit the scope of the conflict in order to impose a *fait accompli* and decisively defeat Ranariddh. Hanoi backed this position, invoking ASEAN's norms to try to prevent intervention occurring. Alatas recalls Vietnam asking,

'Is this not foreign interference? Why are we now putting certain conditions to an entry of a Southeast Asian country into ASEAN, while we have not done so in the past? We have never had pre-conditions for membership in ASEAN...' But in the end the over-whelming view was... we cannot face the world and say: 'business as usual; this is an internal affair; they are welcome as members anyway' (Alatas, 2008).

The CPP nonetheless resisted ASEAN intervention. Many FUNCINPEC MPs had already deserted Ranariddh, preferring to working with the CPP to share of the spoils of state power. They quickly elected a new party leader, Ung Huot, who immediately replaced Ranariddh as 'first prime minister'. Hun Sen pledged to hold the 1998 elections as planned, and there was a marked improvement in political stability. The CPP and its FUNCINPEC allies strenuously resisted external attempts to widen the scope of Cambodia's political crisis in a way that could only benefit Ranariddh's faction. Before the Troika had even visited Phnom Penh, Hun Sen publicly denounced ASEAN's plans to 'interfere in [Cambodia's] internal affairs', threatening to withdraw Cambodia's membership application. 'ASEAN countries must let us solve our problems on their own,' he stated. 'Please stay out of our internal business' (*Financial Times*, 1997). Alatas (2008) recalls the Troika's first meeting with Hun Sen, who 'was livid with rage... He said, "This is foreign interference! This is against ASEAN's own principles! What are you doing here? You have nothing to do with what is happening to Cambodia! I don't want to become a member of ASEAN, not with that kind of organization!"'

ASEAN was ruffled, but not deterred, and soon joined with extra-regional powers to impose foreign intervention on Cambodia. ASEAN first denied the legitimacy of Cambodia's internal attempts to resolve the process, refusing to recognise Ung Huot as Ranariddh's successor by claiming, rather nonsensically, that 'ASEAN member states recognise states, not governments' (ASEAN, 1997a). Meanwhile, Western donors, marshalled by the US, suspended their aid to Cambodia. This was a serious blow, since foreign aid constituted 70 per cent of the state budget, and government expenditure was escalating to combat the KR-FUNCINPEC insurgency (Kevin, 2000, pp. 595–6). The Western donors and the ASEAN Regional Forum (ARF) endorsed ASEAN's lead role in resolving the Cambodian crisis. US Secretary of State Madeleine Albright emphasised that foreign aid was now conditional upon ASEAN intervention, stating that 'cooperation with ASEAN mediation... is essential if Cambodia is to fully rejoin the international community' (ST, 1997). Washington intensified the pressure in September by pushing for Cambodia's UN seat to be assigned to Ranariddh. The seat was ultimately left vacant, stripping the government of its capacity to represent Cambodia internationally. Consequently, Hun Sen was forced to accept ASEAN mediation, affording ASEAN the convenient fiction that it was practising 'intervention with approval', as Malaysia's foreign minister put it (FEER, 1997). In reality, Cambodia had obviously been coerced, enabling ASEAN to become the gate-keeper for Cambodia's international rehabilitation.

ASEAN mediation took the form of a creeping set of conditions for membership in the Association. The Troika's implicit goal was to restore a stable power-sharing agreement between Ranariddh and Hun Sen. However, given that Cambodia was a democracy and elections were pending, this substantive goal could not be openly stated. Instead, ASEAN set various procedural conditions that had to be met before Cambodia could join the Association, such as the holding of elections. However, these conditions were repeatedly met without the coalition being restored, forcing ASEAN to repeatedly change the conditions – hence, 'creeping conditionality'. The break this involved from ASEAN's supposedly binding norms is clear, given that in no other case have membership conditions been imposed beyond very minor, technical criteria.[2]

The ASEAN Troika's first proposal, issued on 19 July, was for Ranariddh to be reinstated and for both co-prime ministers to appoint representatives to run a 'caretaker government' until the May 1998 elections. Hun Sen rejected this. ASEAN therefore called instead for 'free and fair elections' involving 'all political parties', offering technical assistance, while pressing Ranariddh to declare a ceasefire and participate in the polls. ASEAN also lobbied self-exiled FUNCINPEC and SRP legislators to return for the elections, persuading the UN to provide them with protection if they agreed to do so. Progress was, however, repeatedly stalled by Hun Sen's insistence on prosecuting Ranariddh for his treasonous activities.

As the Troika struggled to break the impasse, the region was hit by the Asian financial crisis, which Hun Sen seized upon to try to terminate ASEAN's intervention. Mocking the hypocrisy of ASEAN's crisis-ridden, illiberal regimes seeking to dictate terms to Cambodia, he declared ahead of a scheduled Troika visit in January 1998:

> I would recommend to the ASEAN nations, please do not worry so much about the situation in Cambodia. Instead, they should solve their own economic crises first... I will not welcome the troika delegation... Please do not come and teach us any more about human rights and democracy in Cambodia.

Hun Sen particularly criticised Alatas for acting as if 'he is a foreign minister of Cambodia' (Kyodo, 1998b). He also threatened again to withdraw Cambodia's application to join ASEAN, playing up China's continued aid to the country and its non-interventionist stance. However, since the restoration of his government's international legitimacy and foreign aid depended on cooperating with ASEAN, he had little choice but to suffer continued intervention.

With the region in disarray, Thailand was left to do most of ASEAN's diplomacy. To break the log-jam, Japan proposed that Ranariddh be tried but receive an automatic pardon from King Sihanouk. Thailand's deputy foreign minister, Sukhumbhand Paribatra, shuttled repeatedly between the parties to press them to accept this plan, offering to host and mediate direct talks in Bangkok. Thailand also called for the elections to be postponed from May to create time for the ceasefire and trial to be implemented and for self-exiled politicians to return. All sides eventually agreed, despite Ranariddh trying to exploit the situation by holding out for further concessions. ASEAN governments then pledged to send eight election monitors each and to mobilise international finance for the elections, which were now scheduled for July 1998 (Jones, 2007, p. 539).

Despite being declared 'free and fair' by all foreign observers, the elections did not settle Cambodia's political crisis. The CPP won 41 per cent of the votes, FUNCINPEC, 43 per cent, and the SRP, 14 per cent. Hun Sen immediately proposed a grand coalition, but Ranariddh and Rainsy declared the poll invalid, fleeing the country with many other legislators so as to prevent the National Assembly reaching quorum. Both parties again called for foreign intervention, with an SRP rally in Phnom Penh demanding a US invasion to topple Hun Sen.

This situation stemmed directly from the long-term internationalisation of Cambodia's political conflicts. The parties now holding Cambodian politics hostage were the rebranded guerrilla groups which ASEAN had backed in the CGDK. As longstanding exiles and foreign-educated elites lacking a mass base, they had failed to mobilise sufficient support to defeat the CPP decisively. They therefore fell back on the tried and tested method of using external intervention to manoeuvre themselves into power. They could do so only because Ranarridh had successfully expanded the scope of Cambodian politics to shift the balance of forces against the CPP. The interventionist attention fixed on the country by ASEAN and Western donors allowed them to reject the election results and refuse to cooperate with the CPP in an effort to extract further concessions for their own benefit.

The failure of the elections to restore power-sharing between Ranariddh and Hun Sen prompted ASEAN to again shift its conditions for Cambodian membership. ASEAN officials had repeatedly said that Cambodia would have no difficulty joining the Association after the elections, which would be final clincher for its admission (Jones, 2007, p. 539). Now, however, Singapore's foreign minister, then head of the ASEAN Standing Committee, demanded that Cambodia first form 'a new government that fulfils the aspirations of the Cambodian people *and the desire of the countries in the region*' (Xinhua, 1998, my emphasis). Sukhumbhand resumed his shuttle diplomacy, pushing for negotiations. Talks were eventually convened by Sihanouk, and a coalition agreed on 13 November. Ranariddh held out for half of all ministerial posts for FUNCINPEC and, thanks to the leverage afforded by foreign intervention, the position of president of the national assembly for himself. Because this deal would displace a CPP grandee from this lucrative sinecure, however, the parties also agreed to create a new senate and install him as its chair.

At this point, significant divisions emerged within ASEAN as to whether conditionality should creep forward yet again. Following an AMM held the day after the coalition agreement, Thailand's foreign ministry declared that Cambodia's ASEAN membership would now be made conditional upon the constitutional amendment required to create the senate being approved (Kyodo, 1998a). Manila and Singapore both favoured this move. Philippine Foreign Secretary Domingo Siazon worried that without the amendment in place, the power-sharing agreement might break down into 'another [round of] fighting... [and] we will have to resolve it again. Others are saying, "didn't we get burned there already?" We were ready to accept them and then, days before, they started fighting' (AFP, 1998b). Singapore was also concerned about admitting a 'complete basket-case' that was still potentially 'falling apart', since there would always be 'the expectation that you should do something' in the event of any future political breakdown, 'internally, within ASEAN, as well as externally' (Kausikan, 2008). This indicated the expectation that, even after Cambodia joined ASEAN, it would not really benefit from 'non-interference'.

Amidst serious social, economic and political unrest elsewhere in the region, however, other ASEAN state-managers were increasingly uncomfortable with creeping conditionality. Growing inter-elite tensions complicated policy coordination and eventually curtailed ASEAN's intervention in Cambodia. Despite the official dilution of Surin's 'flexible engagement' proposal earlier that year, ASEAN's involvement in Cambodian politics, including its unprecedented electoral observation mission, reflected the degradation of ASEAN's respect for member-state sovereignty in practice. The Indonesian government, despite having led the ASEAN Troika, was now rediscovering the utility of non-interference as it was beset by intervention from the IMF and foreign pressure over East Timor. Foreign Minister Alatas now opposed creeping conditionality, asking

> since when should ASEAN sit in judgement about how govern-ments work and make it a condition for entry[?] Did we do that when Vietnam entered, or Laos, or Myanmar, or before that Brunei Darussalam? We never said, 'Well, I hope your government works and we will just see first...' I mean, this is an additional conditionality that moves towards [*sic*] internal interference (AFP, 1998a).

The Malaysian government, struggling to contain the scope of its struggle against the *reformasi* movement, agreed with Alatas, as did Vietnam and the newly-admitted member-states, Laos and Burma.

A divided ASEAN thus produced a strange compromise whereby Cambodia was technically admitted, but its formal admission ceremony continued to be postponed until the final condition was met – the estab-lishment of the senate. Sukhumband embarked on yet another round of diplomacy to press the parties to pass the required constitutional amend-ment. Having established a new senate, Cambodia was finally admitted to ASEAN on 30 April 1999. This was nearly two years after the 'coup', and several months after the Western powers had resumed international aid and restored Cambodia's UN seat to the government in Phnom Penh. ASEAN intervention had thus even outlasted that of the West.

Concluding remarks

This chapter has shown that the social conflicts animating ASEAN states continued to set the parameters of 'non-interference' towards Cambodia after the Cold War. This case particularly illustrates the importance of the non-coherence of state apparatuses on sovereignty regimes. The interests of powerful new business elites created a strong impetus towards settling the conflict, particularly in Thailand, but this was resisted by state-business networks which profited from its perpetuation, generating con-tinued intervention. When the conflict was settled, through a large-scale UN intervention, it largely embodied ASEAN states' interests, paving the way for the exploitation of Cambodia's resources and markets. After the settlement, the nature of ASEAN states' engagement with Cambodia, and the degree to which Cambodian sovereignty was respected, continued to be set by the relationships between those states and powerful business interests. ASEAN states encouraged political stability and managed democracy to serve the interests of their investors. Yet the influx of politically-mediated capital exacerbated the rivalry between the two main Cambodian parties. Thailand's state-business networks particularly undermined Cambodia's stability by working with the KR, which was thereby maintained as a significant military force, whose loyalty the coalition parties fought to acquire. This rivalry escalated into outright military confrontation in 1997. ASEAN governments then intervened to impose creeping conditionality on Cambodia's ASEAN membership, becoming the gatekeeper of the country's international rehabilitation. The case also illustrates the impact of inter-elite conflicts on ASEAN's sovereignty regime. As the newer members grew in number and as the financial crisis began to destabilise the societies, economies and polities of key ASEAN states, the inter-elite consensus required to maintain the intervention in Cambodia disintegrated, resulting in its termination.

The effects of these interventions were very severe. ASEAN's plan for a 'comprehensive political settlement' permanently impaired the sovereignty of the Cambodian state. Even as the settlement was being implemented, the actions of ASEAN's state-business networks continued to fuel civil conflict in the country, playing recklessly into Cambodia's power struggle. When the situation degenerated back into civil war, the resumption of formal foreign intervention denied the government aid and development assistance for nearly two years. Cambodia suffered massive capital flight and lost 16 per cent of compound economic growth from 1997–1999 (Kevin, 2000, pp. 595–7). Exacerbating the impact on a population whose per capita annual income was just $300, severe cuts followed in healthcare, education and infrastructure spending. Tourism revenues also fell by a quarter (Curtis, 1998, p. 58). Finally, thanks to the socialisation of Cambodia's socio-political conflict, the balance of forces was coercively altered, which led both to state structures being changed through the creation of a new senate, and the restoration to power of the very forces which had precipitated the crisis in the first place. Ranariddh, who had after all conspired with the KR to overthrow the elected government, escaped accountability and returned to public office. Far from helping to create political stability in Cambodia, the overall effect of ASEAN's meddling was actually the exact opposite.

7
East Timor: Interdependence and Intervention

> East Timor is none of our business. It is a consensus among the ASEAN countries that they will not interfere in each other's internal affairs... we should not get involved.
> – *Thai Prime Minister Chuan Leekpai, 1994* (Inbaraj, 1995, p. 143)

> We wish to see... overwhelming ASEAN forces, coming to help restore the deteriorating situation in East Timor.
> – *Indonesian Defence Minister Wiranto, 1999* (Surin, 2002)

After East Timor vanished from the international agenda in the early 1980s, it did not re-emerge for another decade. FRETILIN's armed resistance to Indonesia's occupation gradually waned through the 1980s in the face of brutal counterinsurgency operations, its armed wing reduced to a rump force operating in the eastern mountains. However, by the turn of the decade, a new generation of resisters had emerged in urban areas in response to high unemployment and the iniquities of Indonesian rule. The army's typically inhumane response – particularly a massacre of pro-independence youths at the church of Santa Cruz in Dili in 1991 – drew international attention back to the territory. In the context of the West's 'new interventionism', Jakarta was pilloried for abusing human rights and came under renewed pressure to settle the conflict peacefully. When the Indonesian state was further weakened by the Asian financial crisis, Jakarta offered the Timorese a referendum on their political future in 1999. When they voted overwhelmingly for independence, the Indonesian army and its allied local militias razed the territory, precipitating a major humanitarian crisis. The UN authorised an International Force for East Timor (INTERFET) to intervene and restore order, then initiated a statebuilding intervention. East Timor regained its independence in 2002.

The conventional view of ASEAN's role in these events is that they simply did nothing, strictly adhering to the non-interference principle (Huntley and Hayes, 2000; Sebastian and Smith, 2000). Most constructivists emphasise how ASEAN was paralysed by its norms against 'intrusive regionalism' (McDougall, 2001, p. 172). As Acharya (2009a, p. 290) puts it, 'non-interference thwarted ASEAN's ability to respond to the East Timor crisis'. English school adherents also attribute ASEAN's 'inability to act' to its 'basic norms and general inclinations', particularly its attachment to sovereignty (Narine, 2002, p. 174; 2005, p. 478). Realists further claim that strict adherence to non-interference hobbled ASEAN-led institutions like the ARF (Emmers, 2004).

However, a few authors have recognised that such claims are difficult to square with ASEAN states' involvement in both INTERFET and subsequent UN interventions. The Association's secretary-general at the time suggests that ASEAN's inability to collectively engage in peacekeeping was 'not so much because of its policy of non-interference as because of its member-states' aversion to investing the Association with any kind of supranational power, particularly one involving military force' (Severino, 2006, pp. 130–1). In a rare scholarly critique, Cotton (2004, pp. 84–5) goes further, arguing that ASEAN's norms were 'systematically ignored' over East Timor, constituting a serious challenge to the 'security community' thesis. Constructivist scholar Jürgen Haacke (2003, pp. 201–4) even describes East Timor as a 'significant moment in the evolution of the "ASEAN way"' (though, typically, its significance is almost immediately downplayed: 'participation [in intervention] has neither amounted to nor automatically heralds a major change in the "ASEAN Way"'). Yet, as with Cambodia in 1997, the explanations offered for ASEAN states' involvement in East Timor tend to be *ad hoc*, ranging from the need to help Jakarta 'save face' to the supposed liberal-democratic identities of some member-states.

This chapter offers a more coherent understanding of ASEAN states' policies. Unusually, it begins well before the 1999 intervention to show how the application of 'non-interference' to East Timor was not simply an automatic product of binding norms. Rather, it was coercively enforced by the Suharto regime and its allies in neighbouring countries' oligarchic classes, as a means of limiting the scope of conflict over East Timor. The second section then considers ASEAN's response to the 1999 humanitarian crisis, showing that core states did far more than is generally acknowledged. It argues that this was principally due to their fear of contagion from the social and economic unrest spreading from Indonesia. The third section then explores differences between the ASEAN states in some depth, showing how they related to the specific linkages between their own socio-economic and political orders and Indonesia's.

The early 1990s: Enforcing 'non-interference'

During the Cold War, ASEAN had worked assiduously to help insulate East Timor from external support by deploying the non-interference principle, defining the invasion as an act of 'decolonisation' and thereby branding further debate as intervention in Indonesia 'internal' affairs. With Western connivance, the issue faded from the UN's agenda after 1982. It returned with a vengeance in the 1990s, in the dangerous context of the 'new interventionism'. Chapter 5 argued that 'non-interference' was essentially redeployed in the post-Cold War period against this threat to established political and economic power relations. However, as this section shows, this redeployment was far from smooth or automatic. Without the shared threat of communist insurgency, ASEAN states' policies lacked a unifying goal and began to diverge. Coercive Indonesian intervention, mediated through emerging transnational business relationships, was required to again marshal ASEAN behind Jakarta.

As Indonesia's foreign minister lamented, the end of the Cold War terminated Jakarta's usefulness as a 'bulwark against communist expansion', producing a stark reversal in Western policies on East Timor. Their earlier support for Suharto was now replaced by vocal concerns for 'good governance... democratisation, [and] human rights' (Alatas, 2006, p. 239). This reversal began in 1988, when Portugal successfully lobbied the European Economic Community (EEC) to adopt a common position on East Timor and began boycotting the inter-regional Asia-Europe Meetings (ASEM), vetoing the upgrading of cooperation agreements. The following year, East Timor returned to the UNCHR's agenda.

Unlike ASEAN's other Cold War-era interventions, Indonesia could not simply withdraw from East Timor once the anti-communist rationale of the original intervention had become obsolete. It had been formally incorporated into the Indonesian republic and its 'decolonisation' was now firmly part of the New Order's nationalist mythology. Moreover, very powerful domestic interests were at stake. As Chapter 3 noted, the Indonesian military had largely captured the Timorese economy for their own benefit. They had also established patronage networks involving Timorese elites in order to stabilise their rule over the territory. These entrenched interests made it impossible to simply pull out of East Timor. Instead, Indonesia sought to defuse Western criticism by 'opening up' the territory to international trade, investment and tourism, in an attempt to showcase its 'development'.

This decision had ironic consequences. Widespread corruption and the monopolisation of economic opportunities by the military, Indonesian transmigrants, and local collaborationist elites had produced very low rates of economic growth and very high rates of youth unemployment, which led to growing urban unrest. By the late 1980s, this had been harnessed by the Timorese resistance, which recruited up to 10,000 urban youths into a clandestine network to resist Indonesian rule. The 'opening up' of East Timor encouraged this movement to try to connect with the West's 'new interventionism'. They repeatedly staged rallies and stunts timed to coincide with visits by Western personalities or international events like Asia-Pacific Economic Cooperation (APEC) summits, in order to persuade the Western powers to intervene (Pinto and Jardine, 1997). The Indonesian army moved to forcibly suppress the resistance, massacring 271 youths at Santa Cruz in November 1991. This prompted a furious Western reaction. The US Congress restricted military aid to Indonesia, instructing President Clinton to pressure Jakarta bilaterally and in multilateral forums. Washington subsequently spearheaded action at the UNCHR. The Netherlands, which headed the main international aid consortium for Indonesia, which had just pledged $4.8bn in aid, suspended all assistance to Jakarta. Other Western states followed, and the European parliament also demanded an international arms embargo. The 'new interventionism' had suddenly turned its gaze on Indonesia. From the Suharto regime's perspective, this gave dangerous encouragement not merely to the Timorese resistance, but also to student groups associated with the pro-democratic opposition within Indonesia itself, which were now also demanding an end to the 'fake process of integration' (Aditjondro, 1994, p. 83).

Jakarta made limited strategic concessions to assuage Western anger while retaining control over East Timorese politics. It appointed a commission of inquiry to investigate the massacre, created a tame human rights commission, and pensioned off a number of military officers. This largely involved purging General Murdani's faction and replacing them with members of Suharto's own network. Suharto's family and close cronies thereby seized control of much of the local economy, which only strengthened the regime's determination to retain East Timor (Aditjondro, 1999; Taylor, 1991, pp. 125–7; Gunn, 1997, pp. 32–7). The rotation of military personnel did not abate counter-insurgency operations in the territory, which actually intensified. Meanwhile, a forum called the 'All-Inclusive East Timor Dialogue' (AIETD) was created to promote 'national reconciliation' talks among pro- and anti-Indonesian Timorese elites. The AIETD presented the problem in East Timor as one of intra-Timorese divisions rather than Indonesia's occupation. The 'all-inclusive' talks were actually stuffed with hand-picked collaborators and led by Suharto's daughter, Siti. They were tightly controlled to prevent the scope of the conflict being widened by its participants. Siti largely used it, alongside other lobby groups, to promote her business interests with Portugal (Aditjondro, 1994, pp. 48–9). Indonesia's concessions were, therefore, very limited. They were, nonetheless, sufficient to restore much Western aid. Continued protests from states like Portugal and Ireland were overridden by other Western governments keen to acquire a slice of the 'Asian economic miracle'.

ASEAN's role in this period was to assist Jakarta in preventing the expansion of the scope of conflict in East Timor. ASEAN diplomacy was directed towards keeping the Timor issue off the agenda of multilateral forums and thereby to limit its scope to an entirely local level where the New Order had the upper hand. This would buy Jakarta time to settle the conflict in a way commensurate with dominant interests. ASEAN's willingness to assist was obviously no longer driven by shared concerns about 'communism' in East Timor. Rather, ASEAN elites were concerned that, given the large numbers of regional conflicts inside Indonesia, Western intervention might lead to its 'Balkanisation', with disastrous consequences for social, economic and political stability in their own territories (Severino, 2008).

ASEAN states therefore lobbied vociferously at the international and regional level to block consideration of East Timor. At the UN, member-states like Thailand tabled annual motions to postpone debates on the issue, thereby containing it in fruitless bilateral talks between Portugal and Indonesia (Singh, 1996, p. 356). ASEAN states also pressed Western powers to downgrade UNCHR resolutions to weaker, non-binding chairman's statements. Malaysia even tried to have the annual resolution scrapped altogether in 1993, claiming it violated UN Charter principles on 'non-interference in the domestic affairs of states'.[1] ASEAN was most successful at the inter-regional level. The 1994 ASEAN informal summit condemned Portuguese efforts to include East Timor in the inter-regional agenda, with Mahathir threatening to suspend dialogue with Europe if Lisbon did not desist. ASEAN also thwarted Portugal's attempt to raise the issue at the ASEM summit in 1996, and that year's APEC summit in Manila (Inbaraj, 1995, pp. 178–9). Finally, faced with threats of expulsion from the ARF, the EU relented. By the time of the Asian crisis, therefore, ASEAN had helped limit the scope of the conflict over East Timor to a level which best suited powerful Indonesian interests.

Just as this application of 'non-interference' was far from neutral, nor was it automatic. Rather, it emerged out of a coercive struggle involving states, business groups and civil society organisations. While Indonesian elites wanted to localise the issue, the Timorese resistance had every incentive to internationalise it as far as possible, to bring in external allies and resources to boost their relatively weak position. Their main external representative, José Ramos-Horta, had declared 'all-out diplomatic war' on Jakarta in 1992, trying to widen the conflict's scope by extending it to other ASEAN societies. He particularly sought support from liberal civil society organisations in neighbouring states by drawing them into a series of discussion forums called the Asia-Pacific Conference on East Timor (APCET). Manila was selected as the first host city in May 1994, to exploit its active civil society, its relatively free media, and the presence of many fellow Catholics. President Ramos's government initially indicated that the Philippines' liberal-democratic status meant that APCET could proceed.

However, a series of crude, coercive Indonesian interventions eventually convinced Ramos to try to suppress APCET. Upon hearing about the planned conference, Jakarta immediately threatened to suspend its efforts to mediate a solution to the Muslim insurgency in Mindanao, in the southern Philippines (Kyodo, 1994a). Like many secessionist wars in Southeast Asia, the Mindanao insurgency is rooted in conflicts over land, resources, and control over state patronage, which have acquired an ethno-religious dimension. Manila was unable to suppress the insurgency, and so the withdrawal of Indonesian mediation, which was being used to help settle the conflict on terms favourable to dominant Philippine interests, threatened a return to civil war. Furthermore, Jakarta withdrew from bilateral trade talks and an East-ASEAN Growth Area business conference being hosted by the Philippines, and cancelled three business delegations, sabotaging $700m in expected joint ventures and investment deals. Indonesia also began impounding Philippine trawlers operating in its waters (Singh, 1996, p. 216; Inbaraj, 1995, p. 215). The force of these moves was enhanced by the increasingly important position of Indonesian state-linked capital in the Philippines. The Suharto family itself was involved through the First Pacific Group, which owned 'significant chunks of the Philippine economy', including major public infrastructure projects run by Suharto's daughter, Siti (Bello and De Guzman, 1999).

Indonesia's intervention partly operated through oligarchic networks of businessmen and politicians who worked to have APCET suppressed. A hurriedly-formed 'Philippine-Indonesian Friendship Society', comprised of leading business and political elites, successfully persuaded a Philippine court to ban the conference (Miclat, 1995, pp. 13–14; Green Left Weekly, 1994). When the Supreme Court overturned this ruling, President Ramos used extraordinary presidential powers to ban foreign participants from attending. He explained that the 'national interest' was at stake, citing lost business opportunities, the Mindanao talks, and maritime stability (Kyodo, 1994b). Manila was quickly rewarded for this decision. The peace talks resumed, the business summit went ahead, and a Siti-led company pledged $2bn in new investments. Suitably chastened, Ramos promised never to allow such events to be staged again, banning all future domestic attempts to discuss Timor, such as Ramos-Horta's plans to stage events alongside the 1996 APEC summit. Liberal civil society activists and politicians were enraged but powerless, given the oligarchic domination of Philippine politics.

Far from ASEAN states automatically acting on the basis of a cherished norm, then, the scope and application of non-interference was actually determined by its exact opposite: crude Indonesian meddling in another state's internal affairs. Norms had not, apparently, transformed the interests and identities of ASEAN states. Rather, it was Jakarta's capacity to influence the Philippines' socio-political stability and economic prosperity, and to mobilise one powerful section of Philippine society – a network of businessmen and political elites – against a less powerful part – civil society groups – that was decisive in this instance.

Similar events transpired whenever civil society groups tried to raise East Timor in ASEAN states. Thailand was disciplined in 1994 when Ramos-Horta planned to attend a human rights seminar timed to coincide with an AMM being held in Bangkok. A threat from Indonesian Foreign Minister Alatas that Jakarta would take a stance 'like what we had shown to Manila' persuaded Bangkok to ban the seminar (Antara, 1994). Thailand's foreign minister explained that to otherwise would 'strain relations' and 'threaten joint investment' (Xinhua, 1994). Bangkok later harassed other human rights conferences dealing with East Timor, including APCET III (Kraft, 2000, p. 9). APCET II was staged in Kuala Lumpur in November 1996. Government ministers urged the civil society groups involved to cancel their plans, citing their fears of Indonesia 'reacting negatively'. When the conference went ahead, it was attacked by a 200-strong mob led by UMNO's youth wing, under the clandestine direction of the deputy home minister. The conference was broken up by police, and its foreign participants deported (NST, 1996b; IPS, 1996; MalaysiaKini.com, 2007). Public invocations of 'non-interference' were coupled with private explanations from government sources that Malaysian government investments in Indonesia had been at risk (NST, 1996a).

The operation of 'non-interference' during this period was thus neither neutral nor automatic. Rather than being a genial norm of regional order, non-interference appears clearly as a strategy of rule used to control the scope of social conflict. ASEAN formed a *cordon sanitaire* against the 'new interventionism' which helped localise and de-internationalise the issue, creating a favourable environment for entrenched Indonesian interests to resolve the East Timor conflict in a way that best served their priorities. This assistance was partly out of fears about the potential impact of the 'new interventionism' on Southeast Asia's post-Cold War social, economic and political orders. It was also partly due to crude bullying from Jakarta, which was required to 'activate' the principle and set its scope of application. Indonesian influence was mediated through emerging transnational politico-business networks, which were mobilised to help suppress liberalising forces represented by civil society organisations.

ASEAN's support for humanitarian intervention in East Timor

As a result of Jakarta's strategic concessions and ASEAN's service as a *cordon sanitaire*, by 1997, Indonesia's position on East Timor was rightly described by UN Special Envoy Jamsheed Marker (2003, p. 26) as 'obviously dominant'. The Asian financial crisis, however, dramatically reversed this position. Suharto's fall from power and the state's sudden total dependency on Western aid persuaded Jakarta to stage a referendum on independence in East Timor. When the Timorese overwhelmingly voted for independence, the Indonesian army and its local militias razed the territory, precipitating a major humanitarian crisis. This section shows that, contrary to conventional analyses, ASEAN did not stand idly by as these events unfolded, but became progressively more involved. Indeed, core ASEAN states actively encouraged and participated in a humanitarian intervention in East Timor.

The Asian financial crisis had a devastating impact on Indonesia which led directly to changes in its East Timor policy. Following the widespread unrest leading to Suharto's downfall, new president Jusuf Habibie inherited a deeply discredited regime, and a state in profound fiscal crisis whose survival depended entirely on Western donors. Habibie was forced to make significant concessions on democracy, human rights and East Timor to enhance the government's credibility with domestic opponents and Western creditors. Flexibility on East Timor in particular was promoted by the network of Muslim intellectuals with which Habibie was associated, and who were now appointed to state offices. Lacking any personal stake in East Timor, they saw an opportunity to rid the government of this 'nuisance' and focus on Indonesia's economic recovery (Crouch, 2000, pp. 152–9; Alatas, 2006, p. 135). In January 1999, after a very limited period of internal debate, Habibie decided to offer the Timorese the choice between very weak regional autonomy or full independence, with a vote scheduled for mid-1999.

This move was only possible because the Indonesian political, military and business networks whose interests were deeply entrenched in East Timor (and other outlying provinces where separatist insurgencies might be expected to take inspiration from Timorese independence) were convinced that they could manufacture a majority vote for autonomy. That this was thought possible reflected these elites' self-delusion that the resistance had little following and was backed only by meddling outsiders (Alatas, 2006, pp. 210–11; Marker, 2003, pp. 110–19, 188). To maximise their room for manoeuvre, however, the army vetoed the deployment of international peacekeepers to maintain order prior to and during the vote. Led by Suharto's son-in-law, General Prabowo, the army began working with Timorese collaborationist elites and militias to intimidate the population into voting for autonomy, backed by senior New Order figures who remained in government in Jakarta, including the defence minister, General Wiranto (Tanter *et al.*, 2006).

Far from standing aloof, as the literature uniformly suggests, ASEAN states were gradually drawn into the situation in East Timor. After discussions about ASEAN's role, Thailand provided a base in its embassy in Lisbon for Indonesian diplomats to negotiate with Portugal over the modalities of the vote. Thailand, the Philippines, Singapore and Malaysia also joined the UN's 'Friends of the Secretary-General' group on East Timor, which was established in January 1999 to 'put pressure on both sides – [but] more on the Indonesians', as Marker (2008) put it. Bangkok and Manila agreed in April 1999 to send personnel to oversee the ballot (Nation, 1999b; Kyodo, 1999d). Ultimately, the task was assigned to the UN Mission in East Timor (UNAMET), to which ASEAN states contributed significantly. UNAMET's chief political officer was Singaporean, while Malaysia and Thailand contributed military liaison officers and, with the Philippines, police officers (UN, 1999). However, UNAMET's security apparatus was limited to only 400 civil police officers, so when violence orchestrated by the Indonesian army flared up in April 1999, the need for international peacekeepers was again raised internationally. Bangkok quickly offered its personnel for this purpose, although Indonesia again rejected the suggestion (AP, 1999f). Meanwhile, as the region began exploring post-ballot scenarios, ASEAN ambassadors met resistance leader Xanana Gusmão in prison (Antara, 1999). Ramos-Horta was also hosted in Manila where, despite making inflammatory remarks about the Indonesian government, he met the foreign secretary and received a pledge of $250,000 for the UN's East Timor trust fund (Manila Standard, 1999b).

None of this bears out the usual unqualified assessment that 'the Indonesian leadership was initially reluctant to involve ASEAN... [and] regional governments were also reluctant to become involved' (Haacke, 2003, p. 197). Certainly, ASEAN states did not send armed peacekeepers to East Timor, but then neither did any other state. Australia, the most activist state on this issue, constantly reiterated that 'invading' East Timor was impossible and, with the US, emphasised diplomacy as the only viable route. Thus, ASEAN states did not appear any more constrained by 'non-interference' than other states. In fact they became increasingly involved in Indonesia's 'internal' affairs.

Escalating violence in East Timor led to the ballot being delayed until August, but did not alter the inevitable result: a 99.6 per cent turnout, with 78.5 per cent voting for independence. When the results were announced on 3 September, pro-integration militias, supported by Indonesian police and military units, immediately went on the rampage, apparently to create the impression of a renewed civil war and thereby overturn the outcome. Forcibly evacuating the pro-Indonesian leadership and population to West Timor while attempting to liquidate the pro-independence leadership, they looted and razed East Timor. Within days, most of the population had been displaced and 80 per cent of buildings had been destroyed or damaged. This precipitated an enormous humanitarian crisis.

ASEAN states did not simply stand silently by, as the literature suggests. The typical view is that they 'found it difficult to respond... let alone criticise [Indonesia] publicly' and 'restricted themselves to "solidarity in silence about a military response to Indonesian military atrocities"' (Haacke, 2003, p. 199). In fact, ASEAN states quickly demanded that the ballot outcome be respected and rapidly began preparing for a peace-enforcement intervention, committing their forces *before* Western states did. Mahathir, for instance, flatly stated as the post-ballot violence broke out: 'they have chosen freedom. The authorities should accept that decision' (AP, 1999b). Three days after the results were announced,

Malaysia and Thailand became the first countries in the world to publicly offer troops for an international intervention force, and were quickly joined by the Philippines and Singapore (Bernama, 1999; Kyodo, 1999f; AFP, 1999e; BBC SWB, 1999). By contrast, the US was still denying that it intended to send any forces to East Timor.

The stance taken by core ASEAN states is all the more remarkable given the considerable danger that any intervention force would face. The New Order establishment had whipped up a ferocious backlash against the UN and others within Indonesia. Many nationalist legislators were already refusing to ratify the outcome, claiming UNAMET had been biased. New Order political elites, including presidential candidate Abdurrahman Wahid, blamed Western powers and the UN, with some declaring a 'jihad' and making lurid threats to attack anyone engaging in 'foreign intervention' (ST, 1999c, 1999d). Martial law had also been declared in East Timor, and rumours abounded that General Wiranto was about to seize power in a coup. Indonesia's UN ambassador had declared that peacekeepers would have to fight their way in; war had been threatened with Australia if it landed troops without Indonesian consent; and three days after ASEAN states had offered peacekeepers, Foreign Minister Alatas was still warning, 'Do not talk about peacekeeping... unless you want to shoot your way into East Timor' (Alatas, 2006, pp. 208–9; Cotton, 2000, p. 8; Advertiser, 1999).

Despite the considerable risks ASEAN states took in offering peacekeepers, scholars often incorrectly depict them as being limited by 'non-interference' by emphasising that 'ASEAN governments... would not have joined INTERFET had it not been for Jakarta's explicit consent' (Haacke, 2003, p. 200). However, this was also the position of virtually every other state. An APEC summit held in Auckland from 9–12 September discussed the East Timor crisis, and every Western state emphasised the need for Indonesian consent (AsiaWeek, 1999a, 1999b). Identical positions were adopted at a UN Security Council meeting on 11 September. Five days after ASEAN states had first offered troops, many Western states now pledged contributions, while Australia offered to lead an intervention force. Yet, while their strident condemnations of Indonesian atrocities certainly exceeded ASEAN states' remarks, Western ambassadors still emphasised that Indonesian consent was necessary.[2]

The Security Council meeting did, however, illustrate that ASEAN was internally divided over East Timor. Here, the newer member-states spoke up for the first time, issuing rather bland statements that indicated little sense of urgency or desire for international intervention. Cambodia's ambassador said he was 'very concerned about the recent

violence', urging Indonesia to restore order. Nonetheless, he emphasised Indonesia's difficult, ongoing political 'transition' and asked the
Council not to act before receiving the report of an ambassadorial
mission that had been despatched to Jakarta. Vietnam, similarly 'very
concerned' and hoping that the situation would soon 'stabilise', also
stressed the situation's 'complicated' nature and Jakarta's 'considerable'
efforts to restore order. Laos echoed this view, echoing Jakarta's claim
that it was 'striving vigorously and in all due earnest to rectify the situation', suggesting that the UN 'allow the Indonesian Government
to shoulder its own responsibilities'.[3] However, the Indochinese states
did not invoke the non-interference principle. It was left to other
states to attack the notion of intervention *per se*, such as Libya, which
claimed that intervention poured 'fuel on hot, burning flash points'
and criticised the use of 'threats and coercion, including this very
meeting'.[4]

By contrast, the original ASEAN member-states were clearly on
the pro-intervention side of the argument. Malaysia's ambassador had
joined the Council mission to persuade Jakarta to accept foreign intervention, telling Wiranto that the army's conduct betrayed Indonesia's
'historical role in and contribution to national peace and regional
stability' (Wheeler and Dunne, 2001, p. 820). The Philippine ambassador told the Security Council that the ballot 'should not be derailed'
and that 'the people of East Timor [must] be given a chance... to chart
their future'. Manila was, he said, 'greatly concerned' by the violence,
which 'tarnished' Indonesia's efforts to resolve the situation in East Timor
and had to be 'stopped immediately'. While 'fully understand[ing]' Indonesian requests for more time to restore order, the situation required
'further determined action'. The Philippines reiterated its offer to contribute to a UN intervention force.[5]

Singapore's ambassador was particularly forthright, stating that his
government was 'shocked and outraged' by events in East Timor. The
decision to hold a referendum was criticised as one 'taken precipitately
without broad national consensus', despite its 'serious implications for
the unity of Indonesia'. This 'did not seem the proper way to settle the
fate of 800,000 people'. 'The authorities should have taken more effective
precautions' to prevent violence; instead, militia had 'been allowed to
go on a violent rampage'. Singapore reiterated that the ballot result
was 'legitimate and unambiguous', warning that the UN risked a 'grave
precedent' if it failed to uphold the outcome and protect its personnel in
the field. While accepting Indonesia's 'primary responsibility' for security
and urging it to fulfil this responsibility, Singapore commended UN

efforts to 'convey a powerful message' to Indonesia, telling Jakarta 'to consider these sincere offers of assistance in the same spirit as they have been offered'.[6]

Thailand did not speak at the Council meeting, but was already rallying troop contributions for the anticipated intervention force. Then-Foreign Minister Surin Pitsuwan explained that 'because Thailand was the chair of ASEAN', Prime Minister Chuan had convened an ASEAN leaders' meeting on the sidelines of the APEC summit in Auckland. Here, Indonesia's representative appealed for ASEAN contributions. Surin was then despatched to Jakarta. Despite being tasked with organising ASEAN support for international intervention in Indonesia, he told the media he was there merely as 'a foreign minister of a neighbouring country, who [just] happens to be the chair of the Standing Committee of ASEAN... in order to give the impression that I am not here violating any ASEAN principle'. Wiranto asked Surin to secure 'overwhelming ASEAN forces', saying, 'come in large numbers. We want to see our neighbours here in East Timor to help us'. Habibie also added: 'take the commandership of the force, if possible'. Surin, doubting that ASEAN had the 'resources' or 'technology' to do so, was urged instead to have a Nordic country selected, rather than Australia (Surin, 2008b).

These private discussions indicated that Indonesian officials had accepted the inevitability of foreign intervention in East Timor. On 11 September, the IMF, under Western donors' instructions, had suspended the aid on which the Indonesian state was relying to remain afloat. The government consequently had little choice but to accept intervention, announcing its decision the following day. What had been achieved was 'consent by political blackmail' (Haacke, 2003, p. 161). Alatas now urged the Security Council to give 'particular consideration... to ASEAN countries' participation in the composition of... a multinational force'.[7] Why? The New Order establishment had by now whipped up considerable unrest against Australia, the likeliest leader of the force. ASEAN troops were therefore necessary to dilute Australian forces and make the intervention 'palatable to the Indonesian public' (Surin, 2008b). The Australian force commander later emphasised that it 'had to be a coalition operation. It would [have been] politically and militarily impossible for Australia to act alone'. Without ASEAN, INTERFET could have faced a violent nationalist backlash and military resistance: indeed, Canberra genuinely thought that war with Indonesia was possible (Cosgrove, 2006, pp. 167, 176).

Once the inevitability of intervention had been accepted, ASEAN states contributed significant personnel. Surin (2008b) urged them to do so 'because it is our region'. Although the CLMV states declined, troops from ASEAN's original members comprised a quarter of INTERFET's 9,900 troops, and a Thai general was appointed as its deputy commander (Dupont, 2000, p. 167). When INTERFET was replaced by the UN Transitional Administration in East Timor (UNTAET) in February 2000, ASEAN personnel comprised around a fifth of its peacekeeping force, which was commanded first by a Philippine and later a Thai general (UNTAET, 2000).

There is therefore little evidence to support the notion that ASEAN states were paralysed by 'non-interference' and thus did nothing to resolve the East Timor crisis. Typically, even those who concede that ASEAN played some role in 1999 nonetheless assert that prior to this 'ASEAN adhered to its long-standing position that East Timor was purely an Indonesian domestic matter' which 'reflects ASEAN's traditional reluctance to interfere in the domestic affairs of its member states' (Dupont, 2000, p. 163). Conversely, this section showed that ASEAN's original member-states were drawn in long before the ballot. Thereafter, they played an important role in pressing Jakarta to accept a post-ballot intervention force, and enabled that force to deploy in the face of a nationalist backlash within Indonesia by diluting the presence of Western troops. We now need to explain why ASEAN states violated their supposedly 'cherished principle' of non-interference.

Why did ASEAN states (not) intervene in East Timor?

Despite the ubiquitous references to 'non-interference' in the literature on ASEAN and East Timor, some scholars do recognise ASEAN states' contributions to INTERFET, offering *ad hoc* explanations based around ASEAN's reputation and the identities of individual states. This section explores the limits of such explanations and advances an alternative analysis based on perceived interdependencies between social, economic and political order in Indonesia and core ASEAN member-states. These states essentially intervened to contain the unrest and disorder in Indonesia and limit its impact on their societies. The CLMV states, which were comparatively unaffected by the Asian financial crisis, felt no such sense of interdependence and thus no compulsion to intervene; indeed, their interests lay, if anything, in the opposite direction. ASEAN's corporate stance was therefore limited not by 'non-interference' but by the difficulty of reconciling states' divergent policies. Moreover, the extent to which individual ASEAN states could intervene was ultimately limited by conflicts within their own societies.

Let us first consider the existing explanations offered for ASEAN states' participation in humanitarian intervention. As with the Cambodian case, these tend to be *ad hoc*, because the theoretical tools required to explain the selectivity of non-intervention are underdeveloped. Some scholars suggest that ASEAN simply wanted to help Jakarta 'save face' (Dupont, 2000, p. 166). This seems a somewhat thin explanation for the violation of the supposed *sine qua non* of the 'ASEAN way'. It also seems rather Orientalist in implying that ASEAN policies are determined by cultural concerns for 'saving face'. Cultural or psychological factors are not required to explain Indonesian leaders' preference for ASEAN troops over Australian ones. The national backlash whipped up against intervention, and Australia in particular, is more persuasive. The CLMV states' refusal to respond to Indonesia's request also suggests that a desire to help Jakarta did not emanate from any shared Asian norms.

A more sophisticated explanation concerns the political identity of the ASEAN states involved. Some constructivists and others have argued that the member-states which championed the intervention were Thailand and the Philippines, which were 'at the democratic end of the spectrum' (McDougall, 2001, p. 172). These countries, it is also emphasised, were those which had recently 'argued in favour of "intrusive regionalism"', i.e., flexible engagement (McDougall, 2001, p. 172; see also Dupont, 2000, p. 165; Narine, 2005, pp. 478–9; Acharya, 2009a, p. 134). A maximalist interpretation claims that member-states were motivated by liberal-humanitarianism. Tow (2004, p. 258) argues that 'ASEAN states proved that they were willing to intervene on human security grounds... the sanctity of state boundaries was violated on the basis of saving lives'. These arguments reflect the general view, critiqued in Chapter 5, that there is a significant split between 'democratic' and 'non-democratic' ASEAN members. However, such explanations cannot account for the interventionist behaviour of Malaysia and Singapore, states not generally considered to be at the 'democratic end of the spectrum' and which had opposed 'intrusive regionalism'. Moreover, as we will discuss below, even Thailand and the Philippines were not principally motivated by humanitarianism.

These explanations are unsatisfactory because scholars lack analytical tools to interpret events that their theoretical presuppositions lead them to believe to be empirical near-impossibilities. That is, they are so used to describing ASEAN as a group of countries that never interferes that when intervention does occur, they have to resort to *ad hoc* explanations of dubious validity. It is not that the explanations offered are always incorrect. For instance, Haacke (2003, pp. 66–8) explains ASEAN states' participation in INTERFET by citing their sense of solidarity with Indonesia, a need to defend ASEAN and Indonesia's reputation and to demonstrate ASEAN's capacity to react, fears for the stability of Indonesia and the region, and a Thai bid for 'moral leadership'. As we shall see below, some of these factors were indeed at play. However, they mostly do not emerge from the interstate norms or culture that constructivists typically foreground in explaining ASEAN's behaviour at other times. And extant constructivist scholarship, even in pluralist approaches like Haacke's which refer to domestic interests and geo-politics as well as norms, does not provide a systematic account of why norms should apply at one moment and not another.

ASEAN states' policies are best explained by the relationship between events in East Timor (and Indonesia more broadly) and the social, economic and political order of each member-state. The core ASEAN states, which had been most badly affected by the Asian crisis and the growing unrest in Indonesia and East Timor, were those which felt compelled to intervene to contain the problem and limit its further contagion to their own territories. Conversely, the CLMV states, which were least affected, felt the least need to get involved.

The state managers of core ASEAN member-states felt that the fate of their societies and economies was bound up with events in East Timor for two basic reasons. First, as the financial crisis had already demonstrated, investors viewed the region *en bloc*. Social and political upheaval in Indonesia and East Timor exacerbated capital flight from the region and further damaged weakened regional currencies, with central bankers and finance ministers all blaming the Timor crisis. As Surin later observed,

> We have been very much affected by the atmosphere of uncertainty, the lack of confidence. Because people from outside perceive the area as being one rather than different countries. The economy certainly has been affected. The investment atmosphere has been affected. Investment already committed to projects in some of those economies has been withdrawn... The immediate impact has already been felt on all the currencies of the region (Newsweek, 1999).

This was clearly exacerbated by the IMF and World Bank's decision to halt aid to Indonesia, which imperilled the financial survival of the state.

Second, state managers were afraid that Indonesia's internal social unrest could easily spread to their own unstable societies, with crippling political consequences. A Philippine government document leaked in May 1999 summarised these fears of contagion:

> Should the situation... further deteriorate, an exodus of a new wave of 'boat people', this time Indonesians, be they East Timorese, Javanese or Sumatrans, is not farfetched. The immediate surrounding countries like Malaysia, Brunei, Thailand, the Philippines and Australia will be the most accessible destinations for the fleeing refugees... Ethnic violence, especially against the Indonesians of Chinese descent, will have serious implications for neighbouring Singapore, Malaysia and Australia, not to mention China... Indonesia's role as the natural leader of ASEAN will now be in doubt and the other countries could be left floundering in the absence of a uniting force and an economically and politically weakened partner... [This] may well make [ASEAN] more distracted, inward-looking and less cohesive. Long-standing rivalries within ASEAN may resurface and the substantial economic weaknesses now revealed within [ASEAN] states will make the grouping as a whole more susceptible to penetration by external powers (Kyodo, 1999c).

The key to understanding ASEAN's reaction, therefore, is the perceived interdependence of the region's socio-political and economic orders, which had recently been underlined by the Asian financial crisis. Core ASEAN states intervened in order to contain the unrest within Indonesian territory and to prevent its further contagion to their fragile, domestic orders. CLMV state managers, by contrast, saw no such need to intervene due to absent or different linkages between their domestic social orders and events in Indonesia.

The CLMV states

The CLMV states generally experienced very little internal upheaval stemming from either the Asian crisis or events in Indonesia. Without the fear that Indonesia's unrest could spread to their own societies, there was little reason for these states to involve themselves in East Timor. They were instead preoccupied, Surin (2008b) found, with the risk of establishing 'the precedent of sending in foreign troops to tame violence and tension and conflict'. This essentially thwarted Surin's attempt to secure a corporate ASEAN response to the crisis.

Burma's military government was the first to demur. The junta stated:

> We... greatly regret the loss of lives and destruction of property. We fully sympathise with our Indonesian brothers. Myanmar and Indonesia have always enjoyed a special relationship dating back to the days of the struggle for independence... The decision of some ASEAN countries to be involved in peacekeeping operations in East Timor is not a coordinated ASEAN position and accordingly we would not like to comment on it (AFP, 1999d).

Rangoon's reasoning was clear enough. As Chapter 8 shows, ASEAN had encouraged Burma to model itself on Suharto's regime, and the New Order's implosion must therefore have profoundly alarmed Burma's generals. Moreover, the junta had no interest in helping the East Timorese independence movement, which had repeatedly expressed solidarity with Burma's democratic opposition, mingled with its separatist leaders, and even pledged that an independent East Timor would support these struggles. Burmese dissidents were also calling for INTERFET-style intervention in their own country. The regime thus had every interest in maintaining 'non-interference' as a means of controlling the scope of conflicts within Burma and limiting external assistance to opposition forces. Relatively unaffected by the Asian crisis and events in Indonesia, there was no countervailing pressure to prompt participation in INTERFET.

The Indochinese states were also reluctant to establish any additional precedents of regional intervention. Vietnam did not criticise Surin's efforts to raise ASEAN peacekeepers but declined to provide troops since it had 'no experience and has never sent any military force to join such activities' (Vietnam News Agency, 1999). However, it also continued referring to Timor as Indonesia's 'internal affair', emphasising the need for INTERFET to cooperate with Jakarta and hoping that 'there will be no intervention in Indonesia's internal affairs' (AFP, 1999g). It would be difficult to ascribe this position to Vietnam's 'socialisation' into ASEAN norms, since it had only been a member for four years. Hanoi's emphasis on 'non-interference' is best explained by the tensions arising from its internal reform processes, described in Chapter 5. Serious rural unrest arising from these reforms had only recently been suppressed and reactive leadership changes were underway within the VCP. Furthermore, as Vietnam had been insulated from the worst effects of the Asian crisis, it did not share the core ASEAN states' sense of profound crisis. It was also unaffected by events in East Timor and thus, like Burma, saw far more risk in weakening the useful principle of non-interference than in violating it.

Cambodia's position was more complex, with clear divisions between its main political parties. The liberal-nationalist SRP opposition immediately recognised Timor's independence after the ballot result, urging the government to follow suit and facilitate its entry to ASEAN (Kyodo, 1999a). FUNCINPEC, part of the governing coalition restored after ASEAN's 1997–1999 intervention, took a similar line, with Prince Ranariddh welcoming Timor's independence and his party's defence minister pledging to contribute to INTERFET (AFP, 1999a). However, CPP Prime Minister Hun Sen quickly retracted this offer, saying that while Cambodia 'fully welcome[d]' the peacekeeping deployment and 'truly desired to participate', the country's 'economic and social problems' and ongoing 'multi-sector reforms, especially that of the armed forces' meant it had 'no ability to send her forces to join the operation' (Xinhua, 1999a). The same reasons were later cited to explain Cambodia's non-involvement in UNTAET.

Cambodia thus invoked its poverty and internal weaknesses, rather than 'non-interference', to justify its non-participation. This was not unreasonable, given the severe costs of renewed civil war in the wake of the July 1997 crisis. However, the clear divide between the political parties suggests an additional logic at work. Notably it was the parties which had benefited most from recent foreign intervention, the SRP and FUNCINPEC that were most keen to participate, while the CPP, which had so recently been disciplined by Western and ASEAN intervention, was much more reluctant. Hun Sen's fury at ASEAN's meddling in Cambodian politics probably sufficed to make him wary of establishing further precedents for ASEAN interventionism. In addition, since the military forms a significant part of the CPP's powerbase and patronage network, and given that the CPP's dominance was still being reconsolidated in the wake of the 1997–1999 crisis, Hun Sen may have been reluctant to send any units abroad.

The core ASEAN states

It was thus ASEAN's original members, which had supposedly been 'socialised' for decades into the 'ASEAN way', that were most involved in the intervention in East Timor. This was *not* because, unlike the CLMV states, they were unconcerned about domestic unrest or 'regime security'. If anything, they had more immediate and concrete concerns, but as we have seen, concern for 'regime security' does not, contrary to received wisdom, necessarily dictate a cast-iron attachment to sovereignty, thus limiting the concept's analytical usefulness. In circumstances where the stability of a particular domestic order depends on certain conditions being satisfied abroad, intervention may well be used to secure these conditions. In this case, the fear that unrest in Indonesia and East Timor could further upset the socio-political and economic stability of the core ASEAN states compelled these governments to intervene to help contain the problem.

Thailand

Thailand's motivations are typically ascribed to its supposedly liberal-democratic identity and political institutions, and the government's desire to lift 'Thailand to a higher ground of international morality, responsibility and credibility' (Haacke, 2003, p. 201). We need to be wary of explanations like this since, as we have seen, formally democratic institutions are entirely compatible with illiberal policies. Such explanations would be more persuasive if they referred to the temporary ascendancy of liberalising forces in Thailand in the wake of the Asian crisis, as discussed in Chapter 5. The Democrat foreign minister, Surin Pitsuwan, for example, was openly committed to 'the protection of rights beyond borders and intervention to promote and safeguard humanitarian ideals and objectives'.[8]

Nonetheless, there are still good reasons to doubt that humanitarianism really drove Thai policy. The Democrat administration had shown scant regard for the East Timorese as recently as March 1998 when government forces had harassed APCET III and other Timor-related civil society conferences in Bangkok. The Democrats had attracted fierce criticism from liberal commentators, who accused them of focusing on persuading Suharto to follow IMF strictures. This suggests a greater commitment to a neoliberal economic agenda than a liberal political one. Furthermore, even with INTERFET on the ground, Thailand joined the rest of ASEAN in opposing the convening of a special session of the UNCHR on East Timor, and in voting against a resolution to establish a commission of inquiry into the violence there.[9] According to Thailand's then-UN ambassador, it was Indonesia, not East Timor, which was seen as a 'friend in need' (Asda, 2008).

Thailand's prime motivation was actually to limit the scope of the unrest in East Timor and Indonesia and prevent its contagion to the rest of the region, in line with the reasoning behind 'flexible engagement'. As we saw above, Surin had particularly emphasised the impact of Timor on regional markets. The Democrat appointee as army commander, General Surayud, also underlined that Thai involvement in INTERFET was necessary 'to protect our own national interests... our prosperity depends to a certain extent on a stable environment in the region' (ST, 1999e). The Democrats' promotion of intervention in East Timor was thus linked to their insistence that domestic crises had to be addressed regionally for Southeast Asia to recover its political and economic stability and for ASEAN to restore its credibility and capacity to engage external powers on favourable terms. As Surin's senior aide, Noppadon Pattama (2000, pp. 35–6), later explained, Thailand intervened

> to maintain regional peace and stability, since unrest and instability in East Timor could impact on regional security... unless each country in the region... puts its house in order, domestic instability could continue to affect the region as a whole. In a world of greater inter-dependence, each country has the responsibility to foster greater transparency and accountability, so that rising expectations at home could be met and domestic problems could be contained within national boundaries. This is the challenge that ASEAN has to face so that it remains relevant and coherent.

Surin (2008b) was also 'concerned about the image of ASEAN' and its perceived capacity to manage regional problems. He told his counter-parts: 'a fire is burning in our backyard... And we can't do anything? That would certainly affect ASEAN credibility'. Surin insisted that 'we should come in, even individually, even as neighbours – then ASEAN would gain'.

The Democrats thus assessed events in Indonesia in terms of their consequences for regional strategies of rule in the wake of the Asian crisis. Their effects on markets endangered the strategies being pursued to restore investor confidence and resume capital accumulation. Their political effects threatened state managers' strategy to re-engage ex-ternal powers to re-secure access to the markets, investment and resources necessary for economic growth and domestic political stability. These effects had to be contained, even if this required the bypassing of non-interference.

The limits of Thai intervention were, however, ultimately set by dom-estic social conflict. Oligarchic forces opposed to the Democrats' domestic neoliberal reforms seized on Thailand's participation in INTERFET and UNTAET to attack the government. An alliance of business oligarchs, the Thai Star Group, condemned Thai involvement as yet another instance of

Chuan 'pandering to the West', warning this could 'fracture the [ASEAN] alliance' (AFP, 1999f). Military leaders resisting Democrat budget cuts also briefed against the government, attacking it for wasting resources and ignoring military advice, and demanded an extra 400m baht to finance the INTERFET contingent, forcing the government to seek external funding (Surin, 2008b; Kyodo, 1999e; ST, 1999b). The parliamentary opposition, led by the politico-businessman General Chavalit, rehearsed these accusations in a no-confidence debate designed to topple Chuan's government in December 1999 (AP, 1999d). These charges had little foundation and merely represented an opportunistic use of the issue by forces opposed to the Democrats' domestic agenda. Nonetheless, this struggle constrained Thai intervention in East Timor. Bangkok rejected Australia's urging to take command of UNTAET, instead halving its troop commitment, and only took command when the Philippines was forced to withdraw in mid-2000. Thailand's decision to intervene and the limits to that intervention were thus intimately bound up with struggles over the country's political economy.

The Philippines

As with Thailand, explanations of Philippine behaviour are often simplistically ascribed to its 'liberal-democratic' status. Certainly, like his Thai counterpart, the Philippine foreign secretary lamented the 'horrendous human suffering' in East Timor and insisted at the UN that 'state and individual sovereignty must converge'.[10] However, there are also reasons to doubt humanitarianism as Manila's guiding motive. Like Thailand, the Philippines had also suppressed APCET. Manila also officially led ASEAN's denunciation of the UNCHR special session and voted against the proposed commission of inquiry, arguing that any investigation should be left to Indonesia. At the special session, it explained its participation in INTERFET not with reference to humanitarianism but by saying that, 'as a friend of Indonesia' it felt bound to 'come to the aid of that peace-loving country' – a designation supposedly proven by its mediation efforts in Mindanao.[11] Faced with criticism from domestic liberals, President Estrada justified this stance by invoking the 'policy of the ASEAN that we do not interfere in the internal problems of each country' – even as ASEAN states' troops were landing in Timor (BusinessWorld, 1999a).

Manila's real concern was to overcome socio-economic and political instability in Indonesia and limit its contagion to the wider region, especially to the Philippines. The Department of Foreign Affairs warned that limiting the East Timor investigation to a national level was 'crucial if the stability and integrity of Indonesia is to be maintained', arguing that internationalising the inquiry would threaten Indonesia's democratisation and economic reform, thus destabilising the wider region (Kyodo, 1999b). An international inquiry risked identifying the New Order figures behind the violence in East Timor, including individuals like General Wiranto, who remained in government and in a position to launch a coup. A military takeover would have exacerbated Indonesia's instability, escalating the risks of contagion identified in the leaked memorandum quoted above. Manila thus strove to avoid this outcome, even mollifying Wiranto personally by awarding him medals for contributing to the Mindanao peace talks, three years after their conclusion (AP, 1999a).

Mindanao was clearly central to the Philippine state's calculations over East Timor. Ruling elites' fears that events in East Timor would foster domestic separatism in Mindanao were immediately borne out when the 8,000-strong Moro Islamic Liberation Front (MILF) declared that the East Timor ballot had inspired it to resume its struggle for independence and demanded that the UN organise a referendum (AP, 1999c). Furthermore, the government feared that continued political upheaval in Indonesia might compromise Jakarta's long-standing support for Manila's efforts to contain the scope of the Mindanao conflict and suppress the long-running insurgency. Suharto's regime had been instrumental in severing external support for the rebels through its influence with other 'Muslim' states like Libya. However, with the flames of nationalism and Islamism being fanned by New Order elites as they scrambled for position in the post-Suharto dispensation, there was concern that transnational Muslim or Malay solidarity might come to trump ASEAN's longstanding inter-elite pact on the necessity of containing conflicts within existing territorial borders. UNTAET's first commander, the Philippine General Jaime de los Santos (2001, p. 82), explained that since 'the prevailing internal security situation in the Philippines has serious international repercussions', it was crucial 'to promote the Philippines' friendly relations with its neighbours so as to solidify support to the campaign to suppress ideological struggles that threaten the security and stability of the country'. Philippine political leaders thus constantly emphasised that the purpose of their contributions to INTERFET and UNTAET was to 'pay back' Jakarta for its past support over Mindanao.

Philippine elites and their ASEAN counterparts also shared a general fear that East Timor could be the first of many separatist successes that could lead to the disintegration of Indonesia and an outflow of social unrest and economic upheaval. Manila's acting foreign secretary analysed

East Timor as a 'complex situation that could affect the central policy of the [Indonesian] government on Irian Jaya, Aceh, and other provinces'. If Jakarta decided to let these secede, too, the resultant unrest could generate enormous refugee outflows to Malaysia and the Philippines and be seized upon by Mindanao's rebels (Manila Bulletin, 2000). Thus, when President Habibie's successor, President Wahid, floated the idea of an independence referendum in Aceh in November 1999, ASEAN states rushed to criticise the proposal, totally disregarding 'non-interference'. The Philippine foreign secretary warned of a 'disease of separatist turmoil' spreading across Southeast Asia (Huxley, 2002, p. 75). Singapore's Lee Kuan Yew cautioned that 'if Aceh gets a referendum… Indonesia is at risk… Nobody wants that to happen'. Malaysia's foreign minister likewise expressed concern 'about the stability of Indonesia… if there is chaos in Indonesia, Malaysia will be the first recipient of illegal immigrants. We have many now and we do not need more' (Scotsman, 1999). Surin agreed that this 'concern is quite legitimate', urging a 'period of reflection and adaptation' (Sydney Morning Herald, 1999). ASEAN states insisted that Jakarta must maintain its grip over the archipelago and implement internal reforms to contain the spread of socio-political upheaval beyond its borders. Wahid subsequently backed down. However, he had so rattled his ASEAN counterparts that when he offered to mediate in Mindanao, he was rebuffed for fear that, as one senior Philippine senator put it, 'MILF could be infected with the "Balkan virus"' (BusinessWorld, 1999b).

As with Thailand, the limits of Philippine intervention were ultimately set by domestic social conflict. Ironically, participation in INTERFET/ UNTAET diverted military resources precisely at the moment when the MILF insurgency had restarted. Some politicians and commentators had always cautioned that the military, with its 100bn-peso budget deficit and antiquated equipment, could not undertake both peacekeeping in Timor and counter-insurgency in Mindanao, warning that the former could 'indefinitely drag on and conceivably undermine the country's own fragile political and economic balance' (Manila Standard, 1999a). By spring 2000, MILF had linked up with the Moro National Liberation Front and the communist New People's Army. The army's inability to cope was blamed on the diversion of resources to East Timor, and Manila had to hurriedly repatriate its troops to deal with the upsurge in domestic unrest. From April to June 2000, its UNTAET contribution shrank by 40 per cent, forcing Thailand to take command of the mission (De Los Santos and Burgos, 2001, p. 65). As in Thailand, the motivations for and limits of the Philippine intervention had been set by the contours of domestic social conflict.

Singapore

The illiberal and undemocratic Singaporean state also pushed for an intervention in East Timor and was harshly critical of Indonesia. Its concern was clearly for the impact of Indonesia's potential unravelling on the region's socio- economic stability. Singaporean officials believed that the unrest in East Timor would 'have a spill-over effect' on Indonesia's other restive provinces, leading ASEAN to try to 'at least contain that problem so the bigger issues could be dealt with' (Kausikan, 2008). As an entrepôt and financial centre, the city-state was especially vulnerable to the economic shocks caused by the Timor crisis. Prime Minister Lee Hsien Loong warned that Singapore's economic recovery after the Asian crisis depended on whether Indonesia stabilised to allow trade and investment to return to the region (Radio Australia, 1999). Unrest had already reached Indonesia's Batam island, just 20km from Singapore, where major Singaporean investments were now physically imperilled. Furthermore, the city-state was refuge to thousands of ethnic-Chinese Indonesians who had fled the pogroms whipped up by New Order forces. If the situation degenerated further, the Singaporean state feared an influx of refugees that could overwhelm its resources and infrastructure and cause serious tensions with the Indonesian government (Huxley, 2002, pp. 81–2). Like other ASEAN states, then, Singapore saw its future social and economic stability as bound up with the chaos in East Timor.

However, Singapore's position on who should intervene was more complex. According to its then-UN ambassador, Bilahari Kausikan (2008), Singapore's view was that ASEAN 'had no capability' to restore order in Timor, lacking the 'level of professionalism, the doctrine, the level of inter-operability' required for successful peace-enforcement. Singapore therefore insisted that the UN, not ASEAN, should take the lead. However, this was not 'a non-interference thing at all... you need the UN... we did not think that this thing could be held together any other way'. Moreover, the 'UN flag' provided vital 'political cover' to avoid bilateral backlash from 'political groups in Indonesia'. Singapore thus lobbied for a prolonged UN presence in East Timor, to restore order and build a viable independent state. It contributed forces to INTERFET because 'you've got to at some point put your money where your mouth is, and you've got to send some troops'.

Unlike Thailand and the Philippines, the Singaporean state had no domestic unrest to contend with; the extent of its intervention in East Timor was largely set by inter-elite tensions between the city-state and Indonesia, which had been revived by Habibie's attacks on the 'red dot'. Its INTERFET contributions were deliberately limited to medical and logistics personnel in order to avoid any potential military clashes with Indonesian forces. Later events suggested that Singapore's caution was well-placed. In November 2000, Senior Minister Lee Kuan Yew criticised a planned Indonesian crackdown against West Papuan separatists as 'risky' and 'unthoughtful'. Lee urged Jakarta to 'learn the lessons' of East Timor and hinted that President Wahid – then embroiled in a corruption scandal – would soon leave office. Wahid responded explosively, heaping vitriol on Singapore, threatening to connive with Malaysia to sever its water supply and to leave ASEAN to form a new regional organisation (The Age, 2000; AFP, 2000b). Despite making meaningful contributions to the UN missions in East Timor, Singapore only took a leadership role when inter-elite tensions had eased somewhat. Singapore's Major-General Huck Gim Tan commanded the peacekeeping element of the UN Integrated Mission in East Timor (UNMISET) for a year from August 2002.

Malaysia

Like their counterparts elsewhere, Malaysia's state managers had both general and specific fears about the spread of unrest from East Timor and Indonesia. Their general concerns were very similar to those outlined above. Their specific worries stemmed from two ways in which Indonesia's political unrest was being transmitted into Malaysia (Huxley, 2002, pp. 75, 79). First, because both countries' populations are predominantly Malay-Muslim, political currents travel particularly easily through ethno-linguistic ties transcending territorial state boundaries. Malaysia's UMNO-led government was fighting a rearguard action against a *reformasi* movement that was drawing direct inspiration and material support from its Indonesian counterpart. Indonesian Islamists were also emerging as a serious political force in the wake of Suharto's fall from power and UMNO feared their potential influence on the opposition Pan-Malaysian Islamic Party (PAS). The interdependence of the two societies was felt so strongly that one Malaysian commentator compared the regional impact of Indonesia's democratisation to the impact of the French revolution on Europe. Secondly, due to this cultural similarity and geographical proximity, hundreds of thousands of Indonesian refugees and economic migrants had travelled to Malaysia looking for work. They were blamed for a wide range of social ills. Malaysia's deputy defence minister thus observed that 'security matters in East Timor will undoubtedly have an effect on Malaysia', since refugee numbers would only rise further 'if there is no stability in that country' (NST, 2000). Malaysia's ruling elite thus had as much interest in containing unrest in Indonesia as that of any other core ASEAN state.

However, the universal consensus in the literature is that Malaysia tried to thwart intervention in East Timor. Scholars claim that Malaysia questioned UNAMET's impartiality, tried to dilute UN resolutions against Indonesia, and opposed intervention in solidarity with Jakarta. They emphasise Malaysia's tokenistic contribution of thirty personnel to INTERFET and UNTAET, its refusal to criticise Jakarta, and its lurid attacks on Australia and the West for trying to 'break up' Indonesia (McDougall, 2001, p. 554; Dupont, 2000, p. 165). Notwithstanding the Malaysian state's nationalistic and xenophobic rhetoric, it is inaccurate to interpret its position as anti-interventionist. The struggle was really over who should be intervening, and Malaysia's clear preference was for ASEAN. As Surin was rallying contributions for INTERFET, Malaysia's deputy prime minister agreed that it should have 'a large ASEAN presence' (ST, 1999a). Mahathir and former Philippine President Ramos agreed on the need for 'maximum ASEAN cooperation' to help Indonesia and, as Ramos put it, 'prevent the outflow effects of political instability in Indonesia' (Xinhua, 1999b). Malaysia's decision to send only a handful of personnel and its hostility to Australia surfaced only *after* Canberra had been given command of INTERFET – a post Malaysia had coveted for itself. Malaysia pushed repeatedly to supplant Australia's leadership, its defence minister insisting that UNTAET should have 'an ASEAN commander' since 'we can understand the problems of our neighbouring countries better because we are ASEAN. We know the culture of ASEAN' (AFP, 1999c).

Malaysia's ambitions for itself and ASEAN were limited not by the non-interference principle, or fear of generating supranational authority, but by Timorese resistance. José Ramos-Horta threatened unrest if 'any ASEAN country... accomplices of Indonesia [tried to] impose them-selves on us', specifically threatening any Malaysian commander with 'total civil disobedience' (AFP, 1999b; IHT, 1999). This hostility to ASEAN, and Malaysia in particular, is only comprehensible in the light of ASEAN's role in supporting Indonesia's annexation and occupation of East Timor. In the long-run, however, Malaysia was able to win over the Timorese, sending business delegations to explore investment opportunities, sup-plying larger peacekeeping contingents, and eventually commanding UNMISET from August 2003 to May 2005.

The wide variation in individual ASEAN countries' positions explains why a unified ASEAN response to the Timor crisis was impossible. The explanation is not provided by 'ASEAN norms', nor by *ad hoc* factors like the presence or absence of democratic institutions, or concerns for separatism. Those states with least experience of ASEAN 'socialisation' felt most uncomfortable with violating non-interference, and vice-versa. If ASEAN's 'we-feeling' meant anything in this case, it meant rallying around Jakarta to *violate* a key ASEAN norm. 'Non-democratic' Malaysia and Singapore were as interventionist as 'democratic' Thailand and the Philippines. Burma and the Philippines both suffered from domestic separatism, yet the Philippines' separatism compelled it to intervene, rather than leading it to fear the dilution of sovereignty. Only considering the situation from the viewpoint of domestic social conflicts and their relationship to events in Indonesia allows all these factors to be reconciled and coherent explanations provided for ASEAN states' interventions in East Timor and their limits. Ultimately, it was the inherent impossibility of combining the resulting divergent policies into a coherent stance, not 'non-interference', which explains why ASEAN did not intervene *en bloc*.

Concluding remarks

The general consensus that ASEAN did not intervene in East Timor because of its norm of non-interference is clearly incorrect. Prior to 1999, ASEAN states maintained their political *cordon sanitaire* to help Jakarta prevent the expansion in the scope of the conflict in East Timor desired by the Timorese resistance. The application of non-interference was determined not by 'consensus' or 'socialisation' but, where necessary, by Indonesian coercion, made possible by the illiberal, oligarch-dominated nature of ASEAN societies. As the Asian financial crisis destabilised Indonesian society and Jakarta's grasp on East Timor, ASEAN states moved quietly to help solve the problem. In response to the humanitarian crisis of September 1999, the core ASEAN states encouraged and participated in a peacekeeping intervention to contain the political, social and economic unrest emanating from Indonesia. Those states least affected by the crisis distanced themselves from the intervention, precluding a corporate response. But it was those states that were supposedly best 'socialised' into the 'ASEAN way' that led the move to intervene. This suggests that the central role of states in maintaining particular social orders is a more accurate guide for explaining state behaviour than reference to abstract 'cherished principles'.

In addition to having significant consequences at the time – effectively enabling an Australian-led force to land – ASEAN's involvement in and experience of the East Timor intervention carried significant consequences for Southeast Asia's sovereignty regime. ASEAN's inability to handle the situation alone prompted early calls for the development of regional peacekeeping capabilities. Malaysia's foreign minister suggested that ASEAN develop 'a mechanism for us to be able to come together quickly, to be able to have some rapid deployment force for peacekeeping purposes under UN operation' so ASEAN could 'handle matters pertaining to our region in our way' (Han, 2000, p. 69). Singapore's defence minister also proposed closer defence cooperation along similar lines, his 'main if unspoken objective' being 'to help the Indonesian authorities stabilise their own country, and thereby to prevent communal violence from spilling over into other parts of the country' (Dosch, 2009, p. 73). In 2003, Indonesia itself proposed that ASEAN develop a regional peacekeeping force as part of an 'ASEAN Security Community'. This was rejected by Vietnam – probably for reasons similar to those given above – and by Singapore which foresaw practical difficulties with the scheme and, now the danger of Indonesia's dissolution had passed, did not wish to expend its resources (Kausikan, 2008).

Despite this, the 2003 proposal signalled serious changes within Indonesia with significant consequences for the wider region. It reflected both the partial liberalisation of the Indonesian polity, and a renewed recognition by Indonesian state managers that selective regional intervention might be used to help stabilise rather than disrupt domestic social order. This was expressed most clearly in the Yudhoyono administration's policy on Aceh. In the wake of the 2004 Asian tsunami, ASEAN states' security forces were admitted to Aceh to provide disaster relief. This unprecedented development led directly to the conclusion of the ASEAN Agreement on Disaster Management and Emergency Response in 2005. In 2006, a joint ASEAN-EU Monitoring Mission oversaw the implementation of a comprehensive peace deal negotiated with Aceh's separatist movement.[12] ASEAN's participation was vital to securing the acquiescence of the Indonesian military, without which the settlement could not have been implemented.

Caballero-Anthony (2005, p. 272) has argued that such practices indicate 'a radical shift from the regional norms constituted in the ASEAN way', providing 'emerging examples of how member states... are adopting the "pooling of sovereignty" approach beyond that of "protecting sovereignty" that is characteristic of the "ASEAN way"'. This is, to some extent, overstated, since it is not qualified by social conflict analysis. As Chapter 5 showed, entrenched interests will continue to limit this 'pooling', generating a highly selective sovereignty regime. Nonetheless, Cabellero-Anthony comes closer here than most to recognising the dynamic nature of ASEAN's sovereignty regime after the Asian crisis. As we shall see in the next chapter, Jakarta's new openness to intervention is certainly reflected in its policy towards Burma: both disaster relief missions and Aceh-style regional monitors have been proposed for ASEAN's pariah member.

8
Burma: ASEAN's Image and the 'Regional Interest'

> We don't set out to change the world and our neighbours. We don't believe in it. The culture of ASEAN is that we do not interfere.
>
> – *Goh Chok Tong, Singaporean Prime Minister, 1992*
> (*Economist*, 1992)

> ASEAN is trying to democratise Myanmar.
>
> – *Nguyen Dy Nien, Vietnamese Foreign Minister, 2004*
> (Kyodo, 2004)

The most serious challenge to ASEAN's international standing since the Cold War has been its inclusion of Burma as a member. Burma, which has been ruled by a military regime since 1988, is widely regarded in the West as a pariah state, home to widespread human rights abuses, the use of child labour, and drug trafficking, whilst the opposition leader, Aung San Suu Kyi, is hailed as popular, pro-democracy icon.[1] Western commentators and journalists consistently lambaste ASEAN for failing to intervene in Burma to address the problems caused by military misrule. Academic studies have generally reinforced this popular perception. Scholars have overwhelmingly argued that ASEAN states have not intervened at all for fear of legitimising intervention in their own countries. Instead, they have lent the shield of 'non-interference' to the Burmese regime and thereby 'legitimised illiberalism' (e.g. Than, 2005; Severino, 2006, pp. 134–48; Martinez-Kuhonta, 2006; Rahim, 2008). Constructivist scholar Amitav Acharya (2009a, pp. 127–34, 258) argues that Western pressure on ASEAN to do something about the regime may have 'tested' non-interference, but while ASEAN policy has shifted somewhat, 'it has not significantly departed from the non-interference doctrine'. Realists similarly emphasise the importance of ASEAN's 'cherished norm' of non-interference in constraining its ability to deal with Burma (Ganesan, 2006).

However, mounting evidence of ASEAN's attempts to insert themselves into Burma's domestic political processes has recently led a few scholars to begin reassessing such judgements. Constructivist scholars Jürgen Haacke (2010) and Christopher Roberts (2010) have both recognised departures from non-interference from 2003 onwards. For both authors, this is mostly due to external, particularly US, pressure, though both also cite transnational security challenges and democratisation in some ASEAN states. Having earlier emphasised the essential continuity of non-interference (Haacke, 2005), Haacke now observes that ASEAN 'has felt it necessary and appropriate to focus on and be critical of developments in Myanmar, despite the longstanding ASEAN norm of non-interference'. He states:

> the limits of ASEAN's flexibility in practising non-interference... have been set by a shared interest in anchoring Myanmar in the ASEAN community, different levels of motivation to promote democracy and human rights... economic interests, geopolitical considerations, political prudence... and a perceived need to preserve regional cohesion and unity (Haacke, 2010, p. 174).

This apparently implies that the extent of ASEAN's adherence to non-interference is now set by a range of non-normative political and economic factors. This contradicts the usual constructivist view that norms themselves direct state behaviour. Roberts, whose unusual goal is to assess how far ASEAN behaves like a security community, goes far further, arguing that 'the Association's repeated practice of contradicting, neglecting, or ignoring its so-called "inalienable principles" whenever convenient, has resulted in an organisation... best characterised by an ASEAN style of self-deception' (2010, p. 110).

This emerging recognition of the gap between ASEAN principles and practice over Burma is very welcome, but clearly remains limited in some crucial ways. First, it generally applies only to post-2003 events: typically, authors still reassert the prior power of non-intervention in ASEAN (Haacke, 2010, p. 159; Roberts, 2010, p. 217). Inadequate attention is still, therefore, being paid to historical practices of intervention, producing faulty assessments of the evolution of ASEAN's sovereignty regime. As this chapter argues, understanding ASEAN's *pre*-2003 efforts to promote political change in Burma is crucial to comprehend what comes after 2003. Second, the idea that adherence to non-interference is apparently determined by non-normative, political factors, or simply by 'convenience', is not accompanied by a coherent theory that explains what these factors are, or when and why it becomes 'convenient' to abandon the 'ASEAN way'.

This chapter tries to resolve these shortcomings using social conflict analysis. Its basic argument is that ASEAN states have been promoting political and economic liberalisation inside Burma for nearly 20 years. The limits to their activism are set not so much by a 'cherished norm' but rather the interests, ideologies and strategies of domestic social forces and the difficulty of reconciling these through inter-elite coordination into a coherent stance. In the period prior to the Asian financial crisis, ASEAN states pushed for limited reforms inside Burma that would serve the interests of their powerful business classes. After the crisis, Burma was pressured far more intensely by Thailand due to the ascendancy of the liberalising Democrats, but Bangkok was relatively isolated. In the longer term, core ASEAN states have increasingly recognised that the junta's reluctance to reform seriously endangers the credibility of their post-crisis reforms, both domestically and abroad. They have therefore adopted a more coercive approach, trying various means to insert themselves into Burma's domestic political processes and seeking to discipline Burma through the creation of new regional institutions. Their ability to do so has been constrained less by 'non-interference' than the regime's refusal to accept any external involvement, the continued business interests of some ASEAN (especially Thai) oligarchs in Burma, and the increasingly difficulty of achieving inter-ASEAN consensus.

The chapter proceeds in four sections. Section one analyses ASEAN's policy of constructive engagement as an attempt at 'Asian values'-style regime change. Section two examines post-crisis policies towards Burma, with a focus on Thailand. Section three explores a period of relative cooperation and success for ASEAN policy due to domestic realignments in key ASEAN states. This ended with a backlash by Burmese regime hardliners in 2003, to which ASEAN reacted extremely critically. The last section considers ASEAN's policies towards Burma from 2005 onwards. It argues that ASEAN's attempts to intervene in Burma have become increasingly coercive – though no less successful – and that the ASEAN Charter represented, in important part, an attempt to gain leverage over the regime by weakening non-interference.

Constructive engagement: Asian values-style regime change

ASEAN states generally describe their policy towards Burma as 'constructive engagement'. By evoking US policy towards South Africa in the 1980s and China in the 1990s, ASEAN sought to emphasise that its political and economic interaction with Burma would help to bring about positive political change there. Analysts typically dismiss such claims derisively, dubbing the policy 'destructive engagement' (Rahim, 2008). Conversely, this section argues that ASEAN has indeed promoted political and economic liberalisation inside Burma. Without recognising this, ASEAN's later anger towards the regime for not reforming cannot be properly understood. However, the scope of 'constructive engagement' was fundamentally limited by the interests of ASEAN's state-linked business classes and the illiberal character of ASEAN regimes. As with Cambodia, the shift from Cold War confrontation to constructive engagement was also resisted by powerful military-business interests, which continued to meddle unconstructively across Burma's borders.

Before considering ASEAN's policies, we need to appreciate Burma's situation at the end of the 1980s. Burma has suffered severe internal unrest since decolonisation in 1948. The ruling Burmese Socialist Programme Party was almost immediately beset by serious communist and ethnic separatist insurgencies. The Thai ruling elite was highly suspicious of the 'socialist' government in Rangoon and fearful that the powerful Chinese-backed Burmese Communist Party (BCP) would link up with the CPT, which was principally active in north and northeast Thailand. They therefore sponsored several ethnic rebel groups along the border to create a buffer force against the Burmese government and the BCP, which fomented further instability inside Burma. In the 1980s, the Burmese government experienced a serious debt crisis and was forced to adopt neoliberal reforms which further weakened the state. The reforms culminated in a currency crisis in 1988 which provoked widespread urban unrest. The government quickly collapsed, and the military seized control. A junta calling itself the State Law and Order Restoration Council (SLORC) organised elections in 1990, but its front party came a very weak second to the pro-democratic National League for Democracy (NLD) led by Aung San Suu Kyi. The military refused to relinquish power, arguing that otherwise the country's ethnic insurgencies would tear the country apart. Suu Kyi was instead placed under house arrest.

Since then, the basic problem has been the impasse caused by the military's inability to simply impose its preferred political solution on the rest of Burmese society and the inability of opposition forces to overthrow the regime. The army has tried to impose what it calls 'discipline-flourishing democracy', a system of rule that would guarantee Burma's territorial integrity, maintain the domination of the main ethnic group, the Bamar, within that territory, and preserve a leading political role for the army. They cultivated support for this system by co-opting social groups into a long-running 'national convention' tasked with drafting a new constitution (finally issued in 2008). The military's hand was significantly strengthened in 1989 by the collapse of the BCP and the alliance of ethnic rebel groups it had long headed. Subsequently, many of the rebels signed ceasefires with the state, turning instead to developing economically the areas under their control. However, these ceasefires are not universal and have frequently degenerated back into armed conflict. The development of the border regions has also created an independent power base for former and current rebel leaders opposed to the military's plans. The pro-democracy opposition has also impeded the regime's grand design. Although too weak to seize power itself, the main opposition party, the NLD, and its figurehead Aung San Suu Kyi enjoy significant popular support and strong Western backing. The resultant impracticality of excluding these forces from a settlement has prolonged Burma's ongoing power struggles. The Burmese military has thus faced serious obstacles in its efforts to territorialise the Burmese state and to create a political system that satisfies the opposition while leaving fundamental power relations intact.

The enormous difficulty of achieving this goal in such a deeply divided society explains why the junta was so keen to join ASEAN after the Cold War and benefit from the umbrella of 'non-interference'. Sovereignty norms help contain the scope of conflict within Burma's existing borders, where the army enjoys a relative advantage over the fragmented opposition forces and can at least attempt to impose its will by force. Normalising relations with ASEAN and opening the country to foreign investment and trade, the army felt, would also help tilt the domestic balance of forces by redirecting foreign economic engagement away from Burma's rebel groups and towards the Burmese state. From ASEAN states' perspective, this opening came at a highly propitious moment since, as we have already seen, domestic business classes had begun agitating for policy changes to allow them to access untapped markets and resources in Burma and Indochina. Given the victory over communism, the ethnic insurgencies supported by Thailand no longer served a useful function for the new rich, and could be discarded.

As with Cambodia, therefore, Thailand's Chatichai administration promoted *rapprochement* with Burma in the late 1980s. Bangkok essentially abandoned its old clients among Burma's ethnic rebel groups in a series of deals mediated primarily by General Chavalit. In exchange for lucrative fishing and logging concessions, Thailand granted the Burmese military permission to pursue rebel forces onto Thai soil. The Thai army also helped suppress the insurgents, while Bangkok cut off their arms supplies and pressed them to agree ceasefires with Rangoon (Silverstein, 2001, pp. 121, 129). Further deals brokered between Burmese and Thai elites followed in areas like natural gas and fisheries. Warming interstate relations were underpinned by the personal profit-mongering of politico-business figures. Telecommunications tycoon Thaksin Shinawatra, for example, used a 1995 stint as foreign minister to acquire lucrative contracts for his ShinCorp subsidiary, Sattel (Pasuk and Baker, 2004, p. 213). By this time, the majority of Burma's ethnic rebel groups had been forced into ceasefires, bilateral trade was valued at over $500m, and Thailand had become the fourth largest investor in Burma (Than, 2005, p. 95; UNCTAD, 2003b, p. 13).

State-linked business interests from other ASEAN countries also rushed to seek profits in Burma. In the 1990s, Malaysian firms sunk $587m into Burma, including oil and gas investments by the state-owned Petronas corporation (UNCTAD, 2003b, p. 13). Many of Suharto's cronies, including family members and long-standing business partners like Bob Hasan, also exploited their political connections to secure deals in Burma. They invested hundreds of millions of dollars in fields like telecommunications, agriculture, logging, manufacturing, and infrastructure development (Green Left Weekly, 1997). As SLORC opened Burma's economy to foreign participation, there was a veritable scramble for a slice of the action. As Malaysia's then-UN ambassador recalls, ASEAN states rushed to seize opportunities 'before the West, before the Chinese... and the Indians' could monopolise them (Razali, 2008). By 1995, ASEAN countries accounted for 39 per cent of investment in Burma and 44 per cent of its foreign trade (Than, 2005, p. 95; UNCTAD, 2003b, p. 13).

As was also the case with Cambodia, the transition from Cold War subversion to post-Cold War *rapprochement* was far from smooth. Reflecting the incoherence of states, the creation of a new sovereignty regime was contested by entrenched forces with an interest in the old one. Powerful Thai military-business complexes along the border fought to preserve their lucrative relationships with Burmese rebel groups. They continued selling arms to the rebels – an estimated $25m-worth from 1990–1992

– and smuggling goods through them, perhaps as much as $2.1bn-worth in 1992 alone. Thai army units could even reportedly be bribed by the Burmese military and rebel groups to intervene selectively in battles across the border (Myoe, 2001, pp. 58, 50–2). This naturally continued to create instability within Burma, bolstered the position of several rebel groups, and doubtless reinforced SLORC's siege mentality.

Perhaps more important for our purposes was that economic re-engagement was also always overlaid with the political objective of liberalisation in Burma. ASEAN promoted ASEAN-style political and economic governance reforms for several reasons. First, the ramshackle arrangements existing in Burma were neither compatible with socio-political stability there nor with the interests of ASEAN merchants and investors. Promoting political and economic reform would, it was thought, benefit both sides. Second, domestic opposition to engage-ment with Burma meant some concessions on the promotion of reform were necessary. The Democrat Party, for example, protested the spill-over of fighting into Thailand in the early 1990s, while Islamist parties were unhappy with the mistreatment of Burma's Muslim minority. Thirdly, Western dialogue partners pushed ASEAN to pressurise Burma after the nullified 1990 elections. It was in reaction to EEC demands at an ASEAN Post-Ministerial Conference in 1991 that ASEAN articulated its policy of 'constructive engagement' with Burma, a stance first for-mulated by Thai foreign ministry officials (Kavi, 2001, p. 122).

Crucially, 'constructive engagement' implied that ASEAN states would not just establish economic relations with Burma and refuse to 'interfere' in its internal politics, but would actively try to persuade SLORC to change its ways. A Thai official explained that the goal was 'to encourage the Myanmarese to move gradually towards democracy and a market economy... We want to encourage those in the Yangon regime who believe there should be more liberalisation'. An Indonesian official similarly emphasised that ASEAN was pushing for change: 'we are telling them very quietly, in a Southeast Asian way, without any fanfare, without any public statements: "Look, you are in trouble, let us help you. But you have to change, you cannot continue like this"' (ST, 1992). The need for the regime to reform was officially expressed as early as 1992, when ASEAN and the EEC jointly called on Burma to 'make further progress towards political and economic reform' (ASEAN, 1992).

Just how far ASEAN was willing to go, however, was determined by powerful domestic interests and ASEAN state managers' post-Cold War geopolitical strategies. First, the intimate relationships being established between the politico-economic elite of ASEAN and Burma ensured that the interests of the 'new rich' would be promoted above all else. To avoid disrupting lucrative trade and investment links necessitated a moderate, non-coercive approach to promoting political reform. This was reinforced by ASEAN's ruling forces' own illiberal predilections. Largely favouring social stability over political liberty, many of the region's governments sympathised with the Burmese junta's struggle to suppress the country's internal unrest and develop the country's economy. Their preferred approach was to encourage Burma to adopt ASEAN-style governance arrangements which could maintain prevailing power relations within the formal trappings of democratic institutions. Another concern for some ASEAN states was that if SLORC was pressed too hard, it might retreat into isolation and thus become heavily dependent on China. This would clearly damage ASEAN's business interests, but also enhance Beijing's strategic reach at a moment when its long-range intentions were extremely unclear. The worst-case scenario for ruling elites obsessed with maintaining social and political stability was that the Burmese regime might simply collapse, producing a 'failed state' into which India and China might intervene (Jasudasen, 2008). The consequences for ASEAN societies' stability, in terms of refugee outflows and so on, would be very serious.

What emerged in practice, then, was 'Asian values'-style regime change – a real attempt to encourage political and economic liberalisation, but one conditioned by the illiberal ideology and oligarchic interests animating ASEAN states. ASEAN strongly encouraged the Burmese regime to adopt Indonesia's mode of governance. Lee Kuan Yew frequently travelled to Rangoon to promote this idea, while Indonesian and SLORC ministers engaged in many reciprocal visits (Kesavapany, 2008; Harsono, 1997). Senior generals visited Jakarta to study the Indonesian military's constitutionally protected political role, translating the New Order constitution into Burmese to serve as a model for their own country (Sundhaussen, 1995). The junta also developed a mass organisation called the Union Solidarity and Development Association, modelled on Suharto's GOLKAR party, which could be mobilised to support the regime's goals (Steinberg, 2000, p. 276). Thai ministers also periodically visited Rangoon to push for progress on constitutional reform and Suu Kyi's release. Singapore devoted considerable resources to 'constructive engagement' through the Singapore Cooperation Programme, training over 5,000 Burmese government officials by 2007 (Xinhua, 2007). Its former ambassador to Rangoon explains that the purpose was to educate elite youths so that they would return home to implement 'good governance' and economic growth, gradually displacing their backwards elders. In keeping with the PAP's elitist, technocratic vision, Singaporean elites (misguidedly) believed that this was 'really going to change the place'. Mass involvement in political change was apparently unnecessary, since 'democracy is a luxury'. Singapore and Malaysia also promoted investment in Burma, believing that this too would 'lift the country up' (Jasudasen, 2008).

Despite the limited nature of the reforms they were promoting in Burma, ASEAN states nonetheless did criticise the regime when it strayed from the path prescribed for it. In 1992, 170,000 members of Burma's Muslim minority, the Rohingyas, were forcibly displaced into Bangladesh. This not only caused an international outcry but also enraged Southeast Asia's Islamists, particularly in Malaysia where the Pan-Malaysian Islamic Party was the leading opposition party and Islam was playing an increasing role in UMNO's legitimising discourse. The Malaysian foreign ministry summoned the Burmese ambassador and instructed Burma 'to immediately cease the oppression... and be prepared to accept them back' (Kyodo, 1992). A ministry official also appeared to threaten sanctions, warning that 'any move now by ASEAN against Burma may mean economic devastation for that country' (IPS, 1992). Brunei, Indonesia and Singapore also criticised Burma's behaviour.

Malaysia particularly sought to punish Burma through international institutions. It backed the appointment of a UN Special Rapporteur on human rights in Burma, vetoed Burma's accession to the TAC and blocked its attendance at ASEAN meetings until the situation improved. Malaysia also urged ASEAN to insist on a timetable for Burma's internal reform to 'stimulate' change. The Association subsequently despatched the Philippine foreign minister as its special envoy, which the regime protested as an act of interference (Acharya, 2009a, pp. 111–12; Kavi, 2001, p. 122; Silverstein, 2001, p. 129). This illustrates that even in the early days of 'constructive engagement', ASEAN states were willing to lecture and reprimand Burma publicly, in violation of 'non-interference'. The Rohingyas episode also shows that collective criticism by ASEAN is not restricted to the post-2003 period. Moreover, this appeared to bear fruit: Burma agreed to repatriate the Rohingyas. Coupled with other concessions, such as the release of Suu Kyi from house arrest in 1995, this encouraged those in ASEAN states who saw constructive engagement as a valid strategy to bring about political change in Burma.

In practice, however, ASEAN's intervention was actually strengthening forces in Burmese society that would resist meaningful reform while weakening those who promoted it. Burma's political economy was such that the regime benefited directly from ASEAN's economic engagement. During the Cold War, the government had expelled the ethnic-Indians who constituted the bulk of Burma's bourgeoisie, and nationalised most of the economy. By the 1990s, state-owned enterprises accounted for half of all exports and 40 per cent of imports, and provided 40 per cent of government revenues (Steinberg, 2001, p. 46). A large proportion of ASEAN trade and investment was therefore mediated directly through the military-dominated state, yielding both tax revenues to finance state coercion and patronage resources for SLORC. In 1989, a make-or-break year for military rule, the teak trade with Thailand alone yielded $112m for the state (FEER, 1990).

While this might be seen as an unintended side effect of economic interaction, other aspects of ASEAN engagement recklessly and intentionally supported SLORC. ASEAN states invested directly in infrastructure projects that could be used for internal suppression (Selth, 2000, pp. 30–1). They also provided direct aid to the regime, either to clear obstacles to profit-making, or to deliberately enhance the regime's stability. Thailand, while pressing anti-regime forces along the border to demobilise, also sent annual cash payments to SLORC, which peaked at around $2.3m in 1997 (Kavi, 2001, p. 124). Government-linked corporations in Singapore and Indonesia funnelled arms and ammunition to SLORC, bypassing Western embargoes. Singaporean state-linked banks also provided large loans for down-payments on Chinese arms. Singaporean training for Burmese officials extended to intelligence and secret police officers. Moreover, Singapore upgraded the defence ministry's espionage and black operations capabilities and helped Burma develop a domestic arms industry in exchange for the prioritisation of Singaporean investments (Selth, 2000, p. 31; Aditjondro, 1997, pp. 44–5).

The net effect of 'constructive engagement' by the time of the Asian financial crisis was therefore to reinforce the military's dominance *vis-à-vis* the forces opposing it. By 1997, SLORC had made relatively few concessions. Its National Convention had been so tightly stage-managed that the NLD had walked out in 1995. SLORC simply rebranded itself the State Peace and Development Council (SPDC), conveying its resolve to cling to power. The illiberal ideology and oligarchic interests behind ASEAN's intervention in Burma clearly contributed to this outcome and thus actually undermined the objectives of constructive engagement. Even Acharya (2009a, p. 133), who tries to play down ASEAN's approach as merely 'testing' non-interference, thus has to admit that constructive engagement 'could not be regarded as strict non-interference' which 'would have meant taking a neutral position... At best, it implied a kind of interference in support of the regime'. The social conflict analysis above helps us explain this selective approach to ASEAN norms.

The post-crisis push for 'flexible engagement'

Although constructive engagement had achieved little by 1997, its basic premise – that interaction with ASEAN would encourage political and economic reform – was reinforced when Burma was accepted as a member in outright defiance of the Western powers. ASEAN was subsequently hit by a Western boycott of ASEAN activities right in the middle of the Asian financial crisis. This section focuses on Thai policy towards Burma to illustrate the way in which social conflict powerfully shapes the practice of non-interference within ASEAN, and to illustrate the beginning of serious post-crisis divergences among ASEAN states. In the wake of the crisis, Thailand's new Democrat government pushed for 'flexible engagement', which sought to prevent Burma using 'non-interference' to preclude ASEAN states intruding into its internal affairs. Despite severe international and domestic constraints, the Democrats cooperated with Western states to offer incentives to the Burmese regime to reform. When this failed, they resorted to an increasingly confrontational and interventionist approach. However, the Democrats ultimately overreached against oligarchic interests, which regrouped to defeat them in the 2001 elections, resulting in a return to business-as-usual with Burma.

The decision to admit Burma to ASEAN attracted fierce international condemnation. Western states had imposed sanctions on the country in response to a large-scale crackdown on the domestic opposition in 1996. Prior to Burma's scheduled admission in July 1997, they pressured ASEAN heavily to exclude the regime, arguing that constructive engagement had failed. However, the imperatives to integrate Burma into the region remained very strong. Despite doubts being raised in some quarters, Malaysia, then ASEAN's chair, managed to persuade its partners to stay on-course. Western states were outraged, cancelling the biannual US-ASEAN Dialogue and the EU Joint Cooperation and ASEAN-EU finance and economic ministers' meetings, despite the onset of the Asian crisis. The EU also refused to admit any of ASEAN's new members to ASEM.

Importantly, however, Burma's entry into ASEAN did *not* imply the extension of non-interference to cover the regime. Instead, the goals of constructive engagement were reinforced. Malaysian Prime Minister Mahathir justified Burmese membership by arguing that it would 'have a very positive effect on them' by exposing the regime to how 'Malaysia manages its free market and its system of democracy'. This would make the junta less 'afraid of the democratic process' and 'over time, they will tend to give more voice to the people... They become a member first, then put their house in order' (AsiaWeek, 1997). This imperative was only underscored by the West's reaction, which marked the beginning of ASEAN's long struggle to re-engage extra-regional powers on favourable terms. Crucially, Western states indicated that they would now hold ASEAN directly accountable for the pace of reform in Burma. US Secretary of State Albright stated that 'by admitting Burma as a member, ASEAN assumes a greater responsibility, for Burma's problems now become ASEAN's problems' (AP, 1997). Western states now expected ASEAN to manage the domestic situation in Burma, and had indicated their willingness to punish the Association if it failed to do so.

The task of constructive engagement was principally taken up by Thailand in the wake of the Asian crisis. The Malaysian government, which had previously led the push alongside Singapore, was heavily distracted by its struggles against its *reformasi* and Islamist opposition. In Thailand, however, the fall of the oligarchic Chavalit government brought to power the Democrat party which, ideologically hostile to Burma, had opposed its entry to ASEAN. Finally freed from coalitional arrangements with pro-Burmese oligarchs, they wanted to seize the opportunity to really push the SPDC to change its ways. Surin's promotion of 'flexible engagement' was partly designed to unleash Thailand from any constraints imposed by 'non-interference' on this goal. As Surin stated, 'our membership in ASEAN and ASEAN's principle of non-interference should not hamper us from expressing our views' (Acharya, 2009b, p. 129). By weakening the standing of non-interference, the foreign ministry hoped to prevent the SPDC invoking it to fend off Thai intervention.

The Democrats faced considerable obstacles, however, in marshalling support for a forceful implementation of constructive engagement. The first set of obstacles emanated from the non-coherence of the state and the continued power of oligarchic forces. Politico-business leaders interested in maintaining good relations with Burma still wielded tremendous influence over the state, being present in parliamentary opposition parties and interpenetrated with various state apparatuses. Surin (1998a) recognised this as a severe constraint:

> [While the Democrats' supporters] urge Thailand to move more quickly and aggressively in pressing for greater democracy and human rights in the region... there are also others, including border business interests and some in the bureaucracy, who stand to lose out from such a course of action. The task of balancing the interests between the more progressive and entrenched establishment interests is a delicate one. Foreign policy cannot get ahead of social factors. Foreign policy... must reflect the existing social structure altogether... if our policy of promoting human rights and democracy hurts the interests of our traders along the border, the policy will encounter domestic political resistance and be ultimately unsustainable.

A moderate approach was therefore still necessary, but even this faced resistance. In May 1999, for example, despite having approval from Surin's foreign ministry, an International Conference of Free Trade Unions conference on 'Democracy for Burma' was sabotaged by the labour ministry's refusal to issue visas for foreign participants. The ministry, which was controlled by an ally of General Chavalit, argued that the conference would damage relations with Burma (Nation, 1999a).

Difficulty in coordinating regional inter-elite agreement on how to deal with Burma also constrained the Democrats. ASEAN states generally agreed that Burma had to be pressed to change its ways. For Indonesia's foreign minister, in relation to Burma, flexible engagement 'was the same policy' as constructive engagement: 'we had flexible engagement already, *vis-à-vis* Myanmar'. In this respect, it was 'controversial only to the degree of the name... my sense of flexible engagement is, you apply it to outsiders. [For] insiders, you must find a better word' – hence the adoption of 'enhanced interaction' (Alatas, 2008). However, ASEAN states were reluctant to deprive themselves of the strategic device of non-interference at the height of the Asian crisis. The norm was therefore officially retained, permitting Burma to wield it against Thailand. In 1999, for example, Prime Minister Chuan proposed that ASEAN retain the 'troika' mechanism used in Cambodia as a formal regional instrument, clearly hoping to deploy it in Burma. However, the other member-states would only agree to this in cases where the target-state gave its consent, thereby neutering the troika. This led

Haacke (2005, p. 190) to conclude that there had been 'no major development of ASEAN's diplomatic and security culture overall because they still upheld the status of norms like non-interference'.

However, it is crucial to recognise that although the lack of regional support constrained what the Thai government could do, this did *not* mean that Thailand remained bound by non-interference. In fact, the 'ASEAN way' appeared to exercise little influence over Bangkok. The Democrats largely bypassed ASEAN to form alliances with similarly-minded Western governments to promote internal change in Burma. At an international conference in Britain in late 1998, Thailand – joined by the Philippines – pressed Europe and the US to drop their sanctions on Burma and instead offer the regime incentives to reform. Although they refused to abandon the use of sanctions, they did agree to offer Burma $1bn in World Bank assistance, which was tied to a series of political conditions (AsiaWeek, 2000). The Philippine and Western ambassadors then pressed Rangoon to accept visits from UN special envoy Alvaro de Soto, who had been tasked with promoting this aid-for-reform scheme, threatening tougher sanctions if the SPDC refused. De Soto subsequently visited the country for five rounds of talks, but each time the regime flatly rejected aid conditionality.

The failure of this multilateral approach eventually led the Democrats into taking a much harsher bilateral stance towards Burma. This was also prompted by growing frustration about the Burmese regime's inability to contain and manage the externalities of its rule within its territorial borders, a key demand underpinning 'flexible engagement'. The first concern was with the activity of Burmese rebel forces. The Democrats had taken a remarkably lenient approach to peaceful Burmese dissidents operating on Thai soil, while instructing the army to shell the border to contain armed conflict within Burmese territory. This stance changed in late 1999 when Burmese dissidents seized the Burmese embassy in Bangkok and a hospital in Ratchaburi, demanding that Thailand stop shelling the border and aid their cause. The first crisis was ended peacefully, but the description of the dissidents by a Thai minister as 'student activists fighting for democracy', and their release at the border, enraged Rangoon. The SPDC sealed the border to trade and revoked Thai fishing concessions in Burmese waters. Bangkok retaliated by cracking down on illegal Burmese immigrants working in Thailand. In the second incident, Thai commandoes stormed the hospital, shooting all the rebels dead.

Another major concern was flows of illegal narcotics. Drug production is closely bound up with political economy relations within Burma, particularly its borderlands. Many ex-rebel groups have turned to producing opium and methamphetamines, smuggling them into Thailand with the alleged connivance of both Burmese regional army commanders and some in the Thai army, who take a cut from the lucrative trade. Some ex-rebel leaders have thereby become major tycoons with close ties to the SPDC and foreign investors (Chee, 1997). The Democrats' social base, however, gained nothing from such tangled relationships, and the party was determined to suppress the trade. Again, they pressed the Burmese regime bilaterally to contain the drugs problem within its own borders. Selected generals hostile to Burma were promoted to key positions within the Thai army, including General Wattanachai, appointed to the northern military command, and General Surayud, appointed commander-in-chief. Wattanachai allegedly recruited the rebel Shan State Army-South as a proxy force to fight drug-trafficking groups inside Burma, like the pro-regime United Wa State Army (Irrawaddy, 2002). Surayud branded drugs the primary threat to Thai security in January 2000, accusing Burma of not doing enough to suppress the trade. A vicious public spat followed, with Burmese state media threatening to expose Thai officials involved in narco-trafficking while Bangkok threatened to 'join the international community in expediting justice on dictators and drug barons' after acceding to the International Criminal Court treaty. By mid-2000, Deputy Foreign Minister Sukhumbhand Paribatra had accused the SPDC of sheltering drugs traffickers and, with Surayud, had reportedly backed armed raids into Burma to destroy narcotics factories (Kavi, 2001, pp. 127, 125). As the crisis deepened, the Thai and Burmese armies began clashing along the border.

The SPDC's inability or unwillingness to contain its domestic problems within territorial bounds led the Thai government to seek to govern these issues regionally or internationally. It was at this point that Chuan pushed his troika proposal, without much success. At the International Labour Organisation (ILO) in June and November 2000, Thailand refused to join ASEAN attempts to help Burma avoid sanctions over the use of forced and child labour, which were being promoted by the US. ASEAN had prepared a draft resolution calling for sanctions to be deferred to give Burma a chance to cooperate with the ILO. Thailand refused to support this, instead slamming Burma's use of 'slave labour', calling for the ILO to establish a permanent presence in Burma and for international sanctions to continue until the regime produced results (Nation, 2000).

In taking such a confrontational and interventionist approach, the Democrats not only departed from the 'ASEAN way', but had also wildly overreached their domestic constraints. The serious deterioration in bilateral political and economic ties with Burma badly damaged oligarchic interests already being attacked by the government's neoliberal reform programme, prompting a backlash. In December 1999, the Chavalit-led opposition launched an unsuccessful no-confidence motion in parliament designed to topple the Chuan government, citing the disruption in trade with Burma (AP, 1999d). Oligarchic forces began regrouping around Thaksin's TRT party. As the 2001 general elections approached, the Chamber of Commerce urged the next government to restore ties with Burma using General Chavalit as an intermediary (Snitwongse, 2001, p. 201).

TRT's victory in the elections led to a rapid reversal of Democrat policies and the resumption of 'new look'-esque approaches, reflecting the interests underpinning the new government. Thaksin publicly repudiated the use of Burmese rebel groups as 'buffers', instead announcing that Thai forces would help compel rebels to sign ceasefires with the regime. However, this was initially resisted by those forces within the state apparatus dedicated to confronting Burma. General Wattanachai, for example, continued launching raids across the border. Thaksin therefore purged the bureaucracy and military of Democrat appointees, sidelining Surayud, Wattanachai and others in favour of his own cronies while appointing Chavalit as his defence minister and envoy to Burma (McCargo and Ukrist, 2005, pp. 131–51; Pasuk and Baker, 2004, pp. 184–7). Thaksin also launched a severe crackdown on Burmese dissidents operating in Thailand. The scope of Thailand's counter-narcotics campaign was dramatically contracted, too. Thaksin abandoned the idea of military raids into Burma, offering the regime crop-substitution aid instead, while launching a domestic 'war on drugs' in which over 2,700 people, many of them enemies of TRT, were extra-judicially killed (McCargo and Ukrist 2005, p. 227).

The business class overwhelmingly benefited from these changes. The border was reopened to trade, bans on Thai imports were lifted, and in exchange for infrastructure development aid, fishing concessions were reactivated and expanded. Chavalit's allies hastened to exploit new trading opportunities. In 2002 alone, over 50 Thai generals visited Burma 'for the purpose of conducting (possibly corrupt) business dealings' (Roberts, 2010, p. 92). New investments in Burma were also facilitated by Thailand's state Export-Import Bank. Thaksin's own ShinCorp was a leading beneficiary, signing a telecommunications contract with a firm owned by the son of a senior Burmese general, Khin Nyunt (McCargo and Ukrist, 2005, pp. 54–5).

Focusing on Thailand's post-crisis policy illustrates how attachment to 'non-interference' is determined by conflict among social forces, not state socialisation or 'national interests'. Thailand's longstanding pursuit of positive relations with Burma to advance the interests of its business class was gradually overturned by the neoliberal Democrat government. While facing significant constraints regionally and domestically, the Democrats attacked non-interference and increasingly adopted a confrontational and interventionist policy against the SPDC. However, in so doing they wildly overreached against the business class. The latter's recapture of state power led to a rapid reversal of policy, with Thailand once more intervening against the SPDC's enemies.

Illusive payoffs: The revival of constructive engagement

The return to power in Thailand of a relatively cohesive, self-confident and brazenly corrupt business class was rather at odds with developments elsewhere in the region. As Chapter 5 detailed, many other ASEAN state managers sought to recover from the crisis through 'good governance' reforms designed to consolidate their domestic hegemony and repair their relations with external powers and markets. ASEAN's treatment of Burma has been closely related to this process. In 2000, to re-engage the Western powers, ASEAN essentially staked its battered reputation on its capacity to promote domestic change in Burma. Renewed efforts at 'constructive engagement' initially appeared to pay off, thanks largely to domestic realignments within Burma. The situation was drastically reversed in 2003 following a major crackdown against the NLD. ASEAN responded by openly criticising the SPDC, allowing its opponents to mobilise within their own states, and eventually by effectively stripping Burma of its forthcoming ASEAN chairmanship.

The link between ASEAN's post-crisis revival and the situation in Burma was firmly established in an explicit *quid pro quo* struck with Western states in December 2000. In 1997, ASEAN had been punished by Western powers for admitting Burma and told that it would be held accountable for reforms within the country. Three years later, ASEAN managed to restore inter-regional cooperation with the EU, but the price of inter-regional cooperation restarting was a series of political concessions. In exchange for EU support for ASEAN's regional integration efforts and for backing on issues like Indonesia's territorial integrity, ASEAN agreed to 'promote and protect all human rights' and emphasise 'the importance of popular participation' in future cooperation (ASEAN, 2000). More specifically, a *quid pro quo* over Burma was also quietly established. European representatives reported that Burma had 'openly' agreed to accept a visit from an EU troika, to lift restrictions on Aung San Suu Kyi, and hold 'early talks' with the opposition, and it 'now remained for ASEAN to ensure the junta kept its word' – as it subsequently did. The Dutch delegate rightly noted 'a departure from the non-interference principle' (AFP, 2000a).[2] ASEAN thereby staked its battered post-crisis reputation upon its ability to get Burma to cooperate with Western demands.

The Association's willingness to do so partly reflected a lack of strategic options in its weakened post-crisis condition, but it also expressed declining interest in coddling the SPDC in many ASEAN states. In parts of the region, the financial crisis had disrupted oligarchic networks with a stake in Burma. The fall of the Suharto regime, for example, ejected most business interests with investments in Burma from direct control over state power. More generally, with the crisis having terminated ASEAN's expansionary boom, ASEAN investment in Burma stagnated after 1997. Earlier investments had, in any case, not yielded the fabulous returns expected. Archaic business laws and tight capital controls often left businesses unable to repatriate their profits or investments. Burma was thus no longer viewed as a golden opportunity in many countries. The SPDC's failure to implement the economic and political reforms demanded by ASEAN had also disillusioned key architects of earlier policies. Lee Kuan Yew, for example, was 'disgusted' by the regime's intransigence and was no longer prepared to shield it from criticism (Kesavapany, 2008).

Burma's greater willingness to cooperate with ASEAN and the West, meanwhile, stemmed largely from internal realignments within the military regime. In 2000, Aung San Suu Kyi dropped her confrontational approach towards the SPDC. This apparently enabled a faction led by General Khin Nyunt, which favoured greater cooperation with external powers, to gain temporary ascendancy (Kyaw, 2009). Nyunt successfully persuaded the regime's leader, General Than Shwe, to pursue dialogue with the opposition in order to ease foreign pressure. This strategy was supported by external realignments, notably the relief of pressure from Thailand after Thaksin's election and the West's willingness to moderate its confrontational approach.

ASEAN therefore resumed its policy of constructive engagement, led once more by Malaysia. Having led the charge for Burma's entry to ASEAN, the Malaysian government had assumed particular responsibility for its conduct. With UMNO rule stabilised at home, Prime Minister Mahathir was able to return to this task. Malaysia joined Thailand and the Philippines at a second major international conference on Burma in March 2000 to argue for deeper international engagement with the SPDC to help spur internal reform. The conference requested that the UNHCR and United Nations Development Programme (UNDP) deploy units in Burma, and that the UN appoint a new special envoy (Asia-Week, 2000). A close associate of Mahathir's, Razali Ismail, was subsequently appointed. Mahathir himself also visited Rangoon in January 2001, announcing upon his return a 'blueprint' for Burma's transition to democracy. The regime, he said, had promised elections 'in a few years' – though Mahathir revealed the sort of illiberal, ASEAN-style 'democracy' he was still promoting when warning that these elections would 'have limits' and that people should 'not use elections to undermine authority' (NST, 2001). Mahathir travelled repeatedly to Rangoon in 2001 and 2002, promoting economic liberalisation and a 'gradual shift' to democracy.

For a while, this combination of forces did appear to deliver significant concessions. An ILO mission was allowed to visit Burma in September 2001 and to establish a presence in the country. Mahathir and Razali visited Burma many times, and Razali was credited with persuading the regime to resume talks with the NLD in September 2000 and to reopen some NLD offices. Renewed visits by the UN special rapporteur on Burma also yielded hundreds of prisoner releases, culminating with Suu Kyi's release from house arrest in May 2002. ASEAN happily took part of the credit for these developments (ASEAN, 2001). 'Non-interference' was invoked in this period *not* to excuse ASEAN inaction on Burma but as a justification for, or even a synonym of, its behind-the-scenes approach. For example, the Philippine foreign secretary suggested that 'it's moving in a positive direction because there is non-interference. We can encourage, we can persuade, but we cannot do it with publicity... they know they have to ultimately follow the democratic process' (AFP, 2001). ASEAN's support for Burma in international institutions remained implicitly conditional upon the delivery of reform. Harsh UN resolutions on the human rights situation, for instance, were opposed only because 'progress' was being made and condemnation might 'hamper efforts towards national reconciliation'.[3]

The continuation of this progress fundamentally rested on the balance of forces within Burma, and when this shifted, 'constructive engagement' was thrown into disarray. This occurred in May 2003, when a Union Solidarity and Development Association mob – apparently directed by

SPDC hard-liner General Maung Aye – violently attacked Suu Kyi's convoy at Depayin, killing several NLD activists. Suu Kyi was quickly returned to house arrest. The backlash against the NLD, which had returned to a policy of confrontation with the regime, also signalled a reversal in Khin Nyunt's fortunes – within months he had been demoted and sidelined, and he was later purged from the junta on corruption charges. A hard-line faction had resumed control.

ASEAN's reacted quickly and sternly to Depayin in a way that was inconsistent with 'non-interference' but which reflected the way in which its standing with key external powers had become inexorably tied to Burma's domestic politics. Mahathir bluntly demanded that Suu Kyi 'be released immediately' (Bernama, 2003a). Malaysia's foreign minister, Syed Hamid Albar, emphasising the threat to 'ASEAN's reputation and image', demanded a timetable for her release (Bernama, 2003b). ASEAN foreign ministers met soon afterwards to 'urge' Burma to free Suu Kyi and restart 'national reconciliation' (ASEAN, 2003). East Timor's foreign minister, an observer at this meeting, reported that the ministers were 'all deeply upset' and had demanded that Burma 'get out of the pariah status' no later than 2006, when it was scheduled to take up the chairmanship of ASEAN (AFP, 2003a). Burma resisted the deployment of an ASEAN troika, proposed by both the Philippines and Indonesia, but did agree to release Suu Kyi quickly and draw up a new constitution during 2004.

This sharp and critical intervention was necessary because of the way in which the Association was now being held accountable for events within Burma. As the Philippine foreign secretary explained, having admitted Burma, ASEAN now shared 'accountability to the world about the slow progress of the transition to democracy in Myanmar' and thus had 'a legitimate interest in what is going on in the country, including anything that could affect the image of ASEAN before the world' (New York Times, 2003; Nation, 2003). A number of scholars have rightly noted this concern for ASEAN's 'credibility' in explaining its treatment of Burma, from Depayin to the present day (Haacke, 2005, 2010; Roberts, 2010; Kyaw, 2009). However, ASEAN's reaction also reflected, crucially, the long history of ASEAN leaders' attempts to promote liberalisation in that country, and the specific *quid quo pro* of 2000. Mahathir, who now even floated the idea of expelling Burma from ASEAN, explained that regional leaders had 'done our very best to get them to change their minds', but the SPDC still apparently wished to 'defy the world... We don't criticise member states unless what one state does embarrasses us, causes a problem for us. We are thinking about ourselves as ASEAN... what they have done has affected us, our credibility' (AFP, 2003b).

This concern for 'credibility' had two main aspects. The first related to ASEAN state managers' post-crisis strategy to re-engage external powers and restore access to lost markets, investment, aid and other forms of political support necessary to restore economic growth and help maintain domestic order. As Chapter 5 explained, the strategy chosen placed a particular premium on ASEAN's 'image' because of the disjuncture between its reformist agenda and the entrenched nature of illiberal rule in the region. The second aspect, however, relates to state managers' efforts to restore their domestic hegemony in the wake of the crisis. As Chapter 5 also explored, dominant forces in key states like Malaysia and Indonesia faced severe challenges and were compelled to adopt reformist, quasi-liberal postures on some issues not simply to project an image to foreigners but also to cultivate legitimacy at home. Without grasping these developments, it becomes difficult to understand why ASEAN often appears so obsessed with its reputation and why it has become so susceptible to what is usually simply glossed in the literature as 'external pressure'. It is also difficult to explain variations within ASEAN without reference to the different social conflicts and interests underpinning the trajectories of particular regimes, which requires going beyond brief references to Indonesian democratisation (e.g. Haacke, 2005; Acharya, 2009a, p. 255).

In the immediate post-Depayin situation, ASEAN clearly acted to pre-empt the inevitable international reaction which would severely threaten its international standing. In the months that followed, the SPDC showed no sign of releasing Suu Kyi. Western powers, facing the prospect of Burma taking over the chairmanship of ASEAN in 2006, ratcheted up the pressure, threatening to boycott ASEAN altogether. In 2004, the EU cancelled ASEM finance and economic ministerial meetings, and the ASEM leaders' summit was only salvaged by the Vietnamese foreign minister's assurance that 'ASEAN is trying to democratise Myanmar' (Kyodo, 2004). However, the EU still insisted on various political conditions being met before they would accept Burma chairing ASEAN. US officials also threatened to boycott ASEAN meetings, disrupt trade between ASEAN and Western countries, and terminate funding for regional development projects, with US senators even raising the spectre of secondary sanctions on other ASEAN states.

The chairmanship crisis helped to revive the notion of a 'regional interest', first mooted during the Cold War. As Singapore's foreign minister put it, Burma's 'domestic politics and our interests as a regional grouping have been intertwined' (Yeo, 2005). At stake here was ASEAN's continued ability as a diplomatic community to mediate between the region's weak states and the external powers whose engagement was vital for the political and economic strategies being pursued by ASEAN state managers. A renewed Western boycott could be fatal to ASEAN's credibility and legitimacy as an international interlocutor. Also at stake were economic interests in key member-states which had previously enjoyed cosy relations with Burma. Singapore was deeply concerned about possible US sanctions against its financial centres because of their involvement in laundering Burmese generals' money, and openly distanced itself from the regime (Jones, 2008, p. 285). Even Thaksin felt a need to act in order to preserve good relations with the US. He had been forced into condemning the Depayin massacre in a joint statement with President Bush in order to salvage talks on a US-Thai free trade agreement. In July 2003, his foreign minister also drafted a 'roadmap' for Burma's transition to democracy and convened an international conference to gain foreign support for the idea – apparently without even consulting the Burmese (Jones, 2008, p. 280). The SPDC reacted frostily to this blatant act of interference, issuing its own 'roadmap' instead.

While the international threat to ASEAN's 'credibility' was the main consideration for ASEAN states after Depayin, there was also unprecedented domestic mobilisation over Burma at this time (L. Jones, 2009). In 2004 and 2005, liberal opposition-party legislators formed national caucuses on Burma in Malaysia, Indonesia, the Philippines, Thailand, Singapore and Cambodia, which were networked as the ASEAN Inter-Parliamentary Myanmar Caucus (AIPMC). AIPMC members began agitating against the SPDC in their respective parliaments, national media, and international forums like the Inter-Parliamentary Union. They urged ASEAN to deprive Burma of the chairmanship and to take a more liberal-interventionist stance to bring about democratic change there. The very fact that vocal opponents of a fellow ASEAN government were able to organise not only in their territories but within their own states is highly significant. It contrasts starkly to the forcible repression of the non-governmental APCET less than a decade previously, and illustrates how weakly 'non-interference' was now being applied to Burma.

The AIPMC's influence varied considerably across the ASEAN states, depending on the domestic balance of forces and the presence or absence of oligarchic interests in Burma. The AIPMC's campaign was strongest in the Philippines and Indonesia. As Chapter 5 explained, these states remain dominated by oligarchic forces whose commitment to liberal values is often tenuous. However, since these elements no longer had any significant interests at stake in Burma, they had more to gain domestically and internationally by burnishing their liberal-democratic credentials through criticising the SPDC publicly, as reformist liberals were demanding. Political space was thus available in these states for a vocal minority to campaign on this specific issue, creating additional pressure to 'do something' about Burma. President Arroyo consequently opposed publicly Burma's chairmanship of ASEAN. President Yudhoyono concurred, and also offered to help mediate a solution to Burma's internal political deadlock.

In the other ASEAN states, domestic mobilisation over Burma was far less significant, but nonetheless illustrated the dilemmas that Burma was creating for oligarchic rule in the region. The Singaporean, Cambodian and (until very recently) Malaysian legislatures have long been little more than rubber stamps for authoritarian executives. The Singaporean state strategically relaxed domestic political space to allow a caucus on Burma to form, even encouraging the AIPMC in other countries. However, it rigidly policed this space to ensure that it would not be exploited by domestic opposition groups to draw parallels between PAP and SPDC rule. The purpose of this move was simply to vent the elite's frustration with the Burmese regime and so distance Singapore from it in order to satisfy ASEAN's Western dialogue partners. As one AIPMC member explained, 'a lot of ASEAN leaders, foreign ministers, [were already] very cheesed off with the attitude of Burma... the AIPMC... helped these leaders to let out their frustrations openly' (Kok, 2008). Similar motives obtained in Cambodia. In neither state did the caucuses exercise any independent influence.

In Malaysia, the emergence of the caucus was more significant. It was allowed to form as part of Prime Minister Abdullah's attempts to relegitimise UMNO rule by emphasising democracy, 'good governance' and institutional reforms. However, the space granted to opposition legislators remained limited. Because Malaysian politico-business elites and even the state oil company retained significant interests in Burma, the caucus was not even permitted to call for sanctions against the country. In Thailand, oligarchic interests in Burma were even more deeply entrenched, and TRT's parliamentary dominance ensured that the tiny anti-Burma caucus was thoroughly marginalised. These differences again underline the difficulty of trying to explain ASEAN policies by reference to an 'ideational divide between the authoritarian and relatively democratic members of ASEAN' (Roberts, 2010, p. 230).

As it became clear from 2004–2005 that the SPDC was unable or unwilling to make significant progress on its 'roadmap', ASEAN leaders and ministers publicly stated that Burma must prioritise the 'regional interest' by relinquishing its turn to chair the Association (AltSEAN, 2005). Muted demurrals from Cambodia and Laos were overridden and Burma was thus effectively stripped of the chairmanship. ASEAN ministers thanked the SPDC 'for not allowing its national preoccupation to affect ASEAN's solidarity and cohesiveness' and showing 'its commitment to the well-being of ASEAN and its goal of advancing the interest of all Member Countries' (ASEAN, 2005b).

ASEAN's refusal to tolerate setbacks in Burma's 'national reconciliation' and its determination to govern this issue regionally reflected the region's transformation since the Asian crisis. Internationally, ASEAN had been badly weakened and forced into significant compromises *vis-à-vis* Western states. Domestically, several key states had undergone hegemonic crises which had compelled shifts in governance which granted more space to liberalising socio-political forces. Meanwhile, oligarchic interest in defending Burma had declined in various ways and was overridden by the larger imperative of maintaining sound economic relations with the US and, to a lesser extent, Europe. In the face of these imperatives, 'non-interference' was violated in many ways: demanding the release of the opposition leader and progress towards 'national reconciliation', proposing a roadmap for Burma's transition to democracy, offering to mediate in Burma's internal conflicts, and permitting domestic opponents of the SPDC to mobilise within ASEAN states. Scholars concerned to emphasise continuity in ASEAN's diplomatic culture downplay these events, emphasising that these measures were not all collectively agreed to, or claiming that neither discussion nor formal admonition constituted breaches of non-interference (Haacke, 2005, pp. 197–8). However, this is simply unpersuasive in light of the extremely restrictive understanding of sovereignty typically advanced by ASEAN policymakers and scholars. Indeed, challenged to defend such actions in light of ASEAN's non-interference principle, Malaysia's foreign minister summed up the implications of this period thusly: 'there is no such thing as absolute non-interference' (NST, 2005).

New crises, attempted interventions and the ASEAN charter

Unfortunately for ASEAN, the chairmanship crisis was just the first in a series of serious crises for Burma and the Association. In 2005, Burma was brought before the UN Security Council; in 2007 the regime drew fierce international condemnation for suppressing the 'saffron revolution', a mass protest movement led by Buddhist monks; and in 2008 the SPDC was denounced and threatened with humanitarian intervention for its response to Cyclone Nargis, which devastated large parts of the country. The regime's inability to manage domestic conflict without damaging the 'regional interest' has enraged ASEAN leaders. However, as much as some member-states wished to wash their hands of Burma, ASEAN has been forced to continue trying to intervene in the country's internal affairs to safeguard its own credibility. The regime's intransigent reaction has led core ASEAN states to promote institutional mechanisms to force Burma to give more consideration to their interests. These have included the ASEAN Charter, an ASEAN human rights mechanism, and the dilution of 'non-interference'. However, thus far no workable consensus has emerged, leaving all hopes staked on the outcome of the 2010 elections.

The first post-chairmanship crisis came in November 2005 when the US indicated that it would push for the UN Security Council to debate the situation in Burma. Far from adhering to non-interference, the Philippines, then a non-permanent Council member, agreed to help table a resolution. In response to Burma's plea for ASEAN support, ASEAN sent Syed Hamid to Rangoon to extract concessions from the SPDC, such as the release of Aung San Suu Kyi, to provide 'ammunition' to defend it. However, the SPDC denied him access to the country until March 2006, and no concessions were offered. Consequently, Malaysia and Singapore proposed simply abandoning Burma, and ASEAN did nothing whatsoever to defend it at the UN. A resolution, tabled in January 2007, was eventually vetoed by China and Russia. However, Indonesia, by then a non-permanent member, merely abstained. Jakarta's ambassador explained that while ASEAN did not see Burma as a threat to international security, Indonesia 'and all its fellow members of ASEAN share[d the resolution's] goals... Myanmar must respond to the imperative of restoring democracy and respect for human rights... we will do everything in our power... to bring about positive change in Myanmar'.[4]

Far from rallying around Burma to defend it from external interference, ASEAN states responded to the threat of UN intervention by re-launching their own attempts to intervene. Again, the reason for this was the fear that ASEAN might otherwise be eclipsed. The 2006 summit communiqué emphasised 'the need to preserve ASEAN's credibility as an effective organisation by demonstrating a capacity to manage important issues within the region' (ASEAN, 2007a). The hope was that the brush with the Security Council would frighten the SPDC into finally cooperating with ASEAN. As Syed Hamid warned the regime, to avoid the further 'internationalisation' of its internal affairs, Burma must 'show its readiness to give ASEAN a role to play' (Bernama, 2007). Essentially, the SPDC was being offered the choice of expanding the scope of its internal politics to include the region, or risk it being forcibly expanded to the global level by more hostile extra-regional actors.

In the quest for a 'role to play' for ASEAN, Indonesia has led the way. Prior to the Security Council vote, President Yudhoyono visited Burma to suggest deploying ASEAN monitors in the country, similar to those used in Aceh. After the vote, Yudhoyono also unsuccessfully proposed that an ASEAN troika be deployed in Burma. Foreign Minister Wirayuda next suggested that the junta organise a five-year power-sharing agreement with the opposition to enable a transition to democracy, later proposing revisions to the draft constitution to accommodate the interests of the NLD and the ethnic minorities (Haacke, 2008, p. 363). With these proposals falling flat, in late 2007 Yudhoyono appointed two special envoys to Burma in the explicit hope of securing a mediating role for Jakarta similar to its position during the Cambodian conflict. As Yudhoyono emphasised, it was Indonesia's lack of 'economic interests' in Burma, in contrast to Thailand, Singapore and Malaysia, which enabled it to push for this role (Jakarta Post, 2007). As Haacke (2008, pp. 368–9) points out, however, there are significant differences between Cambodia in the 1980s and Burma today. While ASEAN exercised considerable leverage over Cambodia in the 1980s and 1990s due to its sponsorship of armed resistance movements, its diplomatic centrality, and its alignment with relevant great powers, it has no comparable leverage over Burma. ASEAN has therefore been unable to compel the SPDC to accept its interventionist approaches. Indonesian diplomats and state-linked think tanks have also been directed to lobby India and China to apply pressure on the SPDC, without much visible success (Soesastro, 2008). Despite these repeated violation of ASEAN norms of non-interference and regional autonomy from the great powers, ASEAN has not been able to force Burma to give it a 'role to play'.

Although Burma's persistent refusal to regionalise its internal affairs has led some member-states to propose abandoning the regime, ASEAN has been unable to disengage due to its credibility as a regional organisation being bound up with Burma's internal affairs. Singapore, for example, has long argued that since the regime will not change its ways, Burma should simply be left to the UN and that ASEAN should persuade the West to focus instead on trade and investment. However, as chair of ASEAN in 2007, Singapore was forced to coordinate a response to the SPDC's violent suppression of the 'saffron revolution', a mass protest movement led by Buddhist monks that erupted in August and September 2007. Realising that to stand aloof amid the resultant international outcry would have severely tarnished ASEAN's image, Singapore felt compelled to organise a collective response. In a joint statement, the ASEAN foreign ministers stated that they were 'appalled to receive reports of automatic weapons being used' and 'demand[ed] that the Myanmar government immediately desist', restart national reconciliation and cooperate with the UN. The usual logic applied: ASEAN elites 'expressed their revulsion' due to the 'serious impact on the reputation and credibility of ASEAN' (ASEAN, 2007b). As Roberts (2010, p. 156) rightly observes, the statement breached 'the three primary principles of the ASEAN Way (sovereignty, non-interference, and consensus)'. However, Singapore was unable to go much further. Foreign Minister Yeo held talks with Chinese officials, who promised to follow a 'constructive' ASEAN lead (Chong, 2008). Yet, when Singapore invited the UN special envoy on Burma to brief the ASEAN-organised East Asia Summit later that year, China threatened to boycott the event, earning Singapore sharp rebukes from Malaysia and Indonesia.

The third crisis to hit Burma and the region in recent years was the impact of Cyclone Nargis, which struck the Irrawaddy delta region in May 2008, unhappily coinciding with a referendum on Burma's new constitution. Nargis devastated the area, killing at least 140,000 people and affecting 2.4 million others, rendering many homeless and creating $4.1bn-worth of damage. The scale of the devastation was comparable to that caused by the Asian tsunami, but in stark contrast to Indonesia's cooperation with external relief efforts, the SPDC refused to admit foreign aid workers into the country at such a critical political moment. Outraged Western journalists and governments blasted the regime, with some invoking the 'responsibility to protect' doctrine and calling for humanitarian intervention. Again, ASEAN was forced to try to govern this domestic catastrophe regionally in order to safeguard its image. As Surin Pitsuwan – by now the Association's secretary-general – put it, 'many lives were at stake, and so was ASEAN's reputation' (Surin, 2009, p. xx). ASEAN despatched an Emergency Rapid Assessment Team to Burma, which reported that the government's relief efforts were 'inadequate', and that 'urgent attention and support from the international community' was required (ASEAN, 2008a). An emergency AMM endorsed the report, instructing Burma to 'allow more international relief workers into the stricken areas'. In exchange, ASEAN would head up a 'humanitarian task force', to mediate between the regime, the UN and Western states, to ensure that aid 'should not be politicised' (ASEAN, 2008c).

ASEAN's efforts were limited by its own capacities and the SPDC's defensive response, but nonetheless significantly assisted the Burmese recovery. Sadly, Western governments' volubility was not matched by generosity: only $303m was raised at a donors' conference in July 2008 for immediate relief, and as of January 2010, only $215m more had been committed for long-term reconstruction. Nonetheless, in the immediate aftermath, the 'tripartite core group' of ASEAN, Burma and the UN delivered food aid to one million people, rebuilt 2,500 schools, provided emergency shelter for 1.7 million people, vaccinated 460,000 animals, and arranged over 2,000 visas for foreign aid workers (ASEAN, 2008d). ASEAN Volunteer Programmes remain in Burma running community-based recovery programmes. Whatever the shortcomings of these efforts, as Singapore's prime minister remarked, 'the situation is clearly better than if ASEAN had not intervened' (Lee, 2008). The choice of verb here seems not to be accidental. ASEAN has fairly paraded its post-Nargis intervention, with Surin (2008a) attacking those 'critical of ASEAN' by emphasising that 'we came in full force'.

These repeated crises have exposed and partly been driven by a violent tension between the imperatives forcing ASEAN to intervene in Burma and the SPDC's staunch resistance to giving the Association any role to play. In an attempt to resolve this tension, core ASEAN states have increasingly promoted institutional innovations to protect the 'regional interest' against the use of 'non-interference' by recalcitrant members. Key among these is the ASEAN Charter. ASEAN's deputy secretary-general describes the Charter as imposing a *'responsibility to cooperate'* in order to prevent 'non-interference' being invoked in a way that 'violate[s] the common interest of ASEAN as a whole'. It implies that 'every member must avoid hurting ASEAN's common interest, and cooperate with fellow members in efforts to resolve all situations, domestic or bilateral, that disturb regional peace and harmony or disrupt the Association' (Termsak, 2009, p. 123). The initial draft, produced in 2006 by an 'eminent persons group', sought to empower the grouping to discipline recalcitrant members by proposing the introduction of majority voting and sanctions mechanisms for non-compliance with ASEAN cooperation. These measures were clearly aimed at restricting the SPDC's use of regional norms to block attempts to widen the scope of Burma's domestic conflicts by governing them regionally. As one ASEAN official emphasised, while the Charter would 'govern everyone... the Myanmar issue was the trigger' (ST, 2005).

However, there were severe internal divisions within ASEAN over the Charter, reflecting the divergence in ASEAN state managers' political

and economic strategies since the Asian crisis and the increasing impossibility of reconciling these through inter-elite coordination. In addition to
imposing a 'responsibility to cooperate', the draft Charter made reference
to democracy, human rights, and 'good governance', and proposed creating an ASEAN human rights body. It thus formed part of core ASEAN
states' attempts to recover their domestic and external legitimacy in the
wake of the crisis. However, the newer member-states were less profoundly affected by the crisis, retained more crudely authoritarian governance arrangements and consequently feared that the new mechanisms
would be most likely to target them. Thus, in the talks held to draw up
the final version of the Charter, while the original member-states largely
backed the draft, Vietnam, Laos and Burma repeatedly threatened to walk
out unless it was diluted. Consequently, the proposals for sanctions
mechanisms and majority voting were scrapped (except, potentially, at
the leaders' summit level), and the human rights body was reduced to
an inter-governmental commission. The final document articulated commitments to democracy and human rights alongside traditional ASEAN
principles, including 'non-interference'. This indicated the failure of this
attempt to decisively resolve the conflict between member-state sovereignty on the one hand and their domestic legitimacy and the 'regional
interest' on the other.

Despite continued rhetorical commitment to non-interference as
a binding norm, however, ASEAN's conduct since the chairmanship
crisis has repeatedly violated that principle. ASEAN states have repeatedly intervened or tried to intervene in Burma to support their post-
crisis bid to regain domestic legitimacy and international credibility.
Since 2005, ASEAN states have left Burma isolated at the UN Security
Council, sent numerous special envoys to demand the release of opposition figures, tried on several occasions to deploy the ASEAN troika or
Aceh-style regional monitors, repeatedly demanded a role in Burma's
process of 'national reconciliation', encouraged extra-regional powers
to pressure the regime, and pressured the SPDC to admit foreign aid
in the wake of Cyclone Nargis. Faced with repeated resistance, other
member-states have tried to change ASEAN's procedures and norms
to enable them to exercise greater leverage over the regime. The failure
of these moves cannot, in light of successive attempts to interfere,
logically be attributed to the power of ASEAN's non-interference principle. Rather, it reflects the increasing difficulty that ASEAN states have
in reaching meaningful consensus, which ultimately flows from the
divergent pathways taken by ASEAN societies, economies and polities,
especially since the Asian crisis.

Concluding remarks

This chapter has argued that, far from clinging to 'non-interference' and doing nothing about the situation in Burma, ASEAN states have been promoting political and economic reforms there for the last two decades. While they have only ever promoted their own style of oligarchic 'democracy', reflecting the social bases of their own power, this does not detract from the fact that ASEAN states have repeatedly intervened, and sought to intervene further, in Burma's internal affairs. Their motivations have included a desire to gain access to Burmese markets, a fear that the Burmese state might collapse, suspicion of Chinese intentions, and a need to appease Western dialogue partners. The relative influence of these factors has clearly changed over time. In the period prior to the Asian crisis, the first three concerns overrode the last in the actual execution of policy. The interests of state-linked business groups were prioritised, strengthening the forces in Burma most opposed to genuine change. It is vital to recognise, however, that there were genuine efforts at 'Asian values'-style regime change in this period, because it is otherwise impossible to explain why ASEAN became so frustrated by the regime's inability or unwillingness to reform. Since the Asian crisis, the interests and power of state-linked business groups in relation to ASEAN's Burma policy has declined in various ways in many states. Indonesia, for example, has transformed from a political model and economic partner under Suharto to the state pushing hardest for an interventionist ASEAN role in Burma. Facing domestic legitimacy crises and significant geopolitical shifts that have severely diminished the region's political and economic allure, ASEAN states no longer feel able to simply defy the West over Burma as they did before the crisis. Even Thailand, where business relationships with Burma bucked the trend under Thaksin, was forced to prioritise its relations with the US and Europe in the wake of the Depayin massacre. Nonetheless, the continued persistence of oligarchic interests in places like Thailand complicate any effort to generalise on the basis of whether states are 'democratic' or not.

As noted earlier, the majority of scholars simply do not consider that ASEAN states have seriously tried to encourage political liberalisation in Burma, or would intervene further, given the chance. Even those who do concede some departure from non-interference often seem to minimise its significance. Haacke (2010, pp. 155, 161), for instance, states that 'ASEAN has not yet moved beyond collective criticism' and even argues that, since individual member-states' interventionist initiatives do not reflect regional consensus, 'ASEAN does not have a policy on Myanmar'.

While it is certainly true that ASEAN's corporate stance has lagged behind the initiatives of its most active members, over-emphasising this tends to downplay the significance of the events described above.

First, what ASEAN *has* been able to agree collectively clearly deviates starkly from the restrictive definitions of sovereignty and 'non-interference' typically provided by scholars and policymakers. Second, it is equally clear that ASEAN states feel decreasingly constrained by the 'ASEAN way' in formulating interventionist initiatives against troublesome neighbours. This contrasts with conventional treatments of ASEAN's diplomacy *vis-à-vis* Cambodia in the 1980s, which typically emphasises member-states' strained but ultimately successful adherence to the 'ASEAN way'. The inability of member-states to persuade everyone to adopt a coherent collective stance points not to the continued normative force of non-interference, but rather to the inability of inter-elite coordination to reconcile increasingly incompatible policy positions arising from the divergent trajectories of social conflict across the region.

Even in the absence of consensus, the consequences for ASEAN's sovereignty regime have been significant. While the balance of forces across ASEAN has not tilted decisively in favour of liberalising reformers, even entrenched and illiberal ruling groups have, to some extent, accepted the rationale behind Surin Pitsuwan's 'flexible engagement' proposal. That is, when the region is treated *en bloc* by investors and important external powers, the failure of any individual country to at least display 'mock compliance' with basic international norms will drag the rest down with it. For reformist elements, this should apply across the board as a permanent limitation on member-states' sovereign autonomy. However, the pressure on ASEAN's ruling forces to implement more internationally-acceptable forms of governance, and their capacity to do so, varies dramatically. This creates serious disagreements over the extent to which domestic politics should be subordinated to the so-called 'regional interest'. Consequently, the tension between member-state sovereignty and ASEAN's post-crisis reform process has not been neatly resolved, nor is it likely to be. Rather, it is likely to play itself out in a messy, inconclusive fashion for some time to come.

Conclusions

This study has critically investigated the theory and practice of non-interference in Southeast Asia. Rejecting the dominant consensus in the existing scholarly and journalistic commentary on ASEAN, it has shown that ASEAN members have frequently violated the sovereignty of other Southeast Asian states. However, it has not simply tried to debunk non-interference by citing these violations as proof of ASEAN's 'organised hypocrisy'. Rather, it provided an analytical approach that both recognises the existence of historical sovereignty regimes and enables us to explain when non-interference is transgressed and respected. Sovereignty was theorised as a strategic device, a technology of power used by dominant social forces within ASEAN states to control the scope of political conflicts and to uphold particular forms of social, economic and political order. ASEAN's sovereignty regime can only be properly understood in relation to the social conflicts underpinning ASEAN states, and the wider context of economic and geopolitical transformation in which they are embedded. The historical survey of ASEAN's sovereignty regime since its inception to the present day falsified the notion of 'non-interference' as a timeless, unchanging norm, showing that the principle is actually relatively dynamic, shifting in terms of its content and application as the nature of state power and the challenges faced by state managers have evolved. This concluding chapter sums up the research findings and draws out the implications for our understanding of sovereignty and Southeast Asian politics.

Summary of findings

Part I considered ASEAN and (non)interference during the Cold War. Here the key dynamic of social conflict was between forces committed to upholding the capitalist *status quo*, and those dedicated to its over-throw. ASEAN was founded only when the former had gained ascendancy in all its member-states. 'Non-interference' in this context was an inter-elite pact designed to bolster capitalist social order in two main ways. First, interstate conflict within ASEAN would be managed to avoid creating instability that could be exploited by leftist forces from within and outside the region. Second, 'non-interference' sought to insulate domestic leftists from external sources of support and thus contain domestic social conflict to a level at which the forces of the *status quo* could successfully manage it. Interventions in this period served the same fundamental purpose of conserving non-communist order. Within ASEAN, member-states joined forces to suppress separatist and communist insurgents, while outside ASEAN, a series of 'containment' operations were launched against leftist forces, often in league with external great powers, in Burma, East Timor and Indochina.

ASEAN's Cold War sovereignty regime thus displayed a relatively clear pattern in which intervention and non-intervention expressed a singular logic – the defence of non-communist social order. A politics of scope was at work in which embattled, pro-capitalist elites sought to police the bounds of acceptable politics, denying external support to leftist forces while often welcoming Western intervention and support for their own state projects. Because this anti-communist logic was integrated into the wider context of the Cold War, ASEAN state managers' economic and geopolitical strategies were closely aligned.

By contrast, in the post-Cold War period, considered in part two of the book, the situation was increasingly complicated. ASEAN societies became more varied and the economic and strategic context more fluid and complex, producing contradictory demands on ASEAN states. Over time, the theory and practice of non-interference has consequently become less coherent, often evolving in response to crises. As competing power centres emerged within increasingly variegated ruling classes, struggles emerged over what sort of sovereignty regime should prevail. Interventions designed to promote the immediate interests of powerful forces continued. Increasingly, however, the need for intervention related in a far more mediated fashion to the interests of state managers. Interventions are increasingly launched to defend ASEAN's 'reputation' with external powers – which in turn is required for the success of post-crisis economic accumulation and hegemonic political strategies.

In the period from the end of the Cold War to the Asian financial crisis, a fairly clear picture emerges. The defeat of communism rendered many Cold War-era interventions obsolete. The politically ascendant 'new rich' pushed for these interventions to be terminated, promoting instead the export of ASEAN capital and governance techniques into the CLMV states. Non-interference remained a crucial means by which state managers sought to control the scope of political conflict. Combined with rhetoric around 'Asian values', it was used to insulate domestic opponents from sources of external support in the threatening context of the West's 'new interventionism'. 'Non-interference' was also used to police the regional agenda, to exclude Western concerns and initiatives that might undermine the illiberal and opaque oligarchic networks that now constituted state power.

However, serious social and political contradictions nonetheless created divergences from non-interference in this period. Reflecting the non-coherence of states, established military-business networks, unwilling to relinquish their lucrative relationships with Cambodian and Burmese rebel groups, continued interfering in those countries' affairs. In Cambodia this contributed, along with rivalry over the influx of state-mediated ASEAN investment, to the coalition government's collapse in 1997. ASEAN intervened to restore the coalition largely out of a sense of ownership derived from its previous interventions in Cambodia, upon which its international political standing had largely been established. This standing is always premised to some extent on displaying a capacity to manage regional problems, especially those of interest to powerful external dialogue partners. This imperative also helps explain ASEAN's promotion of reforms in Burma under the rubric of 'constructive engagement', though the limits of this policy were always set by entrenched politico-business interests.

Another important contradiction in this period was that while democratisation processes had largely benefited elite social groups, they had also opened up some space for liberalising forces to attack the *status quo*. Opponents of Indonesia's occupation of East Timor sought to exploit this space by mobilising support in ASEAN states. To avoid the scope of the Timor conflict widening to the regional level, Jakarta resorted to crude coercion, mediated through emerging regional business networks, to ensure that 'non-interference' prevailed. The struggles over APCET indicated again the importance of inter-elite conflicts in shaping the region's sovereignty regime.

The Asian financial crisis had a profound impact on ASEAN, throwing the societies, economies and polities of core member-states into deep disarray and exposing the hollowness of ASEAN's pretensions to manage regional order. By propelling middle-class reformers to power in Thailand, the crisis generated demands for a change to non-interference. However, as protests like the *reformasi* movement spread across the region, state managers in a number of key ASEAN states rediscovered the value of 'non-interference' as a means of containing conflict territorially. There was thus little immediate shift in ASEAN's *official* non-interference principle. In practice, however, interventionist behaviour persisted. Thailand's new government spearheaded a more coercive, interventionist approach towards Burma.

Moreover, ASEAN states found that intervention, as well as non-intervention, remained crucial in containing the scope of socio-political unrest. Following the humanitarian crisis in East Timor in 1999, the core ASEAN states, fearing the contagion of economic, social and political unrest from a potentially disintegrating Indonesia, moved to contain it by promoting and joining a humanitarian intervention force. Intervention was thus used to help maintain territorially-based power within Indonesia and limit the spread of its domestic unrest, helping to contain conflicts elsewhere, such as in Mindanao. Not since the days of shared anti-communist struggle had ASEAN's social orders appeared so interdependent. However, this intra-elite sense of collective destiny did not extend to the CLMV states, whose societies were relatively insulated from the Asian crisis and events in Indonesia. This precluded a corporate response, foreshadowing future limitations on ASEAN's development. ASEAN's sovereignty regime was becoming increasingly uneven and incoherent, evolving in response to crises.

The Asian crisis severely dented the performance legitimacy of core ASEAN states and profoundly damaged its international standing. In its long shadow, dominant forces have had to find new ways to recast their hegemony and re-engage external dialogue partners and investors. The worst-affected ASEAN governments have increasingly embraced the rhetoric of 'good governance', democracy and human rights, seeking to relegitimise oligarchic rule but within terms borrowed from the West and favoured by their own reformist, middle-class constituents. ASEAN discourse has also been reworked to emphasise the region's supposed compliance with the norms of governance favoured by institutions like the World Bank. Although much of the new discourse is 'mock compliance', there are nonetheless powerful domestic and international imperatives to rejuvenate ASEAN's image in this way. The contradiction between ASEAN's reformist ambitions and the reality of regional governance, however, tends to create recurrent challenges for the credibility of the Association's post-crisis commitments which are experienced by state managers as acute threats to ASEAN's image and reputation.

Indeed, this contradiction now appears to be the main force driving developments in ASEAN's sovereignty regime. Whenever domestic or bilateral issues bring ASEAN states' domestic or international standing into disrepute, key ASEAN states now regularly push for the issues to be governed at the regional level, regardless of 'non-interference'. This is true of recent unrest in Thailand, the Thai-Cambodia border dispute and, of course, Burma. Having linked their reputations directly to Burma's democratisation, ASEAN states have repeatedly tried to try to insert themselves into Burma's internal affairs to promote domestic reforms to assuage key Western powers and reformist elements in their own societies. They have even sought to rebalance the rights and responsibilities of ASEAN membership, proposing a regional Charter that would weaken the protections of 'non-interference' and compel the regime to cooperate.

The failure of this attempt to institutionalise a 'regional interest' to which national interests can be subjugated indicates a profound absence of consensus among ASEAN's ruling elites. The significant divergences in processes of social conflict across the region, particularly since the financial crisis, have generated divergent policy positions that are increasingly difficult, if not impossible, to reconcile through inter-elite coordination. During the Cold War, a 'regional interest' emerged organically from a shared anti-communist struggle. Because ASEAN's ruling classes believed that the stability of neighbouring states was crucial to maintaining their own non-communist social orders, they were prepared to make sacrifices and compromise with their counterparts. These conditions no longer obtain. Most regional governments concur on the need for ASEAN to maintain its coherence and relevance so as to maintain the collective bargaining advantages of a diplomatic community. However, the degree of consensus on what this means in practice is very limited. State managers in core ASEAN states also clearly feel that their social orders, economies and political fates are, to some degree, interdependent. But this assessment is not shared to a significant degree among CLMV states' ruling groups. They did not feel particularly threatened by the likely outflows of the crisis in East Timor. They lack the reformist opposition groups that have compelled the core ASEAN states into 'good governance' reforms. They have historically benefited far less from ASEAN than its founding members, and have even been the targets of ASEAN interventions. They are therefore far less convinced of the need to subordinate their basic interest in containing struggles over power and resources within their territorial borders to some supposed 'regional interest'. Consequently, ASEAN's sovereignty regime is increasingly variegated, uneven and incoherent, evolving largely in response to crises. We will consider some of the implications of this in the third section, below.

Despite this incoherence, it is interesting to compare ASEAN's evolving sovereignty regime with the sort of regime promoted by powerful Western states. Typically, scholars emphasise the divergence between ASEAN's desperate attempts to cling onto Westphalian sovereignty and the West's attempts to promote liberal global governance, democracy, and human rights (Stubbs, 2008). While not wishing to claim that there is no conflict between ASEAN and Western agendas, arguably this clash is somewhat overstated. First, it is clear that the core ASEAN states, at least, do not hold to a rigid, 'Westphalian' view of sovereignty in all circumstances. The ASEAN Charter, the attempt to subordinate member-states' interests to a 'regional interest', and the creation of a regional human rights body, indicate attempts to ensure that domestic governance conforms to basic 'international' (i.e., Western) standards. This is done for instrumental reasons – to shore up domestic hegemony and maintain good external relations – and is constrained even in core states by powerful, entrenched interests. Nonetheless, this expresses the belief that the region should be involved in embedding certain governance standards within member-states. This can also be seen, for example, in ASEAN's efforts to govern financial risks (Nesadurai, 2009b). Regionalism is thus still being used to entrench a particular socio-political order within ASEAN countries. Today, the key expectation of ASEAN states towards each other appears to be that they govern their territories in such a way as to maintain political stability and prevent the contagion of domestic problems to the wider region, either directly, through transnational flows of refugees, drugs, etc, or indirectly, through creating domestic or international difficulties for ASEAN states.

How different is this from the contemporary agenda of Western powers? Arguably, the view of divergence between the West and ASEAN is based on a misreading of Western policy and instruments like the 'responsibility to protect' (R2P). Liberal advocates of the R2P imagine that it is primarily about enforcing human rights norms and enabling external forces (i.e., Western states) to intervene when they are violated. From this perspective, Southeast Asia appears very divergent and retrograde. Arguably, however, the R2P actually expressed Western states' retreat from the early 1990s agenda of humanitarian intervention. By emphasising the responsibility of target states, it instead shifted the burden of improving humanitarian outcomes onto them, rather than interveners (Cunliffe, 2006). In practice, then, R2P seems to be about imposing responsibility on these governments to abide by international standards. While the convergence should not be overstated, and agreement will always be constrained by the divergent interests of powerful social forces, there is nonetheless a parallel here with ASEAN practice. One recent article has even analysed the response to Cyclone Nargis as evidence of the R2P in action (Bellamy and Beeson, 2010).

Moreover, in contemporary Western practice, state-building interventions have eclipsed humanitarian ones. These interventions aim to construct states that serve international interests by robustly governing their territories, suppressing insurgency and terrorism, and preventing the 'spill-over' of other transnational 'security threats' from potentially risky, ungoverned spaces (Hameiri, 2010). This is increasingly achieved by embedding international regulations and regulatory agencies within the apparatuses of target states. Particularly since 9/11, the emphasis has shifted decisively from promoting human rights and democracy to promoting stability above all else, and containing (potential) transnational 'threats' within territorial borders. Again, there are perhaps parallels here with ASEAN's attempts to impose a 'responsibility to cooperate' and to manage issues with transnational or international repercussions at the regional level. Again, the extent to which this actually occurs or succeeds always depends on the entrenched interests at play in any given situation, but this applies as much to Western interventions as to ASEAN ones. There are therefore some tantalising parallels between the global sovereignty regime being promoted by Western powers and the regional sovereignty regime preferred by at least some forces within key ASEAN states. More research could uncover greater overlaps than these preliminary remarks can do justice to.

These findings illustrate the usefulness of operating both with an expansive definition of intervention, and a disaggregated understanding of the state. Widening our view of intervention to encompass non-military actions has uncovered a range of means by which states meddle in each other's affairs, many of which would not be captured by narrow definitions. Disaggregating the state, moreover, illustrated how international politics is not simply a matter of interactions between states, conceived of as coherent unitary actors pursuing a 'national interest' or possessing a singular 'identity', as realists and constructivists suggest. Rather, it is profoundly affected by conflicts within and between state apparatuses, transnational relations between classes, class fractions and other social forces, and the instrumental use of parts of the state by powerful social groups, as well as inter-elite conflicts between states. Social conflict within states can give rise to interventionist practices, including by specific parts of state apparatuses in combination with forces formally outside the state, further complicating a region's *de facto* sovereignty regime. More broadly, the 'social conflict' approach shows how the nature of state power fundamentally shapes the conduct of foreign policy. The dominant role of capitalist elites in constituting state power in Southeast Asia gives rise to forms of intervention that traditional IR theory would simply not expect to find, for example.

Implications for understanding 'non-interference' and norms

What does the finding that ASEAN states have frequently engaged in violations of non-interference imply for how we understand of the Association's 'norm of non-interference', and indeed norms in international politics more broadly? This section argues that that, while the constructivist understanding of norms is simply unsustainable, this does not imply a realist disavowal of the importance of institutions, rules or ideologies. Instead, an approach is required that is sophisticated enough to take account of ideas and interests, since both are implicated in any social situation.

The findings and argument of this book are likely to be most difficult for constructivist scholars to accept. They may still wish to argue that the evidence of ASEAN states' interventionist behaviour does not necessarily disprove their claim that the non-interference principle has played a crucial role in Southeast Asian regionalism. On one level, this is an entirely valid argument. I have *not* claimed that the adoption of 'non-interference' was simply a sham, with no consequences. On the contrary, at key moments it has been a very important technology of power for ASEAN's dominant social forces. Essentially, it has been a pact of mutual survival among social forces faced with threats to their social, economic and political power. This pact long helped channel ASEAN cooperation down lines that reinforced rather than undermined these forces' domination, such as cross-border security pacts, counterinsurgency cooperation, denying territory or political space to social groups contesting state power, and so on. This is still relevant today, since there remain active challenges to the profoundly unequal and frequently oppressive power relations that characterise state power in Southeast Asia. Thailand and Indonesia, for example, have both tried to intervene in Burma's domestic politics in recent years, but have forcefully resisted attempts to discuss the violence in southern Thailand or the regional governance of 'haze' arising from Indonesian forest fires. Clearly, 'non-interference' could not perform its strategic function of limiting the scope of conflicts if it was simply a hollow bit of rhetoric.

However, there is a stark contrast between this view and the constructivist theorisation of 'norms'. My argument suggests that the actual social practice of (non)interference is determined by the scope of agreement among and the ideologies, interests and strategies of ASEAN's dominant societal forces and the state managers operating on their behalf. The norm does not, therefore, operate independently to alter state behaviour. Rather, its operation is always determined by the broader social relations it remains embedded within. By contrast, in their quest to prove the frankly unobjectionable view that 'norms matter', many constructivists theorise norms as independent, active, agential subjects which can transform politics. Acharya (2009a, p. 26) claims, for example, that, 'once established, [norms] have a life of their own. Norms are not epiphenomenal or part of a superstructure shaped by material forces... They have an independent effect on state behaviour, redefining state interests and creating collective interests and identities'. Norms thus 'play a determining, rather than secondary, role in foreign policy interactions'. Similarly, Caballero-Anthony (2005, p. 39) proposes that norms 'translate into a social force and are socially causative. Ideas in short can be the driving force of history'.

In my view, there is very little historical evidence for this idealist view of norms. The gravity and frequency of violations of and even explicit attacks on ASEAN's norm of non-interference makes it logically impossible to argue that the norm has reconstituted member-states' identities and interests. Separating norms from the dynamic and unequal social relations in which they are located and positing them as an independent force in their own right leaves us with no explanatory resources to account for violations of norms. Discrepant evidence must therefore be either neglected, played down, or explained away using *ad hoc*, non-normative factors drawn from outside the constructivist theoretical framework. More pluralist constructivist accounts have tried to avoid this trap by making more modest claims about norms, positing their operation alongside geopolitics and domestic interests (Haacke, 2003, p. 13). To date, however, these factors are simply listed and invoked as convenient; they have not been integrated into a clear framework capable of specifying when and why norms operate. Norms continue to be theorised as discrete causal factors, rather than as elements within a broader set of dynamically evolving social power relations that condition how they operate.

A weaker version of constructivist scholarship might concede that norms may not 'constitute' state identities, but can at least independently 'regulate' state behaviour. Quentin Skinner argues that even if an agent is not motivated by the principles they profess, he will 'nevertheless be obliged to behave in such a way that his actions remain compatible with the claim that these principles genuinely motivate him'. This is because the agent possesses a 'standard motive for attempting to legitimate his untoward social or political actions' and to achieve this he must rely on an '*existing* range of favourable evaluative-descriptive terms' which is set by 'the prevailing morality of the society in which the agent is acting'. Consequently, 'he can only hope to legitimate a restricted range of actions' (Skinner, 1988, pp. 110–17). Some IR scholars have used this argument to suggest that state behaviour – including intervention – is norm-governed because of this concern for legitimacy (e.g. Wheeler, 2000). Do sovereignty norms regulate state behaviour in this way?

Clearly, state managers do often seek to legitimise interventions with recourse to prevailing moral standards. For example, the US and UK governments expended considerable resources trying to legitimise their 2003 invasion of Iraq by reference to international law, and their failure to do so incurred international and domestic costs. Constructivists are thus surely correct to criticise realists for simply dismissing 'logics of appropriateness' in favour of 'logics of consequences', as Krasner puts it. Arguably, however, this constructivist-realist debate over which 'logic' really 'matters' is couched in an unhelpful and unrealistic dichotomy, since both of these logics interrelate in a complex social whole.

Legitimacy is not simply an abstract language game, as Skinner seems to imply, but is always constituted within a set of unequal social power relations which condition a society's 'prevailing morality' (logic of appropriateness) and the costs of transgressing it (logic of consequences). To continue the example above, the US and UK stood a far greater chance of legitimising their invasion of Iraq than, say, Iraq did of legitimising its 1990 invasion of Kuwait, by virtue of being powerful states involved in interpreting international law and policing international politics as permanent members of the UN Security Council. The international costs they incurred for failing to do so were far less than those imposed on Iraq, either after 1990 or after 2003. Domestically, in neither the US nor the UK were anti-war movements able to inflict serious costs on the dominant forces occupying state power. This suggests that, as Stinchcombe (1968, p. 150) puts it, 'the person *over whom power is exercised* is not usually as important as *other power holders*' in determining standards of legitimacy and the costs of being seen as illegitimate.

From this perspective, ASEAN states have often been able to violate non-interference with relative impunity because those opposed to their actions have been relatively powerless. East Timor, Burma and the Indochinese states all protested ASEAN interference at various points, but their cries generally went unheeded. By contrast, more powerful states can successfully resist interference. The APCET imbroglio, for example, illustrated the Indonesian regime's capacity to shape the practice of non-interference through its very opposite (and the need to consider power relations within ASEAN far more closely than most scholars do). It was not until the US decisively withdrew its support in 1999 that the regime's ability to reject foreign intervention in East Timor collapsed. Similarly, while Thailand has been able to fend off external involvement in its domestic political crisis since 2006, Cambodia was too weak and dependent on foreign aid to do so in 1997. Domestic power relations are also important here. The APCET imbroglio counterpoised two forms of intervention, corresponding to two opposing sets of social forces. Ultimately the repressive intervention promoted by state-linked oligarchs trumped the liberalising intervention promoted by the reformist, middle-class civil society organisations, reflecting the power relations between these social forces. Similarly, the Thai Democrats' efforts to intervene in Burma and East Timor were curtailed by the resurgence of powerful oligarchic forces.

Domestic social conflicts thus not only give rise to particular forms of intervention, they also define the way in which 'legitimacy' concerns operate in practice. If ASEAN states represented the interests of social groups strongly ideologically opposed to intervention on a principled basis, they might struggle to legitimise interventionist behaviour. Generally, however, they do not. During the Cold War, leftist forces generally opposed counter-revolutionary interventions, and at the peak of their power in the mid-1970s they were able to compel changes in state policy, such as the closure of US bases in Thailand. Yet even then, establishment interests committed to suppressing the left predominated and promoted containment interventions in ASEAN's near abroad. Today, the main opposition groups in Southeast Asia are, in the vein of Western liberals, generally pro-interventionist, creating, if anything, difficulties for ASEAN states in legitimising *non*-intervention – as we saw in the case of the AIPMC. Essentially, then, if attaining legitimacy depends on 'the prevailing morality of the society' in which agents operate, to fully understand the role that legitimacy plays, we need to investigate not just the 'morality' but also 'the society'. Crucially, 'society' is not principally comprised of smooth 'socialisation' and 'interactions' between states conceived of as coherent units with their own identities, as constructivists suggest, but by gross inequalities in power and material resources possessed by real human subjects facing profound structural constraints.

The rejection of a constructivist theorisation of norms, however, should not imply an embrace of realism. Constructivists rightly argue that realists unduly downplay the importance of ideas and ideology. Yet, the answer is not to reify them as agential subjects standing outside of broader social relations as constructivists too often do. To understand the role of norms in international politics requires us to transcend the increasingly stale debate between realists and constructivists that dominates mainstream IR theory and particularly the study of ASEAN. Gramscian approaches provide a useful way forward because their starting point rejects the separation of ideational and material structures that is implicit in mainstream IR theory (Bieler, 2001). For Gramscians, ideas are part of an overall social structure and can thus only be meaningfully understood in relation to the interests, ideologies and strategies of particular social forces struggling against one another within concrete, complex and evolving social, economic and geopolitical contexts. From this perspective, ideas 'only become effective if they do, in the end, connect with a particular constellation of social forces' and 'ideological struggle is part of the general social struggle for mastery and leadership – in short, for hegemony' (Hall, 1986, p. 42).

On this view, the power of 'non-interference' to affect state behaviour does not emerge from its status as a 'cherished principle'; rather, this status is actually what needs explaining. I have argued that we can only understand ASEAN's *selective* attachment to non-interference in relation to the interests, ideologies and strategies of dominant social forces as they struggle against each other. Its content and application can thus only be grasped in relation to this social conflict, which is dynamic and historically evolving. Ideas do 'matter', but they are not agential forces standing outside history or above real human subjects.

Implications for understanding Southeast Asian regionalism

As the introductory chapter illustrated, scholars of all theoretical persuasions rely heavily on 'non-interference' to explain the development of Southeast Asian regionalism and regional states' behaviour. Although a few scholars recognise some limited evolution of the norm, the non-interference principle is generally seen as a stagnant, irritatingly obdurate drag on ASEAN's conduct and evolution, and even on ASEAN scholarship. Jörn Dosch (2006, p. 164) surely speaks for many in remarking that over the last two decades,

> despite the impressive volume of analysis, the discourse on Southeast Asian regionalism has not distinctly progressed. This is not surprising in view of the unchanging nature of the analytical object: ASEAN's lack of institutional evolution, and most member states' reluctance to touch upon the sensitive issue of national sovereignty, make it difficult for students of ASEAN to add any new and original findings to the debate.

This implies that existing scholarly interpretations of ASEAN are essentially correct and that, given the Association's own conservatism, everything that can reasonably be said about ASEAN has already been said. ASEAN states' boring refusal to intervene in each other's affairs translates into a boring academic consensus. However, if, as I have argued, ASEAN *has* intervened and is far from 'unchanging', then this consensus is misguided, and a great deal more scholarly work remains to be done. This section draws out the challenges this study poses for the subfield as a whole. It critiques the 'security community' view of ASEAN, proposing an alternative approach of 'contested regionalism', and critiques the use of 'non-interference' as a catch-all explanation, urging more sophisticated analyses of specific issue areas.

This study has serious implications for the view of ASEAN as a 'security community'. This is the claim that, having been socialised into regional norms and a regional identity, Southeast Asian states have developed sufficient 'we-feeling' to transcend international anarchy, making war among them essentially unthinkable. Although pioneered by constructivists, this view has been so widely adopted that even ostensibly realist scholars refer to ASEAN as a '*de facto* security community' (Chin, 2007, p. 397), and the 'ASEAN Security Community' was launched as an official regional project in 2004. However, according to the original progenitor of the 'security community' thesis, non-interference is 'the single most important principle underpinning ASEAN regionalism' (Acharya, 2009a, p. 57). If, as I have argued, this principle is rather flexible, it seriously calls into question the notion that ASEAN regionalism is ultimately built upon solid normative foundations and a quest for a regional identity.

Furthermore, the evidence considered in this study not only disproves the claim that ASEAN states have been 'socialised' into a norm of non-interference, but also casts doubt on other aspects of the 'ASEAN way'. In the process of violating non-interference, ASEAN states have also overturned other regional norms, such as the prohibition against the threat or use of force in resolving disputes. Indonesia, supposedly a key architect of the 'ASEAN way', has been a major violator. Examples include the crude bullying of its ASEAN partners over APCET, the threat to unleash Malaysian intervention against the Philippines to force President Marcos into signing TAC, and numerous threats against Singapore, including combining with Malaysia to threaten to sever the city-state's water supply. At such moments, other ASEAN states are almost being menaced by the implicit prospect of a return to *Konfrontasi*-esque conflict. During a 2005 territorial dispute with Malaysia in the Sulawesi Sea, for example, Indonesian protestors staged rallies, chanting the *Konfrontasi*-era slogan, 'crush Malaysia', the chair of the Indonesian parliament's foreign affairs and security committee demanded the expulsion of the Malaysian ambassador, and Jakarta despatched three warships to the disputed area with the president onboard. Of course, Indonesia is not the only violator of ASEAN norms. Thailand, for example, has also ignored the principle of the non-use of force *vis-à-vis* Burma and Cambodia. Further critical studies could seriously challenge the existing academic consensus on the 'ASEAN way' by questioning what determines its content and application in practice.[1]

One potential alternative to the 'security community' paradigm is the notion of 'contested regionalism', coined by Carroll and Sovacool (2010) in their recent analysis of the Trans-ASEAN Gas Pipeline Project. This project is supposed to be connecting ASEAN states into an integrated distribution network, to enhance regional harmony, international cooperation and energy security. The project's *goals* are shaped by the high-minded rhetoric and grand plans for cooperation issued by foreign ministry bureaucracies. However, in practice, the project's *outputs* are being powerfully shaped by entrenched relationships between state officials and business groups and the ideological context of economic development. Regionalism in practice is thus 'contested' because state power itself is contested and constrained by structural relationships. Indeed, we might more usefully think about multiple contending 'regionalisms', since different socio-political coalitions typically pursue very different region-building projects, with what emerges in practice being a function of conflicts between and among these coalitions. African regionalism has already been analysed in this way, generating exciting insights into the forces shaping international cooperation (Söderbaum, 2004).

Such insights can only emerge from careful and critical empirical research that insists on a social reality beyond the latest ASEAN communiqué, and disaggregates the state rather than taking it for granted as the basic unit of analysis. Realist critics Jones and Smith (2006, p. 100) rightly argue that a constructivist emphasis on norms, identity and consensus has 'deflected analytical attention' away from intra-ASEAN tensions and 'internal divisions' reflecting 'unresolved ethnic and religious dissonance and opaque networks of corruption and patronage'. However, realists' reluctance to elaborate the constitution of state power and its influence on international politics does not get us very far, either. Adopting the notion of 'contested regionalism' is one way of transcending the limitations of both constructivism and realism.

Viewing regionalism as a contested field would allow us to integrate the politics of scope discussed in this study into our understanding of regional governance. If, rather than assuming that states are coherent actors pursuing a singular region-making project, we emphasise their conflict-ridden and contested nature, regionalism in practice can be seen partly as a struggle between societal forces over the appropriate scale at which to govern particular issues. For example, Hameiri and Jayasuriya (2011) argue that a form of 'regulatory regionalism' is emerging in the Asia-Pacific. They suggest that elements of domestic state apparatuses are increasingly inter-penetrated with international, regional and national institutions in other countries, and are governing particular issue areas in accordance with regionally-agreed priorities and procedures – hence, 'regulatory regionalism'. This is a result of particular interests strategically shifting the governance of specific issues into a regional/international context, thereby insulating it from domestic contestation. Such moves may be resisted by other social forces and state apparatuses with a stake in restricting the scope of conflict over the issue. What emerges in practice is a function of these forces' struggles for power and control. From this perspective, regionalism is not simply a project pursued by states, nor is it a zero-sum game where states must give up authority to supra-national institutions for cooperation to emerge. Rather, regionalism can work through specific societal actors transforming states themselves. What emerges is not supra-national authority but a rescaling of governance to regional spaces located within the state or alongside domestic institutions. Thus, issues like monetary policy in East Asia are increasingly governed in a way that is simultaneously regional and national (Nesadurai, 2009b). Again, such transformations are only visible when adopting a non-statist ontology.

Final thoughts on 'non-interference'

Finally, I want to offer some reflections on 'non-interference' as an explanatory trope, and on the oft-repeated policy recommendation that ASEAN should dispense with non-interference. As the introductory chapter illustrated, ASEAN analysts often use 'non-interference' to explain virtually every limitation of the grouping, from its inability to discipline problematic member-states, to its inaction on transnational security threats. The present study suggests that this is unsustainable, and that scholars must seek deeper causes in the nature of state power in the region. Doing so would reveal that the usual policy recommendation produced by analysts – that ASEAN should abandon the non-interference principle – would not necessarily lead to greater regional peace and cooperation. Indeed, it might lead to the opposite outcome.

If, as I have argued, non-interference is much more flexible and selective than is commonly supposed, it can no longer serve as a convenient catch-all explanation for everything that critics consider to be wrong with ASEAN. For example, instead of blaming 'non-interference' for the lack of cooperation on transboundary 'haze' pollution, one would need to look instead at the entrenched relationships between agribusiness owners, corrupt officials and venal politicians in Indonesia that arguably constitute the real practical impediments to effective international cooperation (Tay, 2009). Some scholars appear implicitly to realise the importance of domestic power relations by, for example, suggesting that some state officials aiding and abetting piracy impedes effective regional cooperation against transnational crime. However, such insights are typically left undeveloped and tend to be accompanied by criticism of 'non-interference' (e.g. Emmers, 2003).

If these state-society relationships are crucial in setting the contours of state policy, then abolishing the non-interference principle, as virtually all commentators urge ASEAN to do, would not necessarily create the conditions necessary for effective regional cooperation. The assumption underlying such demands is apparently that if only state power could be unleashed internationally against a given problem, then the problem could be solved. But what if the problem is *caused* by the nature of state power itself? For example, a US Congressional Research Service Report (2009) recently accused both high- and low-ranking Malaysian officials of involvement in trafficking Burmese migrants. Similar accusations have been levelled at Thai officials. Here, people-trafficking is not a 'security threat' which confronts states, but is in part actually being *produced* by states themselves.

Non-interference, as a technology of power, is partly designed to avoid challenges to precisely this sort of interpenetration of state apparatuses and corrupt and predatory business interests. Abolishing the principle, however, would not automatically dissolve these deeply entrenched relationships. Interlinked and competing state-business networks and related problems, like the abuse of minority populations, are endemic in Southeast Asia. It is therefore by no means certain that exposing any single relationship to external scrutiny and/or attack would produce a cooperative or harmonious outcome. Those under attack might be defeated. However, they might instead work to push the state into isolation, as in Burma, or engage in tit-for-tat retaliation that could rapidly escalate into serious interstate tension, or even conflict. The shrill reaction of ASEAN state managers when their counterparts elsewhere stray into sensitive territory populated by entrenched state-business compacts suggests that the latter is a distinct possibility.

'Non-interference' is clearly designed to limit the scope of conflicts over power and resources to a level that privileges dominant social groups but also, as many conventional analyses of ASEAN often recognise, to a level that is relatively stable and manageable. Stability always privileges the forces of the *status quo* and is thus not automatically desirable. However, advocates of abolishing 'non-interference' need to recognise that what they are actually advocating is a dramatic widening of the scope of social and political conflict which could have unpredictable and even very destructive consequences. Moreover, although Southeast Asian states are not particularly democratically accountable to their own populations, they are nonetheless *always potentially* more accountable than foreign states or remote instruments of regional or global governance. Rescaling governance to the international level removes issues from even the possibility of democratic political contestation. It does not, therefore, have automatically progressive outcomes as many analysts and activists apparently assume.

Even if the networks constituting state power are not directly implicated in any given problem, abandoning 'non-interference' may still not aid in finding a solution. As Chapter 8 showed, ASEAN has tried a wide range of more or less coercive approaches to promote reform in Burma, without success. Despite continued criticism of the limitations of such efforts, it is unclear what more ASEAN could reasonably be expected to do. Calls for the Association to intervene more forcefully in Burma are really attempts to avoid confronting the weakness of foreign intervention as an instrument of political change. ASEAN is far from alone in failing in this respect: Western sanctions are generally judged to have had little effect, successive UN envoys have returned from Burma empty handed, and even the US has recently moderated its stance, hoping that the 2010 elections, however badly rigged, might eventually deliver political change. If, as this book has argued, state forms and state power stem principally from local socio-political struggles, albeit conditioned by global dynamics, the judgement of former UN envoy Razali Ismail (2008) seems fundamentally accurate here:

> External developments cannot bring about change in Myanmar. The job cannot be done by parties outside. For any true-blue trans-formation of society or country... they must have elements within the country willing to do certain things.

Similar judgements could well be made about other parts of the world, such as Iraq and Afghanistan, where the legacy of international inter-vention is even worse. As Western powers are painfully and all-too-slowly learning, democracy cannot be externally imposed on societies.

Contrary to the received wisdom, then, abandoning non-interference in Southeast Asia, rather than solving problems, might well exacerbate and multiply them. Sovereignty and non-interference are used stra-tegically, and are never neutral in the scoping effects they have on political conflict. However, altering the scope of conflict is not necess-arily any more progressive or productive than maintaining it. Indeed, many of the interventions documented in this book have had highly destructive effects. ASEAN's Cold War interventions fuelled insurgency and instability in its near abroad, and in the case of East Timor cost over 100,000 lives. ASEAN's 'constructive engagement' of Burma has, if anything, only helped to entrench military rule. Its post-Cold War meddling in Cambodia helped damage the economy, deepened the oppos-ition's dependency on foreign powers, and restored an unstable coalition that later degenerated anyway, as FUNCINPEC was outmanoeuvred by the CPP. ASEAN's contribution to INTERFET helped stabilise Indonesia and save lives in East Timor, but would have been unnecessary without the earlier Indonesian invasion that ASEAN and others had sanctioned. Moreover, the independent state of Timor-Leste has emerged as a fra-gile entity rife with internal conflicts, which seems unable to stand with-out permanent international involvement. External involvement in domestic problems seems to work best when it is limited to supporting local processes of conflict resolution, such as the Aceh Monitoring Mission, which helped implement a peace agreement to which both the government and rebel forces had already agreed. The capacity of external intervention to simply impose a settlement on domestic social conflicts seems very limited indeed.

Notes

Introduction

1 As Peou (2002) notes, Southeast Asian IR is peculiarly characterised by a significant overlap between realist and constructivist arguments.

Chapter 1   Theorising Sovereignty and Intervention

1 For more on the strategic disavowal of sovereignty, see Adler-Nissen and Gammeltoft (2008).
2 Singapore is a very rare case where society is indeed dominated by bureaucratic elites. However, this can only be explained by virtue of the deliberate and ongoing destruction and forcible disorganisation or co-optation of all rival social forces using a wide variety of coercive, institutional and ideological mechanisms (Rodan, 2006).
3 Etel Solingen (1998, 2004, 2005) similarly argues that regional orders are shaped by the 'grand strategies' of domestic coalitions. My approach differs from Solingen's in several ways. Solingen uses 'ideal type' notions of coalitions whose grand strategy is solely determined by their response to globalisation (which immediately breaks down when applied to ASEAN, leading to references to 'hybrid' coalitions); state institutions are depicted merely as (unexplained) 'constraints' on policy; and outcomes are explained through a rather sparse rational choice model. My approach, informed by historical sociology and Marxist state theory, is far less parsimonious, but is arguably better able to explain how and why coalitions and state power are socially constituted and change, and provides a more flexible framework to track historical developments.

Chapter 2   The Social Foundations of ASEAN and 'Non-Interference'

1 'Memorandum of Conversation', 23 July 1964 (Keefer, 2001, p. 584).
2 'The Huk Resurgence in the Philippines', CIA, 19 April 1967; 'Memorandum From Marshal Wright of the National Security Council Staff to the President's Special Assistant (Rostow)' (Keefer, 2001, pp. 771–2, 783).
3 'Memorandum of Conversation', 26 May 1970; 'Telegram From the Embassy in Indonesia to the Department of State', 29 July 1970 (Lawler, 2006, pp. 632, 578).
4 'Intelligence Note from the Director of the Bureau of Intelligence and Research to the Secretary of State', 26 March 1966; 'Action Memorandum from Assistant Secretary of State for East Asia and Pacific Affairs (Bill Bundy) to Secretary of State', 20 May 1966; 'Telegram from US Embassy in Manila

to Department of State', 25 July 1966 (Keefer, 2001, pp. 807–8, 813–14, 816–18).

5 'Telegram from Secretary of State Rogers to the Department of State', 5 August 1969 (Lawler, 2006, p. 589); 'Memorandum of Conversation', 5 July 1975 (State Department, 1975c).

6 'Memorandum of Conversation', 26 May 1970 (Lawler, 2006, pp. 640–1).

7 'Memorandum from Vice-President Humphrey to President Johnson', 19 October 1966 (Keefer, 2001, p. 636).

8 'Telegram from the Embassy in Indonesia to the Department of State', 2 April 1970 (Lawler, 2006, p. 617); 'Telegram from the Embassy in Indonesia to the Department of State', 15 April 1970 (Lawler, 2006, p. 619); 'Memorandum of Conversation', 26 May 1970 (Lawler, 2006, pp. 634–5); 'Memorandum of Conversation', 26 May 1970 (Lawler, 2006, pp. 640–1); 'Memorandum of Conversation', 1 July 1970 (Lawler, 2006, pp. 663–8); 'Memorandum from the Deputy Assistant to the President for National Security Affairs (Haig) to the President's Assistant for National Security Affairs (Kissinger)', 7 July 1970 (Lawler, 2006, pp. 668–9); 'Memorandum of Conversation', 8 July 1970 (Lawler, 2006, pp. 673–4); 'Indonesian Support to Cambodia', Top Secret Cable from State Department to US Embassy in Jakarta, 24 April 1970 (State Department, 1970).

9 'Telegram from Secretary of State Rogers to Department of State', 5 August 1969 (Lawler, 2006, p. 587).

10 'Telegram from the Embassy in Indonesia to the Department of State', 19 April 1970; 'Memorandum of Conversation', 26 May 1970 (Lawler, 2006, pp. 622, 634–5).

11 'Memorandum of Conversation', 29 July 1969 (Lawler, 2006, p. 39); 'Memorandum from the President's Assistant for National Security Affairs (Kissinger) to President Nixon', 20 October 1969 (Lawler, 2006, p. 66); 'Telegram from the Embassy in Thailand to the Department of State', 3 March 1970 (Lawler, 2006, p. 114); 'Memorandum from the President's Assistant for National Security Affairs (Kissinger) to President Nixon', 26 March 1970 (Lawler, 2006, pp. 122–3); 'Backchannel Message from the Under Secretary of State for Political Affairs (Johnson) to the Ambassador to Thailand (Unger)', 20 May 1970 (Lawler, 2006, pp. 133–5); 'Backchannel Message from the Ambassador to Thailand (Unger) to the Under Secretary of State for Political Affairs (Johnson)', 21 May 1970 (Lawler, 2006, pp. 136–9); 'Memorandum from John H. Holdridge of the National Security Council Staff to the President's Assistant for National Security Affairs (Kissinger)', 5 June 1970 (Lawler, 2006, pp. 141–2); 'Backchannel Message from the Ambassador to Thailand (Unger) to the Under Secretary of State for Political Affairs (Johnson)', 18 September 1970 (Lawler, 2006, p. 183); 'Letter from the President's Assistant for National Security Affairs (Kissinger) to the Ambassador to Thailand (Unger)', 27 October 1970 (Lawler, 2006, p. 197); 'Memorandum from Secretary of Defense Laird to President Nixon', 16 September 1972 (Lawler, 2006, p. 376); 'Memorandum from the President's Assistant for National Security Affairs (Kissinger) to President Nixon', 25 September 1972 (Lawler, 2006, pp. 382–3).

12 'Memorandum from the President's Assistant for National Security Affairs (Kissinger) to President Nixon', 26 March 1969 (Lawler, 2006, p. 566); 'Telegram from Secretary of State Rogers to the Department of State', 5 August 1969 (Lawler, 2006, p. 589); 'Telegram from the Embassy in Australia to the

Department of State', 14 January 1970 (Lawler, 2006, p. 607); 'Memorandum of Conversation', 1 July 1970 (Lawler, 2006, pp. 663–9); 'Memorandum from John H. Holdridge of the National Security Council Staff to the President's Assistant for National Security Affairs (Kissinger)', 13 October 1970 (Lawler, 2006, p. 677).

13 'Memorandum of Conversation', 5 July 1975 (State Department, 1975c, p. 5).
14 'Discussion of President Ford and Lee Kuan Yew on Southeast Asia', Memorandum of Conversation, 8 May 1975 (State Department, 1975a).
15 'Ford-Suharto Meeting', Secret Cable from US Embassy in Jakarta to State Department, 6 December 1975 (State Department, 1975b).
16 'Conversation with Mr Tan Boon Seng', Memorandum from British High Commission, Singapore, to FCO, 1 August 1975, FCO 15/2111/#.
17 Letter from Stuart, A.C., British Embassy, Jakarta, to A.M. Simons, FCO, 9 February 1976, FCO 15/2174/8.
18 'ASEAN and the Bali Summit', Letter from R.A. Woolcott, Australian ambassador in Jakarta, to Australian Foreign Minister, 3 March 1976, FCO 15/2173/56. TAC provided for a 'High Council' to be assembled to resolve intramural disputes, and Marcos had publicly stated his intention to use it to settle the Sabah claim; Malaysia had therefore threatened not to sign the Treaty. The conflict was only settled by Indonesia's aggressive 'mediation' and by effectively neutering the High Council.

Chapter 3   East Timor: ASEAN and Third-World Colonialism

1 'Talk with General Yoga', Letter from Peter Male, FCO, to Mr Wilford, FCO, 16 April 1975, FCO 15/2082/11.
2 A/C.4/31/SR.16, pp. 10–12.
3 A/C.4/35/SR.12, p. 13.
4 'Ford-Suharto Meeting', Secret Cable from US Embassy in Jakarta to State Department, 6 December 1975 (State Department, 1975b); 'Secretary's Meeting with Indonesian Foreign Minister Adam Malik', Memorandum of Conversation, 5 September 1975 (State Department, 1975d).
5 S/PV.1864, p. 13.
6 A/C.4/SR.2180, p. 357.
7 'Your Tel No. 1073: Timor', Cable from 'Norris', British High Commission, Kuala Lumpur, to FCO, 10 December 1975, FCO 15/1707/250.
8 'My Telegram No. 328: Portuguese Timor', Cable from J.A. Ford, British Ambassador in Jakarta to FCO, 5 September 1975, FCO 15/1705/100.
9 A/C.4/SR.2180, p. 358. The draft resolution was A/C.4/L.1125.
10 A/C.4/SR.2186, p. 402.
11 A/C.4/L.1132, introduced at A/C.4/SR.2187, p. 404.
12 *Ibid.*, p. 412.
13 A/C.4/SR.2188, p. 408.
14 S/PV.1864, pp. 19–20.
15 'Portuguese Timor', Cable from 'HE', British High Commission, Singapore, to FCO, 20 August 1975, FCO 15/1705/88.

16   'Visit of Lee Kwan Yew', Letter from A.C. Stuart, British Embassy, Jakarta, to
     C. W. Squire, FCO, 22 September 1975, FCO 30/2765/44.
17   'Singapore and South East Asia: Conversation with Mr Lee Kuan Yew on
     7 February 1976', Letter from Peter Tripp, British High Commission, Singa-
     pore, to Hugh Cortazzi, FCO, 9 February 1976, FCO 15/2159/1; 'Conversation
     with Singapore's Foreign Minister on 13 February 1976', Letter from Peter
     Tripp, British High Commission, Singapore, to Peter Male, FCO, 14 February
     1976, FCO 15/2159/5.
18   'Portuguese Timor' (FCO 15/1705/88).
19   S/PV.1909, pp. 6–7; S/PV.1911, pp. 3–4.
20   E.g., A/C.4/32/SR.27, p. 20; A/C.4/32/SR.31, p. 15; A/C.4/35/SR.11, p. 12.
     See also A/BUR/34/SR.1, p. 12; A/BUR/35/SR.1, pp. 13–14; A/BUR/36/SR.1,
     pp. 16–17; A/BUR/37/SR.2, p. 5.
21   A/C.4/SR.2180, p. 358. See also, e.g., S/PV.1864, p. 11; S/PV.1909, p. 3;
     A/C.4/32/SR.19, pp. 4–5.
22   S/PV.1867, pp. 1–2.
23   A/C.4/32/SR.17, p. 8.
24   A/C.4/35/SR.14, p. 13 (Angola); A/C.4/36/SR.18, p. 20 (Zimbabwe).
25   See, e.g., A/C.4/35/SR.11, pp. 12, 15–16, 18–19. ASEAN's collaboration with the
     ousted Khmer Rouge regime yielded an immediate reversal in its position on
     East Timor. See A/31/PV.16, p. 325; A/32/PV.28; A/C.4/35/SR.23, pp. 11–12.

Chapter 4   Cambodia: Representation, Refugees and Rebels

1   'Visit of President Soeharto to Japan', Letter from G.A. Duggan, British Embassy,
     Jakarta, to J.L. Jones, FCO, 28 July 1975, FCO 15/2082/27, p. 129.
2   A/34/PV.4, pp. 37–8; A/34/PV.4, p. 51; A/34/PV.62, pp. 1195, 1210; A/34/PV.65,
     p. 1251; A/35/PV.34, p. 687, etc.
3   A/35/PV.35, p. 716.
4   A/34/PV.62, p. 1209; A/35/PV.34, p. 689.
5   A/35/PV.35, pp. 704–5, 709–10; A/36/PV.103, pp. 1871–2.
6   S/13724/Add.1; S/PV.2185, p. 5; A/35/484, pp. 2–4.
7   A/35/PV.34, p. 689.
8   Indonesian ambassador Kamil, A/34/PV.65, p. 1251.
9   Philippine ambassador Romulo, A/35/PV.35, p. 714.
10   Cf. A/RES/34/22; A/RES/35/6; A/RES/36/5.

Chapter 5   ASEAN after the Cold War: Capital, Crisis, Conflict

1   A/54/PV.16, p. 7.
2   By 1985 a US government report seriously countenanced 'the emergence of a
     radical, anti-US regime in the Philippines' that could 'threaten the unity and
     pro-Western policies of the ASEAN' (Congressional Research Service, 1985).
3   A/54/PV.16, p. 7.
4   A/C.3/46/SR.46, pp. 8–9.
5   For details see http://www.aceh-mm.org.

Chapter 6   Cambodia: From Cold War to Conditionality

1 In 18 months of daily press coverage in the regional and international media and UN debates, I found about half-a-dozen scattered references to the PPA.
2 These are that new members must deposit an initial $1m in ASEAN's coffers and $250,000 per annum thereafter, and have sufficient English-speaking diplomats to participate fully in ASEAN activities. However, even these conditions had earlier been overlooked to permit the CLMV states to join, underscoring the interventionist nature of ASEAN's behaviour now.

Chapter 7   East Timor: Interdependence and Intervention

1 E/CN.4/1993/SR.69, pp. 2–3. This apparently principled stand was contradicted by Malaysia's sponsorship of over a dozen other resolutions that year, and its urging of Western intervention in the Balkans.
2 S/PV.4043; S/PV.4043 (Resumption).
3 S/PV.4043 (Resumption), pp. 5–6, 9, 17.
4 *Ibid.*, 13.
5 S/PV.4043, pp. 20–1.
6 S/PV.4043 (Resumption), pp. 19–21.
7 S/PV.4045, p. 4.
8 A/54/PV.14, p. 10. Surin later advised the International Commission on State Sovereignty, which drew up the 'Responsibility to Protect' doctrine.
9 E/CN.4/S-4/SR.1, p. 4; E/CN.4/S-4/SR.5, p. 5.
10 A/54/PV.21, pp. 11–12.
11 E/CN.4/S-4/SR.2, pp. 5–6.
12 The two Principal Deputy Heads of Mission were Malaysian and Thai army officers. Military and civilian officials from Malaysia, Thailand, Brunei and the Philippines were deployed throughout Aceh as heads or deputy heads of district offices tasked with disarming the Free Aceh Movement and monitoring and verifying Indonesian force reductions. See http://www.aceh-mm.org.

Chapter 8   Burma: ASEAN's Image and the 'Regional Interest'

1 Burma was renamed 'Myanmar' by the military regime. I use both terms interchangeably but retain original usages.
2 The existence of this explicit *quid quo pro* was confirmed by Severino (2008) and Razali (2008).
3 A/C.3/56/SR.54, pp. 3–4. By contrast, non-ASEAN states such as Egypt continued explicitly to oppose 'any interference in the internal affairs of States on the pretext of investi[gati]ng the human rights situation' – A/C.3/57/SR.54, p. 3.
4 S/PV.5619, pp. 4–5.

Conclusions

1 For one all-too-rare attempt to do this, see Nischalke (2002).

References

Abdullah Badawi, A. (2006a) 'Opening Address to 39th AMM: Forging a United, Resilient and Integrated ASEAN', Kuala Lumpur, 25 July, http://www.aseansec. org/18555.htm, date accessed 12 December 2007.

—— (2006b) 'Preservation and Innovation in Planning the Future of ASEAN', ASEAN Lecture, Kuala Lumpur, 8 August, http://www.aseansec.org/18634.htm, date accessed 25 July 2007.

Abinales, P. N. and Amoroso, D. J. (2005) *State and Society in the Philippines* (Boulder: Rowman & Littlefield).

Acharya, A. (2009a) *Constructing a Security Community in Southeast Asia: ASEAN and the Problem of Regional Order*, 2nd edn (London: Routledge).

—— (2009b) *Whose Ideas Matter? Agency and Power in Asian Regionalism* (Ithaca: Cornell University Press).

Aditjondro, G. J. (1994) *In the Shadow of Mount Ramelau: The Impact of the Occupation of East Timor* (Leiden: Indonesian Documentation and Information Centre).

—— (1997) 'A Poisoned 30th Birthday Present for ASEAN: Suharto's Intimate Relationships with the Burmese Military Junta', in R. Bachoe and D. Stothard (eds) *From Consensus to Controversy: ASEAN's Relationship with Burma's SLORC* (Bangkok: AltSEAN-Burma), pp. pp. 37–47.

—— (1999) 'ABRI, Inc.', *Sydney Morning Herald*, 8 May.

Adler-Nissen, R. and Gammeltoft-Hansen, T. (eds) (2008) *Sovereignty Games: Instrumentalizing State Sovereignty in Europe and Beyond* (New York: Palgrave Macmillan).

Advertiser (1999) 'Stay Out of Our Affairs or You Will Pay', 9 September.

AFP (1997) Agence France Presse, 'ASEAN in Emergency Cambodia Talks as Ousted Prince Seeks UN Help', 10 July.

—— (1998a) 'ASEAN Ministers Wrangle Over Cambodia Membership', 11 December.

—— (1998b) 'Philippines FM Casts Doubts on Cambodia's Early Entry into ASEAN', 21 November.

—— (1999a) 'Cambodia Ready to Participate in Timor Peacekeeping Force: Minister', 13 September.

—— (1999b) 'Free East Timor Wants Nothing to do With ASEAN, Ramos Horta Warns', 15 October.

—— (1999c) 'Malaysia Will Not Take Part in Australian-Led Force to Timor', 16 September.

—— (1999d) 'Myanmar Expresses Solidarity with Indonesian "Brothers"', 13 September.

—— (1999e) 'Philippines Willing to Send Troops to East Timor Under UN Command', 7 September.

—— (1999f) 'Thailand Pandering to West Over Timor: Nationalist Lobby', 26 September.

—— (1999g) 'Vietnamese FM Calls for Respect of Rights of Timor, Indonesia', 15 September.

—— (2000a) 'EU Ministers Hail Progress on Myanmar As They End ASEAN Boycott', 12 December.
—— (2000b) 'Indonesia's Wahid Launches Tirade Against Singapore', 26 November.
—— (2001) 'ASEAN Ministers Kick Off Informal Retreat', 30 April.
—— (2003a) 'East Timor FM Says No One in ASEAN Believes Rangoon "Protecting" Suu Kyi', 17 June.
—— (2003b) 'Mahathir says Burma May Have to Be Expelled from ASEAN', 20 July.
—— (2003c) 'Southeast Asian Quest for Single Market On the Rocks', 22 June.
Agnew, J. (2009) *Globalization and Sovereignty* (Lanham: Rowman and Littlefield).
Alagappa, M. (1993) 'Regionalism and the Quest for Security: ASEAN and the Cambodian Conflict', *Journal of International Affairs*, 46(2): 439–67.
Alatas, A. (2006) *The Pebble in the Shoe: The Diplomatic Struggle for East Timor* (Jakarta: Aksara Karunia).
—— (2008) Interview with the Author, Jakarta, February.
Alexander, R. J. (1999) *International Maoism in the Developing World* (London: Praeger).
AltSEAN (2005) *Pressure Works: Burma Backs Off From ASEAN Chair*, http://www.altsean.org/Reports/ASEANChair.php, date accessed 18 August 2005.
Amer, R. (1992) *The United Nations and Foreign Military Interventions: A Comparative Study of the Application of the Charter* (Uppsala: Dept of Peace and Conflict Research, Uppsala University).
Anderson, B. R. (1995) 'East Timor and Indonesia: Some Implications', in P. Carey and G. C. Bentley (eds) *East Timor at the Crossroads: The Forging of a Nation* (London: Cassell), pp. 137–47.
—— (1998) *The Spectre of Comparisons: Nationalism, Southeast Asia and the World* (London: Verso).
Anghie, A. (2005) *Imperialism, Sovereignty and the Making of International Law* (Cambridge: Cambridge University Press).
Antara (1994) 'Foreign Minister Comments on ASEAN Regional Forum, East Timor', 19 July.
—— (1999) 'Six Envoys Have "Wide-Ranging" Discussion With Gusmão', 25 May.
Antolik, M. (1990) *ASEAN and the Diplomacy of Accommodation* (London: M. E. Sharpe).
Anwar, D. F. (1994) *Indonesia in ASEAN: Foreign Policy and Regionalism* (Singapore: ISEAS).
Anwar I. (1997) 'Crisis Prevention', *Newsweek International*, 21 July.
AP (1997) Associated Press, 'US Denounces Asian Leaders' Decision on Burma', 24 July.
—— (1999a) 'Former Indonesian Military Chief Receives Citation from Philippine President', 9 December.
—— (1999b) 'Malaysia's PM Expresses Concern Over East Timor Violence', 7 September.
—— (1999c) 'Muslim Separatists Find Inspiration in East Timor Vote', 5 September.
—— (1999d) 'Opposition Launches Censure Motion against Thai Government', 15 December.
—— (1999e) 'Report: Malaysia Encouraged Indonesia to Invade East Timor', 20 October.

—— (1999f) 'Thailand Willing to Provide Troops if UN Peacekeepers Set for Timor', 24 April.

—— (2008) 'Malaysia Seeks to Defuse Thai-Cambodia Row', 20 October.

Asda, J. (2008) Interview with the Author, Bangkok, January.

ASEAN (1967) 'ASEAN Declaration', Bangkok, 8 August, http://www.aseansec.org/1212.htm, date accessed 27 March 2007.

—— (1971) 'ZOPFAN Declaration', Kuala Lumpur, 27 November, http://www.aseansec.org/1215.htm, date accessed 27 March 2007.

—— (1976a) 'Joint Communiqué of the Ninth ASEAN Ministerial Meeting', Manila, 24–26 June, http://www.aseansec.org/1239.htm, date accessed 17 March 2008.

—— (1976b) 'Treaty of Amity and Cooperation', Bali, 24 February, http://www.aseansec.org/1217.htm, date accessed 27 March 2007.

—— (1979) 'Joint Communiqué of the 12th ASEAN Ministerial Meeting', Bali, 28–30 June, http://www.aseansec.org/1242.htm, date accessed 27 March 2007.

—— (1980) 'Joint Communiqué of the 13th ASEAN Ministerial Meeting', Kuala Lumpur, 25–26 June, http://www.aseansec.org/1243.htm, date accessed 27 March 2007.

—— (1981) 'Joint Communiqué of the 14th ASEAN Ministerial Meeting', Manila, 17–18 June, http://www.aseansec.org/1244.htm, date accessed 27 March 2007.

—— (1986) 'ASEAN Joint Statement on the Situation in the Philippines', Jakarta, 23 February, http://www.aseansec.org/1612.htm, date accessed 29 August 2007.

—— (1992) 'Joint Declaration of the Tenth ASEAN-EC Ministerial Meeting', Manila, 29–30 October, http://www.aseansec.org/1193.htm, date accessed 11 February 2010.

—— (1997a) 'Joint Press Statement of Special ASEAN Foreign Ministers Meeting', Singapore, 11 August, http://www.aseansec.org/16282.htm, date accessed 10 July 2007.

—— (1997b) 'Joint Statement of the Special Meeting of the ASEAN Foreign Ministers on Cambodia', Kuala Lumpur, 10 July, http://www.aseansec.org/1826.htm, date accessed 10 July 2007.

—— (1998) 'Statement on Bold Measures at the 6th ASEAN Summit', Hanoi, 16 December, http://www.aseansec.org/688.htm, date accessed 10 July 2007.

—— (2000) 'Vientiane Declaration', Vientiane, 11–12 December, http://www.aseansec.org/676.htm, date accessed 10 July 2007.

—— (2001) 'Chairman's Statement of the 8th ASEAN Regional Forum', Hanoi, 25 July, http://www.aseansec.org/538.htm, date accessed 10 July 2007.

—— (2003) 'Joint Communiqué of the 36th ASEAN Ministerial Meeting', Phnom Penh, 16–17 June, http://www.aseansec.org/14833.htm, date accessed 10 July 2007.

—— (2004) 'Vientiane Action Programme 2004–2010', Vientiane, 29 November, http://www.aseansec.org/VAP-10th%20ASEAN%20Summit.pdf, date accessed 10 July 2007.

—— (2005a) 'Chairman's Statement of the 11th ASEAN Summit: "One vision, One Identity, One Community"', Kuala Lumpur, 12 December, http://www.aseansec.org/18039.htm, date accessed 10 July 2007.

—— (2005b) 'Joint Communiqué of the 38th AMM', Vientiane, 26 July, http://www.aseansec.org/17592.htm, date accessed 12 July 2007.

—— (2007a) 'Chairperson's Statement of the 12th ASEAN Summit', Cebu, 13 January, http://www.aseansec.org/19280.htm, date accessed 10 July 2007.

—— (2007b) 'Statement by ASEAN Chair', New York, 27 September, http://www.aseansec.org/20974.htm, date accessed 1 December 2007.

—— (2008a) 'ASEAN Emergency Rapid Assessment Team Mission Report, 9–18 May 2008: Cyclone Nargis, Myanmar', http://www.aseansec.org/21558.pdf, date accessed 12 December 2008.

—— (2008b) 'Charter of the Association of Southeast Asian Nations', http://www.aseansec.org/21069.pdf, date accessed 22 January 2009.

—— (2008c) 'Press Release of the Tripartite Core Group – Six Months after Cyclone Nargis – Continued Need for Relief and Long Term Support', Yangon, 2 November, http://www.aseansec.org/22046.htm, date accessed 12 December 2008.

—— (2008d) 'Special ASEAN Foreign Ministers Meeting Chairman's Statement', Singapore, 19 May, http://www.aseansec.org/21556.htm, date accessed 10 July 2008.

ASEANAffairs.com (2008) 'Talks Ease Tension, Joint Patrols Agreed', 17 October.

AsiaWeek (1997) 'I Am Still Here', 9 May.

—— (1999a) 'APEC '99: Day Three', 10 September.

—— (1999b) 'Day Two: The Missing Agenda', 9 September.

—— (2000) 'Inside "Secret" Meetings', 31 March.

Aubrey, J. (2000) 'Canberra: Jakarta's Trojan Horse in East Timor', in S. Mccloskey and P. Hainsworth (eds) *The East Timor Question: The Struggle for Independence from Indonesia* (London: IB Tauris), pp. 133–49.

Ayoob, M. (1995) *The Third World Security Predicament: State Making, Regional Conflict, and the International System* (London: Lynne Rienner).

Barnett, R. J. (1970) *Intervention and Revolution: The United States in the Third World* (London: Paladin).

BBC SWB (1999) BBC Summary of World Broadcasts, 'Indonesian Finance Minister Discusses Sanctions With Regional Leaders', *Source: Radio Republic Indonesia*, 11 September.

Beeson, M. (2004) 'Southeast Asia', in A. Payne (ed.) *The New Regional Politics of Development* (London: Palgrave Macmillan), pp. 118–44.

Bell, D. A., Jayasuriya, K. and Jones, D. M. (eds) (1995) *Towards Illiberal Democracy in Pacific Asia* (New York: St Martin's Press).

Bellamy, A. J. and Beeson, M. (2010) 'The Responsibility to Protect in Southeast Asia: Can ASEAN Reconcile Humanitarianism and Sovereignty?', *Asian Security*, 6(3): 262–79.

Bellin, E. (2000) 'Contingent Democrats: Industrialists, Labor, and Democratization in Late-Developing Countries', *World Politics*, 52(1): 175–205.

Bello, W. and De Guzman, M. (1999) 'Indonesia's Unravelling: Impact on the Philippines', *BusinessWorld*, 8 October.

Beresford, M. (1993) 'The Political Economy of Dismantling the "Bureaucratic Centralism and Subsidy System" in Vietnam', in K. Hewison, R. Robison and G. Rodan (eds) *Southeast Asia in the 1990s: Authoritarianism, Democracy and Capitalism* (St Leonards, Australia: Allen and Unwin), pp. 215–36.

Bernama (1999) 'M'sian Peacekeepers Ready to Serve in East Timor', 6 September.

—— (2003a) 'Dr Mahathir: M'sia Wants Suu Kyi Released', 10 June.

—— (2003b) 'Malaysia's Hamid says ASEAN Wants Burma to Set Date for Suu Kyi's Release', 15 June.

—— (2007) 'Myanmar is Not a Threat But Must Give Role to ASEAN', 11 January.

Bickerton, C. J., Cunliffe, P. and Gourevitch, A. (eds) (2006) *Politics Without Sovereignty: A Critique of Contemporary International Relations* (London: UCL Press).

Bieler, A. (2001) 'Questioning Cognitivism and Constructivism in IR Theory: Reflections on the Material Structure of Ideas', *Politics*, 21(2): 93–100.

Bolton, K. (1999) 'Domestic Sources of Vietnam's Foreign Policy', in C. A. Thayer and R. Amer (eds) *Vietnamese Foreign Policy in Transition* (Singapore: ISEAS), pp. 170–201.

Booth, A. (1994) 'Repelita IV and the Second Long-Term Development Plan', *Bulletin of Indonesian Economic Studies*, 30(3): 3–39.

Boutros-Ghali, B. (1995) 'Introduction', in *The United Nations and Cambodia, 1991–1995* (New York: United Nations).

BP (2010) Bangkok Post, 'ASEAN Calls for Peace Dialogue', 18 May.

Budiardjo, C. and Liong, L. S. (1984) *The War Against East Timor* (London: Zed Books).

Bunnag, T. (2008) Interview with the Author, Bangkok, February.

Business World (1999a) 'Estrada Justifies RP Vote Against East Timor Probe', 30 September.

—— (1999b) 'Wahid Warned vs Interfering in Mindanao', 24 November.

Buszynski, L. (1994) 'Thailand's Foreign Policy: Management of a Regional Vision', *Asian Survey*, 34(8): 721–37.

Caballero-Anthony, M. (2005) *Regional Security in Southeast Asia: Beyond the ASEAN Way* (Singapore: ISEAS).

Caballero-Anthony, M. (2008) 'Non-traditional Security and Infectious Diseases in ASEAN: Going Beyond the Rhetoric of Securitization to Deeper Institutionalization', *Pacific Review*, 21(4): 507–25.

Capizzi, E., Hill, H. and Macey, D. (1976) 'FRETILIN and the Struggle for Independence in East Timor', *Race and Class*, 17(4): 381–95.

Carroll, T. and Sovacool, B. (2010) 'Pipelines, Crisis and Capital: Understanding the Contested Regionalism of Southeast Asia', *Pacific Review*, 23(5): 625–47.

Case, W. (2005) 'Malaysia: New Reforms, Old Continuities; Tense Ambiguities', *Journal of Development Studies*, 41(2): 224–39.

CAVR (2005) *Chega! The Report of the Commission for Reception, Truth and Reconciliation in Timor-Leste: Executive Summary* (Dili: Commission for Reception, Truth and Reconciliation).

Chachavalpongpun P. (2009) 'Diplomacy under Siege: Thailand's Political Crisis and the Impact on Foreign Policy', *Contemporary Southeast Asia*, 31(3): 447–67.

Chamberlain, E. (2009) *Rebellion, Defeat and Exile: The 1959 Uprising in East Timor*, 2nd edn, http://www.scribd.com, date accessed 1 March 2010.

Chanda, N. (1986) *Brother Enemy: The War After the War* (New York: Macmillan).

Chandler, D. P. (2000) *A History of Cambodia*, 3rd edn (Boulder: Westview).

Chee S. J. (1997) 'Burma and Singapore: Strange Bedfellows', in R. Bachoe and D. Stothard (eds) *From Consensus to Controversy: ASEAN's Relationship with Burma's SLORC* (Bangkok: AltSEAN-Burma), pp. 26–30.

Chin, K. W. (2007) 'Introduction: ASEAN – Facing the Fifth Decade', *Contemporary Southeast Asia*, 29(3): 395–405.

Chong, C. (2008) Interview with the Author, Singapore, February.

Clapham, C. (1996) *Africa and the International System: The Politics of State Survival* (Cambridge: Cambridge University Press).

Clark, R. S. (1980) 'The "Decolonization" of East Timor and the United Nations Norms on Self-Determination and Aggression', *Yale Journal of World Public Order*, 7(1): 2–44.

Congressional Research Service (1985) 'Insurgency and Counterinsurgency in the Philippines', document CPH03036, http://nsarchive.chadwyck.com, date accessed 11 March 2007.

Cosgrove, P. (2006) *My Story* (Sydney: HarperCollins).

Cotton, J. (2000) 'The Emergence of an Independent East Timor: National and Regional Challenges', *Contemporary Southeast Asia*, 22(1): 1–22.

—— (2003) 'Southeast Asia After 11 September', *Terrorism and Political Violence*, 15(1): 147–70.

—— (2004) *East Timor, Australia and Regional Order: Intervention and its Aftermath in Southeast Asia* (London: RoutledgeCurzon).

Cribb, R. (2001) 'Genocide in Indonesia, 1965–1966', *Journal of Genocide Research*, 3(2): 219–39.

Crouch, H. (2000) 'The TNI and East Timor Policy', in J. J. Fox and D. B. Soares (eds) *Out of the Ashes: Destruction and Reconstruction of East Timor* (Adelaide: Crawford House), pp. 151–79.

Cunliffe, P. (2006) 'Sovereignty and the Politics of Responsibility', in C. J. Bickerton, P. Cunliffe and A. Gourevitch (eds) *Politics Without Sovereignty: A Critique of Contemporary International Relations* (London: UCL Press), pp. 39–57.

Curtis, G. (1998) *Cambodia Reborn? The Transition to Democracy and Development* (Washington: Brookings Institution Press).

Dawn (1974) 'Portugal's Forgotten Colony', 4 September.

Dawson, G. W. (1995) 'Historical Reality and the Case of East Timor', in CIIR/IPJET (ed.) *International Law and the Question of East Timor* (London: Catholic Institute for International Relations), pp. 11–20.

De Los Santos, J. and Burgos, A. M. B. (2001) *Restoring Hope: Peacekeeping, The East Timor Experience* (Quezon City: AM Cleofe Prints).

Desker, B. (2008) Interview with the Author, Singapore, February.

Deyo, F. (2006) 'South-east Asian Industrial Labour: Structural Demobilisation and Political Transformation', in G. Rodan, K. Hewison and R. Robison (eds) *The Political Economy of Southeast Asia: Markets, Power and Contestation*, 3rd edn (Oxford: Oxford University Press), pp. 283–304.

Dixon, C. (2004) 'State, Party and Political Change in Vietnam', in D. McCargo (ed.) *Rethinking Vietnam* (London: RoutledgeCurzon), pp. 15–26.

Dosch, J. (2006) *The Changing Dynamics of Southeast Asian Politics* (Boulder: Lynne Rienner).

—— (2009) 'Sovereignty Rules: Human Security, Civil Society, and the Limits of Liberal Reform', in D. K. Emmerson (ed.) *Hard Choices: Security, Democracy, and Regionalism in Southeast Asia* (Singapore: ISEAS), pp. 59–90.

Dunn, J. (1977) *East Timor – From Portuguese Colonialism to Indonesian Incorporation* (Canberra: Parliament of Australia Legislative Research Service).

—— (1983) *Timor: A People Betrayed* (Adelaide: Jacaranda Press).

Dupont, A. (2000) 'ASEAN's Response to the East Timor Crisis', *Australian Journal of International Affairs*, 54(2): 163–70.

Dwipayana, G. and Ramadhan, K. H. (1991) *Soeharto: My Thoughts, Words and Deeds – An Autobiography*, ed. Lestiono, M. (Jakarta: C.T. Citra Lamtoro Gung Persada).

Economist (1992) 'Myanmar's Monsters', 29 February.

Elliot, D. W. P. (1987) 'Deadlock Diplomacy: Thai and Vietnamese Interests in Kampuchea', in D. A. Ablin and M. Hood (eds) *The Cambodian Agony* (London: M. E. Sharpe), pp. 65–92.

Emmers, R. (2003) 'ASEAN and the Securitization of Transnational Crime in Southeast Asia', *Pacific Review*, 16(3): 419–38.

—— (2004) 'Regional Organisations and Peacekeeping: A Study of the ARF', in L. Elliot and G. Cheeseman (eds) *Forces for Good: Cosmopolitan Militaries in the Twenty-First Century* (Manchester: Manchester University Press), pp. 134–49.

Emmerson, D. K. (2009) 'Critical Terms: Security, Democracy, and Regionalism in Southeast Asia', in D. K. Emmerson (ed.) *Hard Choices: Security, Democracy, and Regionalism in Southeast Asia* (Singapore: ISEAS), pp. 3–56.

Evans, G. (1975) 'Portuguese Timor', *New Left Review*, 91: 67–79.

FEER (1990) Far Eastern Economic Review, 'Partners in Plunder: Thailand's Timber Shortage Gives Rangoon its Opening', 22 February.

—— (1997) 'ASEAN Faces New Challenges', 14 August.

Findlay, T. (1995) *Cambodia: The Legacy and Lessons of UNTAC* (Oxford: Oxford University Press).

Finnemore, M. (2003) *The Purpose of Intervention: Changing Beliefs About the Use of Force* (Ithaca: Cornell University Press).

Frost, F. (1991) 'The Cambodia Conflict: The Path Towards Peace', *Contemporary Southeast Asia*, 13(2): 119–63.

Financial Times (1997) 'Cambodia Rebuffed by ASEAN', 11 July.

Ganesan, N. (2006) 'Thai-Myanmar-ASEAN Relations: The Politics of Face and Grace', *Asian Affairs*, 33(3): 131–50.

Gibbs, D. N. (1991) *The Political Economy of Third World Intervention: Mines, Money and U.S. Policy in the Congo Crisis* (Chicago: Chicago University Press).

Gill, S. (1994) 'Structural Change and Global Political Economy: Globalizing Élites and the Emerging World Order', in Y. Sakamoto (ed.) *Global Transformation: Challenges to the State System* (Tokyo: UN University Press), pp. 169–99.

Girling, J. L. S. (1981) *Thailand: Society and Politics* (Ithaca: Cornell University Press).

—— (1992) 'Regional Security in Southeast Asia', in K. S. Sandhu, S. Siddique, C. Jeshurun, A. Rajah, J. L. N. Tan and P. Thambipillai (eds) *The ASEAN Reader* (Singapore: ISEAS), pp. 369–71.

Gomez, E. T. (2002) 'Political Business in Malaysia: Party Factionalism, Corporate Development, and Economic Crisis', in E. T. Gomez (ed.) *Political Business in East Asia* (London: Routledge), pp. 82–114.

Gomez, E. T. and Jomo, K. S. (1997) *Malaysia's Political Economy: Politics, Patronage and Profits* (Cambridge: Cambridge University Press).

Green Left Weekly (1994) 'Ramos Bows to Suharto on East Timor Conference', 1 June.

—— (1997) 'The Suharto Regime and the Burmese Military Junta', 2 July.

Gunn, G. C. (1997) *East Timor and the United Nations: The Case for Intervention* (Lawrenceville, NJ: Red Sea Press).

Haacke, J. (1999) 'The Concept of Flexible Engagement and the Practice of Enhanced Interaction: Intramural Challenges to the "ASEAN Way"', *Pacific Review*, 12(4): 581–611.

—— (2003) *ASEAN's Diplomatic and Security Culture: Origins, Development and Prospects* (London: RoutledgeCurzon).

—— (2005) '"Enhanced Interaction" with Myanmar and the Project of a Security Community: Is ASEAN Refining or Breaking with its Diplomatic and Security Culture?', *Contemporary Southeast Asia*, 27(2): 188–216.

—— (2008) 'ASEAN and Political Change in Myanmar: Towards a Regional Initiative?', *Contemporary Southeast Asia*, 30(3): 351–78.

—— (2010) 'The Myanmar Imbroglio and ASEAN: Heading Towards the 2010 Elections', *International Affairs*, 86(1): 153–74.

Hadiz, V. R. (2004) 'The Politics of Labour Movements in Southeast Asia', in M. Beeson (ed.) *Contemporary Southeast Asia: Regional Dynamics, National Differences* (London: Palgrave), pp. 118–35.

Hall, S. (1986) 'The Problem of Ideology – Marxism Without Guarantees', *Journal of Communication Inquiry*, 10(2): 29–44.

Halliday, F. (1999) *Revolution and World Politics: The Rise and Fall of the Sixth Great Power* (London: Macmillan).

Hameiri, S. (2010) *Regulating Statehood: Statebuilding and the Transformation of the Global Order* (Basingstoke: Palgrave Macmillan).

Hameiri, S. and Jayasuriya, K. (2011) 'Regulatory Regionalism and the Dynamics of Territorial Politics: The Case of the Asia-Pacific Region', *Political Studies*, 59(1): 20–37.

Han F. (2000) 'The East Timor Issue and its Regional Impact: A View from China', in B. Brown (ed.) *East Timor – The Consequences* (Wellington: NZIIA), pp. 64–9.

Harsono, A. (1997) 'Love at First Sight: SLORC meets ABRI', *Inside Indonesia*, 52.

Heinberger, J. E. (1994) *Peacekeeping in Transition: The United Nations in Cambodia* (New York: Twentieth Century Fund Press).

Henderson, J. (1999) *Reassessing ASEAN* (Oxford: Oxford University Press).

Hewison, K. (2000) 'Thailand's Capitalism Before and After the Economic Crisis', in R. Robison, M. Beeson, K. Jayasuriya and H.-R. Kim (eds) *Politics and Markets in the Wake of the Asian Crisis* (London: Routledge), pp. 192–211.

—— (2006) 'Thailand: Boom, Bust, and Recovery', in G. Rodan, K. Hewison and R. Robison (eds) *The Political Economy of Southeast Asia: Markets, Power and Contestation*, 3rd edn (Oxford: Oxford University Press), pp. 74–108.

Hewison, K., Robison, R. and Rodan, G. (1993) 'Introduction: Changing Forms of State Power in Southeast Asia', in K. Hewison, R. Robison and G. Rodan (eds) *Southeast Asia in the 1990s: Authoritarianism, Democracy and Capitalism* (St Leonards, Australia: Allen and Unwin), pp. 2–8.

Hoadley, J. S. (1975) *The Future of Portuguese Timor* (Singapore: ISEAS).

—— (1977) 'Indonesia's Annexation of East Timor: Political, Administrative and Developmental Initiatives', *Southeast Asian Affairs 1977* (Singapore: ISEAS), pp. 133–42.

Hobsbawm, E. J. (1973) *The Age of Revolution: Europe 1789–1848* (London: Cardinal).

242   *References*

Hughes, C. (2003) *The Political Economy of Cambodia's Transition, 1991–2001* (London: RoutledgeCurzon).
Huntley, W. and Hayes, P. (2000) 'East Timor and Asian Security', *Bulletin of Concerned Asian Scholars*, 32(1–2): 67–72.
Hutchison, J. (2006) 'Poverty of Politics in the Philippines', in G. Rodan, K. Hewison and R. Robison (eds) *The Political Economy of Southeast Asia: Markets, Power and Contestation*, 3rd edn (Oxford: Oxford University Press), pp. 39–73.
Huxley, T. (1983) *Indochina and Insurgency in the ASEAN States, 1975–1981* (Canberra: ANU).
—— (2002) *Disintegrating Indonesia? Implications for Regional Security* (London: Oxford University Press).
IHT (1979) International Herald Tribune, Title Unavailable, 7 July.
—— (1999) 'East Timor Leaders Oppose a Malaysian-Led Force', 3 November.
Inbaraj, S. (1995) *East Timor: Blood and Tears in ASEAN* (Chiang Mai: Silkworm Books).
IPS (1992) Inter-Press Service, 'Burma Facing Sanctions from Southeast Asia', 12 March.
—— (1996) 'East Timor Takes Backseat to ASEAN Solidarity', 11 November.
Institute for Policy Research (1997) *Cambodia in ASEAN: Partnership for Peace and National Reconciliation*, http://ikdasar.tripod.com/sa_2000/sea/smc/msc_1.htm, date accessed 27 January 2009.
Irrawaddy (2002) 'Border Blowout', 1 May.
Jakarta Post (2007) 'SBY Pursues Alternative Approach to Myanmar', 21 November.
Japan Times (1981) Title Unavailable, 15 September.
Jasudasen, T. (2008) Interview with the Author, Kuala Lumpur, January 2008.
Jayakumar, S. (1997) 'Opening Statement', 30th ASEAN Ministerial Meeting, Subang Jaya, 24 May, http://www.aseansec.org/4002.htm, date accessed 10 June 2006.
—— (2000) 'Opening Statement', 33rd ASEAN Ministerial Meeting, Bangkok, 24 July, http://www.aseansec.org/3734.htm, date accessed 10 July 2007.
Jayasuriya, K. (2001) 'Globalisation and the Changing Architecture of the State: Regulatory State and the Politics of Negative Coordination', *Journal of European Public Policy*, 8(1): 101–23.
Jessop, B. (1990) *State Theory: Putting the Capitalist State in its Place* (London: Polity).
—— (2008) *State Power: A Strategic-Relational Approach* (Cambridge: Polity).
Jolliffe, J. (1978) *East Timor: Nationalism and Colonialism* (St Lucia: University of Queensland Press).
Jones, D. M. (1998) 'Democratization, Civil Society, and Illiberal Middle Class Culture in Pacific Asia', *Comparative Politics*, 30(2): 147–69.
—— (2009) 'Toward Relative Decency: The Case for Prudence', in D. K. Emmerson (ed.) *Hard Choices: Security, Democracy, and Regionalism in Southeast Asia* (Singapore: ISEAS), pp. 265–91.
Jones, D. M. and Smith, M. L. R. (1997) 'ASEAN, Asian Values and Southeast Asian Security in the New World Order', *Contemporary Security Policy*, 18(3): 126–44.
—— (2006) *ASEAN and East Asian International Relations: Regional Delusion* (Cheltenham: Edward Elgar).

Jones, L. (2007) 'ASEAN's Intervention in Cambodia: From Cold War to Condition-ality', *Pacific Review*, 20(4): 523–50.
—— (2008) 'ASEAN's Albatross: ASEAN's Burma Policy, from Constructive Engagement to Critical Disengagement', *Asian Security*, 4(3): 271–93.
—— (2009) 'Democratisation and Foreign Policy in Southeast Asia: The Case of the ASEAN Inter-Parliamentary Myanmar Caucus', *Cambridge Review of International Affairs*, 22(3): 387–406.
Kausikan, B. (2007) *The Ages of ASEAN*, unpublished manuscript, on-file with the author.
—— (2008) Interview with the Author, Singapore, February 2008.
Kavi C. (2001) 'Thai-Burma Relations', *Challenges to Democratization in Burma: Perspectives on Multilateral and Bilateral Responses* (Stockholm: International IDEA), pp. 117–29.
Keefer, E. C. (ed.) (2001) *Foreign Relations of the United States, 1964–1968*, vol. XXVI (Washington, DC: US Government Printing Office).
Kesavapany, K. (2008) Interview with the Author, Singapore, February.
Kessler, R. J. (1989) *Rebellion and Repression in the Philippines* (New Haven: Yale University Press).
Kevin, T. (2000) 'Cambodia's International Rehabilitation, 1997–2000', *Contemporary Southeast Asia*, 22(3): 594–612.
Khong, Y. F. (1997) 'ASEAN and the Southeast Asian Security Complex', in D. A. Lake and P. M. Morgan (eds) *Regional Orders: Building Security in a New World* (University Park, PA: Pennsylvania State University Press), pp. 318–39.
Khoo, N. (2004) 'Deconstructing the ASEAN Security Community: A Review Essay', *International Relations of the Asia-Pacific*, 4(1): 35–46.
Kiernan, B. (1993) 'The Inclusion of the Khmer Rouge in the Cambodian Peace Process: Causes and Consequences', in B. Kiernan (ed.) *Genocide and Democracy in Cambodia: The Khmer Rouge, the United Nations and the International Community* (New Haven: Yale University Press), pp. 191–272.
—— (2002) 'Introduction: Conflict in Cambodia, 1945–2002', *Critical Asian Studies*, 34(4): 483–95.
Kohen, A. and Taylor, J. (1979) *An Act of Genocide: Indonesia's Invasion of East Timor* (London: Tapol).
Kok, T. (2008) Interview with the Author, Kuala Lumpur, January.
Kraft, H. J. (2000) 'Track Three Diplomacy and Human Rights in Southeast Asia: The Case of the Asia Pacific Coalition for East Timor', paper presented at the Global Development Network 2000 conference, Tokyo, 11–13 December.
Kraisak C. (2008) Interview with the Author, Bangkok, January.
Krasner, S. D. (1999) *Sovereignty: Organized Hypocrisy* (Princeton: Princeton University Press).
Kyaw, Y. H. (2009) 'ASEAN's Pariah: Insecurity and Autocracy in Myanmar (Burma)', in D. K. Emmerson (ed.) *Hard Choices: Security, Democracy, and Regionalism in Southeast Asia* (Singapore: ISEAS), pp. 151–89.
Kyodo (1992) 'Malaysia Demands Myanmar Stop Oppressing Muslim Minority', 10 March.
—— (1994a) 'Indonesia Slams Manila Conference on East Timor', 10 May.
—— (1994b) 'Ramos Defends Decision on East Timor Conference', 1 June.
—— (1998a) 'ASEAN Unlikely to Admit Cambodia in Dec.', 14 November.
—— (1998b) 'Hun Sen Rejects Further Mediation Role for ASEAN', 12 January.

—— (1999a) 'Cambodian Opposition Recognizes E. Timor Independence', 9 September.

—— (1999b) 'Manila Defends "No" Vote on E. Timor', 1 October.

—— (1999c) 'Manila Expresses Concern Over Turmoil in Indonesia', 5 May.

—— (1999d) 'Philippines Willing to Help Indonesia on E. Timor Vote', 21 April.

—— (1999e) 'Thailand Considering Reducing E. Timor Troops', 27 September.

—— (1999f) 'Thailand Ready to Assist UN Peacekeeping, Chuan Says', 6 September.

—— (2004) 'Japan, Vietnam, EU Agree to Find Ways to Resolve ASEM Row', 2 July.

—— (2005) 'ASEAN to Review "Cherished" Noninterference Policy', 13 December.

—— (2008) 'ASEAN Ministers Meet to Offer Mediation on Thailand-Cambodia Dispute', 22 July.

Lawler, D. J. (ed.) (2006) *Foreign Relations of the United States, 1969–1976*, vol. xx (Washington, DC: US Government Printing Office).

Lawless, R. (1976) 'The Indonesian Takeover of East Timor', *Asian Survey*, 16(10): 948–64.

Lawson, G. and Shilliam, R. (2010) 'Beyond Hypocrisy? Debating the "Fact" and "Value" of Sovereignty in Contemporary World Politics', *International Politics*, 46(6): 657–70.

Lee H. L. (2008) 'Opening Address', 41st ASEAN Ministerial Meeting, Singapore, 21 July, http://www.aseansec.org/21759.htm, date accessed 8 August 2008.

Lee Kuan Yew (2000) *From Third World to First – The Singapore Story: 1965–2000* (Singapore: Singapore Press Holdings).

Leifer, M. (1973) 'The ASEAN States: No Common Outlook', *International Affairs*, 49(4): 600–7.

—— (1978) 'Decolonisation and International Status: The Experience of Brunei', *International Affairs*, 54(2): 240–52.

—— (1983) *Indonesia's Foreign Policy* (London: Allen & Unwin).

—— (1989) *ASEAN and the Security of Southeast Asia* (London: Routledge).

—— (1999) 'The ASEAN Peace Process: A Category Mistake', *Pacific Review*, 12(1): 25–38.

Maisrikrod, S. (1992) 'Thailand's Policy Dilemmas Towards Indochina', *Contemporary Southeast Asia*, 14(3): 287–300.

MalaysiaKini.com (2007) 'APCET II: Megat Ordered the Mob Attack', 21 June.

Malik, A. (1980) *In the Service of the Republic* (Singapore: Gunung Agung).

Manila Bulletin (2000) 'RP Concerned by Indon Dev'ts', 1 October.

Manila Standard (1999a) 'Into the Indonesian Quagmire', 14 September.

—— (1999b) 'RP Commits Funds for E. Timor', 29 July.

Marker, J. (2003) *East Timor: A Memoir of the Negotiations for Independence* (London: McFarland).

—— (2008) Interview with the Author, by telephone, July.

Martinez-Kuhonta, E. (2006) 'Walking a Tightrope: Democracy versus Sovereignty in ASEAN's Illiberal Peace', *Pacific Review*, 19(3): 337–58.

Maung A. M. (2001) *Neither Friend Nor Foe: Myanmar's Relations with Thailand Since 1988 – A View from Yangon* (Singapore: IDSS).

McCargo, D. and Ukrist, P. (2005) *The Thaksinization of Thailand* (Copenhagen: NIAS Press).

McDougall, D. (2001) 'Regional Institutions and Security: Implications of the 1999 East Timor Crisis', in A. Tan and J. D. K. Boutin (eds) *Non-traditional Security Issues in Southeast Asia* (Singapore: IDSS), pp. 166–96.

Miclat, A. N. (1995) *Breaking the Silence: The Story Behind APCET* (Quezon City: APCET).

Migdal, J. S. (2001) *State in Society: Studying How States and Societies Transform and Constitute One Another* (Cambridge: Cambridge University Press).

Moller, K. (1998) 'Cambodia and Burma: The ASEAN Way Ends Here', *Asian Survey*, 38(12): 1087–104.

Moon, C. and Chun, C. (2003) 'Sovereignty: Dominance of the Westphalian Concept and Implications for Regional Security', in M. Alagappa (ed.) *Asian Security Order: Instrumental and Normative Features* (Stanford, CA: Stanford University Press), pp. 106–37.

Moravcsik, A. (2000) 'The Origins of Human Rights Regimes: Democratic Delegation in Postwar Europe', *International Organization*, 54(2): 217–52.

Mubyarto, Soestrisno, L., Hudiyanto, Djatmiko, E., Setiawati, I. and Mawarni, A. (1991) *East Timor: The Impact of Integration – An Indonesian Socio-Anthropological Study* (Northcote: Indonesia Resources Information Programme).

Mysliwec, E. (1988) *Punishing the Poor: The International Isolation of Kampuchea* (Oxford: Oxfam).

Nairn, A. (1997) 'Foreword', in C. Pinto and M. Jardine (eds) *East Timor's Unfinished Struggle: Inside the Timorese Resistance* (Boston: South End Press), pp. xii–xxv.

Narine, S. (2002) *Explaining ASEAN: Regionalism in Southeast Asia* (London: Lynne Rienner).

—— (2005) 'Humanitarian Intervention and the Question of Sovereignty: The Case of ASEAN', *Perspectives on Global Development and Technology*, 4(3–4): 465–85.

—— (2006) 'The English School and ASEAN', *Pacific Review*, 19(2): 199–220.

Nation (1999a) The Nation 'Gov't Flayed for Ban on Burma Labour Meet', 22 May.

—— (1999b) 'Thais Respond to Pleas for Timor Poll Aid', 1 April.

—— (2000) 'Thais Oppose ASEAN Bid to Fend Off ILO Move', 16 November.

—— (2003) 'Philippines Demurs as ASEAN Backs Burma', 17 June.

Neher, C. D. (1990) 'The Foreign Policy of Thailand', in D. Wurfel and B. Burton (eds) *The Political Economy of Foreign Policy in Southeast Asia* (London: Macmillan), pp. 177–203.

Nesadurai, H. E. S. (2009a) 'ASEAN and Regional Governance After the Cold War: From Regional Order to Regional Community?', *Pacific Review*, 22(1): 91–118.

—— (2009b) 'Economic Surveillance as a New Mode of Regional Governance: Contested Knowledge and the Politics of Risk Management in East Asia', *Australian Journal of International Affairs*, 63(3): 361–75.

Newsweek (1999) 'The Fallout from East Timor', 18 October.

Nichterlein, S. (1977) 'The Struggle for East Timor: Prelude to Invasion', *Journal of Contemporary Asia*, 7(4): 486–96.

Nischalke, T. (2002) 'Does ASEAN Measure Up? Post-Cold War Diplomacy and the Idea of Regional Community', *Pacific Review*, 15(1): 89–117.

Noppadon P. (2000) 'East Timor: The Consequences for ASEAN', in B. Brown (ed.) *East Timor – The Consequences* (Wellington: NZIIA), pp. 34–9.

NST (1996a) New Straits Times, 'APCET II Organisers Face Action if There is Backlash', 7 November.

—— (1996b) 'NGOs Urged to Reconsider Meeting', 5 November.

—— (2000) 'Malaysia to Continue Monitoring East Timor', 28 January.

—— (2001) 'Myanmar Problem Cannot Be Solved By Confrontation', 29 January.

—— (2005) 'Rethinking ASEAN Principle', 1 February.

New York Times (2003) 'ASEAN Urges Burma to Ease Crackdown', 17 June.

Observer Foreign News Service (1974) 'Crocodile Colony Up For Grabs', 11 November.

Ong, A. (2000) 'Graduated Sovereignty in Southeast Asia', *Theory, Culture and Society*, 17(4): 55–75.

Osiander, A. (2001) 'Sovereignty, International Relations and the Westphalian Myth', *International Organization*, 55(2): 251–87.

Pasuk, P. and Baker, C. (2004) *Thaksin: The Business of Politics in Thailand* (Copenhagen: NIAS).

Peou, S. (2000) *Intervention and Change in Cambodia: Towards Democracy?* (Singapore: ISEAS).

—— (2002) 'Realism and Constructivism in Southeast Asian Security Studies Today: A Review Essay', *Pacific Review*, 15(1): 119–38.

Phnom Penh Post (2007) 'July 1997: Shock and Aftermath', 27 July.

Pinto, C. and Jardine, M. (1997) *East Timor's Unfinished Struggle: Inside the Timorese Resistance* (Boston: South End Press).

Pollard, V. K. (1970) 'ASA and ASEAN, 1961–1967: Southeast Asian Regionalism', *Asian Survey*, 10(3): 244–55.

Poulantzas, N. (1976) *State, Power, Socialism* (London: New Left Books).

Quinn-Judge, P. (1981) 'An Arranged Marriage', *Far Eastern Economic Review*, 11 September, pp. 8–9.

Radio Australia (1999) 'Singapore Leader Warns of Economic Effects of Instability', 17 January.

Rahim, L. Z. (2008) 'Fragmented Community and Unconstructive Engagements: ASEAN and Burma's SPDC Regime', *Critical Asian Studies*, 40(1): 67–88.

Rajaratnam, S. (1980) *From Phnom Penh to Kabul* (Singapore: Ministry of Foreign Affairs).

—— (2006a) 'ASEAN and the Indochina Refugee Problem', in K. C. Guan (ed.) *S. Rajaratnam on Singapore: From Ideas to Reality* (Singapore: World Scientific Publishing), pp. 115–17.

—— (2006b) 'Building Relations with ASEAN's Communist Neighbours', in K. C. Guan (ed.) *S. Rajaratnam on Singapore: From Ideas to Reality* (Singapore: World Scientific Publishing), pp. 100–3.

—— (2006c) 'The Dominoes Did Not Fall', in K. C. Guan (ed.) *S. Rajaratnam on Singapore: From Ideas to Reality* (Singapore: World Scientific Publishing), pp. 104–7.

—— (2006d) 'The Founding of ASEAN', in K. C. Guan (ed.) *S. Rajaratnam on Singapore: From Ideas to Reality* (Singapore: World Scientific Publishing), pp. 90–2.

—— (2006e) 'Highlighting the Soviet Threat', in K. C. Guan (ed.) *S. Rajaratnam on Singapore: From Ideas to Reality* (Singapore: World Scientific Publishing), pp. 47–52.

—— (2006f) 'What is ASEAN About?', in K. C. Guan (ed.) *S. Rajaratnam on Singapore: From Ideas to Reality* (Singapore: World Scientific Publishing), pp. 93–4.

Ramcharan, R. (2000) 'ASEAN and Non-Interference: A Principle Maintained', *Contemporary Southeast Asia*, 22(1): 60–88.

Ramos Horta, J. (1987) *Funu: The Unfinished Saga of East Timor* (Trenton, NJ: Red Sea Press).

Razali I. (2008) Interview with the Author, Kuala Lumpur, January.

Republic of Indonesia (1975) *Government Statements on the East-Timor Question* (Jakarta: Department of Information).

—— (1976) *Process of Decolonization in East Timor* (Jakarta: Department of Information).

Richardson, M. (1982) 'ASEAN and Indochinese Refugees', in A. Broinowski (ed.) *Understanding ASEAN* (London: Macmillan), pp. 92–114.

Roberts, C. (2010) *ASEAN's Myanmar Crisis: Challenges to the Pursuit of a Security Community* (Singapore: ISEAS).

Robison, R. (1986) *Indonesia: The Rise of Capital* (Sydney: Allen and Unwin).

—— (1996) 'The Politics of Asian Values', *Pacific Review*, 9(3): 309–27.

Robison, R. and Hadiz, V. R. (2004) *Reorganising Power in Indonesia: The Politics of Oligarchy in an Age of Markets* (New York: RoutledgeCurzon).

Robison, R., Hewison, K. and Higgott, R. (eds) (1987) *Southeast Asia in the 1980s: The Politics of Economic Crisis* (London: Allen and Unwin).

Robison, R. and Rosser, A. (2000) 'Surviving the Meltdown: Liberal Reform and Political Oligarchy in Indonesia', in R. Robison, M. Beeson, K. Jayasuriya and H.-R. Kim (eds) *Politics and Markets in the Wake of the Asian Crisis* (London: Routledge), pp. 171–91.

Rodan, G. (1993) 'Preserving the One-Party State in Contemporary Singapore', in K. Hewison, R. Robison and G. Rodan (eds) *Southeast Asia in the 1990s: Authoritarianism, Democracy and Capitalism* (St Leonards, Australia: Allen and Unwin), pp. 77–108.

—— (ed.) (1996a) *Political Oppositions in Industrialising Asia* (London: Routledge).

—— (1996b) 'The Internationalization of Ideological Conflict: Asia's New Significance', *Pacific Review*, 9(3): 328–51.

—— (2006) 'Singapore: Globalisation, the State, and Politics', in G. Rodan, K. Hewison and R. Robison (eds) *The Political Economy of Southeast Asia: Markets, Power and Contestation*, 3rd edn (Oxford: Oxford University Press), pp. 137–69.

Rodan, G., Hewison, K. and Robison, R. (2006) 'Theorising Markets in Southeast Asia: Power and Contestation', in G. Rodan, K. Hewison and R. Robison (eds) *The Political Economy of Southeast Asia: Markets, Power and Contestation*, 3rd edn (Oxford: Oxford University Press), pp. 1–38.

Rodan, G. and Jayasuriya, K. (2007) 'The Technocratic Politics of Administrative Participation: Case Studies of Singapore and Vietnam', *Democratization*, 14(5): 795–815.

Roff, S. R. (1992) *Timor's Anschluss: Indonesian and Australian Foreign Policy in East Timor, 1974–1976* (Lampeter: Edwin Mellen Press).

Rosenberg, J. (1994) *The Empire of Civil Society: A Critique of the Realist Theory of International Relations* (London: Verso).

Rüland, J. (2009) 'Deepening ASEAN Cooperation Through Democratization? The Indonesian Legislature and Foreign Policymaking', *International Relations of the Asia-Pacific*, 9(3): 373–402.

Rungswasdisab, P. (2006) 'Thailand's Response to the Cambodian Genocide', in S. E. Cook (ed.) *Genocide in Cambodia and Rwanda: New Perspectives* (New Brunswick, NJ: Transaction Publishers), pp. 73–126.

Saldanha, J. M. d. S. (1994) *The Political Economy of East Timor Development* (Jakarta: Sinar Harapan).

Schattschneider, E. E. (1960) *The Semisovereign People: A Realist's View of Democracy in America* (New York: Holt, Reinhart and Winston).

Scotsman (1999) 'Neighbours Jittery over Aceh Referendum Offer', 10 November.

Sebastian, L. C. and Smith, A. L. (2000) 'The East Timor Crisis: A Test Case for Humanitarian Intervention', in D. Singh (ed.) *Southeast Asian Affairs 2000* (Singapore: ISEAS), pp. 64–86.

Selth, A. (2000) *Burma's Secret Military Partners* (Canberra: ANU).

Senior Singaporean Diplomat (2008) Interview with the Author, Singapore, February 2008.

Severino, R. C. (2006) *Southeast Asia in Search of an ASEAN Community: Insights from the Former ASEAN Secretary-General* (Singapore: ISEAS).

—— (2008) Interview with the Author, Singapore, February.

Shawcross, W. (1984) *The Quality of Mercy: Cambodia, Holocaust, and Modern Conscience* (New York: Simon and Schuster).

Siddique, T. (2008) Interview with the Author, Singapore, February.

Silverstein, J. (2001) 'Burma and the World: A Decade of Foreign Policy under the State Law and Order Restoration Council', in R. H. Taylor (ed.) *Burma: Political Economy under Military Rule* (London: Hurst & Company), pp. 119–36.

Simon, S. W. (1982a) *The ASEAN States and Regional Security* (Stanford: Hoover Institution Press).

—— (1982b) 'Cambodia and Regional Diplomacy', in *Southeast Asian Affairs 1982* (Singapore: ISEAS), pp. 196–207.

Singh, B. (1994) *Bear and Garuda: Soviet-Indonesian Relations from Lenin to Gorbachev* (Yogyakarta: Gadjah Mada University Press).

—— (1996) *East Timor, Indonesia and the World: Myths and Realities*, 2nd edn (Kuala Lumpur: ADPR Consult).

Sit, S. (1995) *ASEAN's Diplomacy vis-à-vis Vietnam: A Study of Foreign Policy Interaction on the Cambodian Problem, 1978–1990*, DPhil thesis, University of Oxford.

Skinner, Q. (1988) 'Some Problems in the Analysis of Political Thought and Action', in J. Tully (ed.) *Meaning and Context: Quentin Skinner and His Critics* (Princeton: Princeton University Press), pp. 97–118.

Smith, M. (1991) *Burma: Insurgency and the Politics of Ethnicity* (London: Zed Books).

Snitwongse, K. (2001) 'Thai Foreign Policy in the Global Age: Principle or Profit?', *Contemporary Southeast Asia*, 23(2): 189–212.

Söderbaum, F. (2004) *The Political Economy of Regionalism: The Case of Southern Africa* (Basingstoke: Palgrave Macmillan).

Soesastro, H. (2008) Interview with the Author, Jakarta, February.

Solingen, E. (1998) *Regional Orders at Century's Dawn: Global and Domestic Influences on Grand Strategy* (Princeton: Princeton University Press).

—— (2004) 'Southeast Asia in a New Era: Domestic Coalitions from Crisis to Recovery', *Asian Survey*, 44(2): 189–212.

—— (2005) 'ASEAN Cooperation: The Legacy of the Economic Crisis', *International Relations of the Asia-Pacific*, 5(1): 1–29.

ST (1975a) Straits Times, 'KL "Yes" to Timor Force', 3 September.
—— (1975b) Title Unavailable, 24 October.
—— (1979) Title Unavailable, 31 July.
—— (1980) 'Lee: Kremlin Backing Carries Risk of Wider Conflict', 26 September.
—— (1981) 'ASEAN's Resolution Offers the Best Solution – Says Son Sann', 19 April.
—— (1982a) 'Musa Promises "All Out" Economic Assistance', 22 June.
—— (1982b) 'The Third Force Must Be Given Beef and Teeth', 11 June.
—— (1992) 'ASEAN Prefers Soft Talk to Threats in Dealing with Yangon', 26 August.
—— (1997) 'Support for ASEAN Move on Cambodia, Myanmar', 28 July.
—— (1999a) 'ASEAN: Members Pledge to Feature Strongly in UN Force', 13 September.
—— (1999b) 'Bangkok Defends Move to Take Part in INTERFET', 1 October.
—— (1999c) 'Gus Dur Blames Violence on Ballot Process', 7 September.
—— (1999d) 'Indonesia Hears a Nationalist Drumbeat', 21 September.
—— (1999e) 'Thais Question Country's Role in E. Timor', 28 September.
—— (2005) 'New Charter to Signal Need for Reform in Myanmar', 13 December.
State Department (1970) 'Indonesian Support to Cambodia', Top Secret Cable from State Department to US Embassy in Jakarta, document CVW00444, http://nsarchive.chadwyck.com, date accessed 6 March 2007.
—— (1975a) 'Discussion of President Ford and Lee Kuan Yew on Southeast Asia', document CKT01616, http://nsarchive.chadwyck.com, date accessed 27 March 2007.
—— (1975b) 'Ford-Suharto Meeting', Secret Cable from US Embassy in Jakarta to State Department, document CKT01843, http://nsarchive.chadwyck.com, date accessed 11 March 2007.
—— (1975c) 'Memorandum of Conversation', Henry Kissinger and Adam Malik, document CKT01690, http://nsarchive.chadwyck.com, date accessed 7 March 2007.
—— (1975d) 'Secretary's Meeting with Indonesian Foreign Minister Adam Malik', Memorandum of Conversation, document CKT01773, http://nsarchive.chadwyck.com, date accessed 7 March 2007.
Steinberg, D. I. (2000) 'The State, Power, and Civil Society in Burma-Myanmar: The Status and Prospects for Pluralism', in M. B. Pedersen, E. Rudland and R. J. May (eds) *Burma Myanmar: Strong Regime, Weak State?* (Adelaide: Crawford House Publishing), pp. 91–122.
—— (2001) 'The Burmese Conundrum: Approaching Reformation of the Political Economy', in R. H. Taylor (ed.) *Burma: Political Economy under Military Rule* (London: Hurst & Company), pp. 41–69.
Stinchcombe (1968) *Constructing Social Theories* (New York: Harcourt, Brace & World).
Strange, S. (1996) *The Retreat of the State: The Diffusion of Power in the World Economy* (Cambridge: Cambridge University Press).
Stubbs, R. (1990) 'The Foreign Policy of Malaysia', in D. Wurfel and B. Burton (eds) *The Political Economy of Foreign Policy in Southeast Asia* (London: Macmillan), pp. 101–23.
—— (2008) 'The ASEAN Alternative? Ideas, Institutions and the Challenge to "Global" Governance', *Pacific Review*, 21(4): 451–68.

Sukhumbhand P. (1984) 'Strategic Implications of the Indochina Conflict: Thai Perspectives', *Asian Affairs*, 11(3): 28–46.

—— (1985) 'Can ASEAN Break the Stalemate?', *World Policy Journal*, 3(1): 95–106.

—— (2004) 'A Regional Perspective on Burma', *Irrawaddy*, 1 July.

Sunday Times (1975) Singapore, 'Malaysia Accepts Indonesian Action', 14 December.

Sundhaussen, U. (1995) 'Indonesia's New Order: A Model for Myanmar?', *Asian Survey*, 35(8): 768–80.

Surain S. (2001) 'The Dual Narrative of "Good Governance": Lessons for Understanding Political and Cultural Change in Malaysia and Singapore', *Contemporary Southeast Asia*, 23(1): 65–80.

Surakiart, S. (2003) *Forward Engagement: Thailand's Foreign Policy* (Bangkok: Ministry of Foreign Affairs).

Surin P. (1998a) 'Thailand's Foreign Policy During the Economic and Social Crises', speech at Thammasat University, Bangkok, 12 June, http://russia.shaps.hawaii. edu/fp/asean/fm02.html, date accessed 13 January 2006.

—— (1998b) 'Thailand's Non-Paper on the Flexible Engagement Approach', Manila, 27 July, http://www.thaiembdc.org/pressctr/pr/pr743.htm, date accessed 10 October 2008.

—— (2000) 'Setting ASEAN's Future Agenda', *Bangkok Post*, 16 July.

—— (2002) 'How East Timor Reshaped ASEAN', *Bangkok Post*, 19 May.

—— (2008a) 'How Did We Get You Here?', Press Statement, 26 June, http://www. aseansec.org/21704.htm, 4 January 2009.

—— (2008b) Interview with the Author, Jakarta, February.

—— (2009) 'Foreword', in D. K. Emmerson (ed.) *Hard Choices: Security, Democracy, and Regionalism in Southeast Asia* (Singapore: ISEAS), pp. xix–xxi.

Sydney Morning Herald (1999) 'ASEAN Set to Discuss Aceh Risks', 18 November.

Tan, P. J. (2006) 'Indonesia Seven Years After Suharto: Party System Institutionalization in a New Democracy', *Contemporary Southeast Asia*, 28(1): 89–114.

Tanter, R., Van Klinken, G. and Ball, D. (eds) (2006) *Masters of Terror: Indonesia's Military and Violence in East Timor* (Oxford: Rowman & Littlefield).

Tasker, R. (1982) 'Trumped-Up Trio', *Far Eastern Economic Review*, 25 June, 8–10.

Tay, S. S. C. (2009) 'Blowing Smoke: Regional Cooperation, Indonesian Democracy, and the Haze', in D. K. Emmerson (ed.) *Hard Choices: Security, Democracy, and Regionalism in Southeast Asia* (Singapore: ISEAS), pp. 219–39.

Taylor, J. (1991) *Indonesia's Forgotten War: The Hidden History of East Timor* (London: Zed Books).

Termsak, C. (2009) 'Institutional Reform: One Charter, Three Communities, Many Challenges', in D. K. Emmerson (ed.) *Hard Choices: Security, Democracy, and Regionalism in Southeast Asia* (Singapore: ISEAS), pp. 91–131.

Terry, F. (2002) *Condemned to Repeat? The Paradox of Humanitarian Action* (Ithaca: Cornell University Press).

Teschke, B. (2003) *The Myth of 1648: Class, Geopolitics, and the Making of Modern International Relations* (London: Verso).

Thakur, R. C. (2000) 'Human Security Regimes', in W. T. Tow, R. C. Thakur and I.-T. Hyun (eds) *Asia's Emerging Regional Order: Reconciling Traditional and Human Security* (Tokyo: UN University Press), pp. 229–53.

Than, M. (2005) *Myanmar in ASEAN: Regional Cooperation Experience* (Singapore: ISEAS).

Thayer, C. A. (1999) 'Vietnamese Foreign Policy: Multilateralism and the Threat of Peaceful Evolution', in C. A. Thayer and R. Amer (eds) *Vietnamese Foreign Policy in Transition* (Singapore: ISEAS), pp. 1–24.

The Age (2000) 'Lee Warns Jakarta on West Papua', 25 November.

Tow, W. T. (2004) 'Alternative Security Models: Implications for ASEAN', in R. C. Thakur and E. Newman (eds) *Broadening Asia's Security Discourse and Agenda: Political, Social, and Environmental Perspectives* (Tokyo: UN University Press), pp. 245–63.

Ukrist, P. (2008) 'A Different Coup D'état?', *Journal of Contemporary Asia*, 38(1): 124–42.

Um, K. (1989) 'Cambodia in 1989: Still Talking But No Settlement', *Asian Survey*, 30(1): 96–104.

—— (1991) 'Thailand and the Dynamics of Economic and Security Complex in Mainland Southeast Asia', *Contemporary Southeast Asia*, 13(3): 245–70.

UN (1991a) United Nations, *Agreement Concerning the Sovereignty, Independence, Territorial Integrity and Inviolability, Neutrality and National Unity of Cambodia*, Paris, 23 October.

—— (1991b) *Agreements on a Comprehensive Political Settlement of the Cambodia Conflict*, Paris, 23 October.

—— (1991c) *Declaration on the Rehabilitation and Reconstruction of Cambodia*, Paris, 23 October.

—— (1999) *UNAMET Fact Sheet*, 9 August, http://www.un.org, date accessed 8 November 2008.

UN Department of Political Affairs, Trusteeship and Decolonization (1976) *Issue on East Timor* (New York: United Nations).

UNCTAD (2003a) *Cambodia Country Profile*, http://www.unctad.org, date accessed 26 January 2009.

—— (2003b) *Myanmar Country Profile*, http://www.unctad.org, date accessed 20 January 2009.

—— (2008) *Handbook of Statistics*, http://stats.unctad.org/Handbook, date accessed 20 January 2009.

—— (2009) *Foreign Direct Investment Database*, http://stats.unctad.org, date accessed 26 October.

UNTAET (2000) *East Timor Update*, March, http://www.un.org/peace/etimor/untaetPU/ETupdateME.pdf, date accessed 8 November 2008.

US Congress (2009) *Trafficking and Extortion of Burmese Migrants in Malaysia and Southern Thailand* (Washington, DC: US Government Printing Office).

Van der Kroef, J. M. (1976) 'Indonesia and East Timor: The Politics of Phased Annexation', *Solidarity*, 10(5–6): 17–28.

—— (1981) 'ASEAN, Hanoi and the Kampuchean Conflict: Between "Kuantan" and a "Third Alternative"', *Asian Survey*, 21(5): 515–35.

—— (1983) 'Refugees and Rebels: Dimensions of the Thai-Kampuchean Border Conflict', *Asian Affairs*, 10(1): 19–36.

Van Dijk, C. (1976) 'East Timor (1)', *Review of Indonesian and Malayan Affairs*, 10(1): 1–32.

Vickery, M. (1987) 'Refugee Politics: The Khmer Camp System in Thailand', in D. A. Ablin and M. Hood (eds) *The Cambodian Agony* (London: M. E. Sharpe), pp. 293–331.

Vietnam News Agency (1999) 'Vietnam: Spokesman Comments on Joining East Timor Peacekeeping Force', 14 September, via BBC Monitoring.

Vincent, R. J. (1974) *Non-Intervention and International Order* (Princeton: Princeton University Press).

Walter, A. (2008) *Governing Finance: East Asia's Adoption of International Standards* (Ithaca: Cornell University Press).

Westad, O. A. (2005) *The Global Cold War: Third World Interventions and the Making of our Times* (Cambridge: Cambridge University Press).

Wheeler, N. J. (2000) *Saving Strangers: Humanitarian Intervention in International Society* (Oxford: Oxford University Press).

Wheeler, N. J. and Dunne, T. (2001) 'East Timor and the New Humanitarian Interventionism', *International Affairs*, 77(4): 805–27.

Widyono, B. (2008) *Dancing in Shadows: Sihanouk, the Khmer Rouge, and the United Nations in Cambodia* (Plymouth: Rowman & Littlefield).

Wight, M. (1978) *Power Politics* (New York: Holmes & Meier).

Wingfield, T. (2002) 'Democratization and Economic Crisis in Thailand: Political Business and the Changing Dynamic of the Thai State', in E. T. Gomez (ed.) *Political Business in East Asia* (London: Routledge), pp. 250–300.

Wurfel, D. (1990) 'Philippine Foreign Policy', in D. Wurfel and B. Burton (eds) *The Political Economy of Foreign Policy in Southeast Asia* (London: Macmillan), pp. 146–76.

Xinhua (1982) 'Thailand Hopes for Political Solution to Kampuchean Problem', 14 June.

—— (1994) 'Thai Army Chief Against SEANET Meeting in Thailand', 19 July.

—— (1998) 'ASEAN Urges All Parties in Cambodia to Avoid Violence', 9 September.

—— (1999a) 'Cambodia Will Not Send Forces to East Timor: PM', 14 September.

—— (1999b) 'Malaysia PM, Former Philippine President Discuss E. Timor', 15 September.

—— (2007) 'Myanmar Leader Meets Singapore FM', 4 April.

Yeo, G. (2005) 'Transcript of Singapore Foreign Minister George Yeo's Media Conference on Myanmar's Chairmanship of ASEAN', Vientiane, 26 July, http://app.mfa.gov.sg, date accessed 25 February 2010.

Index